MARX AFTER MARX

harry harootunian

MARX

AFTER

MARX

history and time in the expansion of capitalism

COLUMBIA UNIVERSITY PRESS   New York

COLUMBIA UNIVERSITY PRESS

PUBLISHERS SINCE 1893

NEW YORK   CHICHESTER, WEST SUSSEX

CUP.COLUMBIA.EDU

Library of Congress Cataloging-in-Publication Data

Harootunian, Harry D., 1929–

Marx after Marx : history and time in the expansion of capitalism / Harry Harootunian.

pages cm

Includes bibliographical references and index.

ISBN 978-0-231-17480-0 (cloth : alk. paper)

ISBN 978-0-231-54013-1 (e-book)

1. Marx, Karl, 1818–1883.   2. Capitalism.   3. Socialism.   I. Title.

HX39.5.H276 2015

335.4—dc23

2015008490

c 10 9 8 7 6 5 4 3 2 1

COVER DESIGN: CHANG JAC LEE

For the memory of my relatives (grandparents, aunts, uncles, cousins), whose names I never knew, who perished as victims of the genocidal excesses of primitive accumulation inaugurating Turkey's drive to transform a failing imperial order into capitalist modernity. They are Walter Benjamin's "nameless," whose memory is honored only through an act of historical construction.

We suffer not only from the living, but from the dead. *Le mort saisit le vif.*
Karl Marx, *Capital*

CONTENTS

ACKNOWLEDGMENTS

In the time I wrote this book, I accumulated a staggering amount of debt to people who helped me along the way. My deepest appreciation and thanks belong to Kristin Ross, with whom I discussed virtually every stage of the book's unfolding and who critically read through an earlier draft, which straightened out arguments for coherence and writing for clarity. My thanks to Hyun Ok Park for the discussions we've carried on over the years on questions and approaches of mutual concern, and for reading an earlier draft. I am particularly grateful to Carol Gluck, who gave me the opportunity to teach the material that constitutes the book before it was written.

I owe a special thanks to the students enrolled in several classes I taught at Columbia University over the past six years that concentrated on Marx's writings, who ultimately gave immeasurable help in shaping the book. I'd like to single out Andy Liu, Adam Bronson, Max Ward, Ramona Bajema, Jack Wilson, Norihiko Tsuneishi, and Michela Durante. I equally owe a great debt of gratitude to Ken Kawashima, not only for suggesting the book's title but for our discussions over the years that have filtered into the making of the book. Thanks also go to Rebecca Karl for her inestimable knowledge of China's modern history, which I've drawn on, and for letting me use the draft of her invaluable essay on Wang Yanan and to Massimiliano Tomba for his important reading of Marx's conception of time.

Thanks too to Hayden White for his critical reading of the early chapters of the book; to Manu Goswami for useful advice and observations based on her command of Marx's texts; to William Haver and Michael Dutton for their generous responses from which I learned a great deal; and to Viren Murthy, whose mastery of Japanese and Chinese intellectual history and Marxism has been an incomparable source of support.

I want to remember Joyce Liu, director and professor of the Graduate Institute for Social Research and Cultural Studies, National Chiao Tung University, Taiwan, for inviting me to deliver a keynote at an International Conference on East Asian Marxisms, which happened to be my first run-through of the problem of deprovincializing Marx. My thanks to the Literature Program of Duke University, and especially Michael Hardt, Rey Chow, and Fredric Jameson, for the opportunity to present the substance of the book at a workshop at the Franklin Center in spring 2013. Thanks also to Anne Allison and Chris Nelson and their colleagues, and to Charlie Piot for a second invitation to present my current work in a workshop (winter 2015); to Katsuya Hirano and William Marotti and their graduate students at UCLA (October 2013) for the opportunity to speak on some of the intellectual and historical issues I've been concerned with in my career; to Moishe Postone, William Sewell, and the Social Theory Workshop at the University of Chicago (February 2012), where I spoke on the problem of deprovincalizing Marx; and to Naoyuki Umemori and his colleagues at Waseda University, Tokyo, for asking me to speak on my current research (November 2014).

Finally, my thanks to the staff of the Columbia University Press, who have eased the path to publication and made it a genuinely pleasant experience—especially Jennifer Crewe, the director of the press; Kathryn Schell, my editor; and Anita O'Brien for her wonderful copy editing. I want also to express appreciation to the Schoff Fund at the University Seminars at Columbia University for its help in publication. The ideas presented have benefited from discussions in the University Seminars on Modern Japan.

MARX AFTER MARX

INTRODUCTION

deprovincializing marx

There have been few more important episodes in the history of Marxism than its provincialization in the figure of what the Soviets named "Western Marxism," to differentiate their own discussions from Georg Lukács's *History and Class Consciousness*. This naming made it clear that the intention was to show how Lukács represented a shift from preoccupations with labor and the production process, as such, to the force of the commodity form to structure thought and culture. In our time, this tendency has become so hegemonic or commonsense among Marxist and non-Marxian interpreters of cultural studies that it has managed to mask its own culturally and politically specific origins and run the risk of making its claims complicit with capitalism's self-representation.[1] This reflection undoubtedly derives from the presumption that the commodity relation has been finally achieved everywhere, signaling the final realization of what Marx named "real subsumption" and announcing the final completion of capitalism's domination of everyday life. The apparent consequence in this changed perspective that assumes capital's completion has been the accompanying conviction that all of society has been subsumed, whereby value has trumped history. This capacity recalls Marx's explanation of how capital "becomes a very mystical being, since all the productive forces of social labour appear attributable to it, and not to labour, as such, as a power springing forth from its own womb."[2] In this narrative the importance of labor has been demoted to residual status, since, as Massimiliano Tomba explains, value is made to appear to proceed directly from the productive process and consumption, and its culture is elastically expanded to fill every pore of society and inform all human activity.

This perspective on Marx was in part produced by the so-called Frankfurt School's earlier (prewar) intervention and appropriation of Lukács's analysis of reification and its successive expansion into cultural disciplines, as well as being reinforced in the later work of Antonio Negri and his followers, who have presumed the final completion of the commodity relation everywhere—the putative realization of "real subsumption"—to reaffirm capitalism's own self-image in the pursuit of progress. Both cases share the common ground of this changed perspective that assumes capitalism's final externalization and naturalization, where it has subsumed the whole of society. With Frankfurt Marxism, it is the explicit transfer to circulation, whereas in Negri, productive labor is envisioned as intellectual and immaterial, expressed now in the sovereign subject of the "General Intellect." What both commonly propose are the unimportance or secondary stature of industrial labor, as such, and the expansion of the commodity relation to mediate all sectors of society. Both, moreover, "submitted history to process, a sort of auto-reflection. Unilinear historical progress allowed the measuring of the level of (Western) civilization attained by populations with histories different from those of Europe, thus justifying the domination of those who were represented as lower down the scale."[3] Deprovincializing Marx entails not simply an expanded geographic inclusion but a broadening of temporal possibilities unchained from a hegemonic unlinearism.

The self-image that calls attention to the completion of the commodity relation—the regime of real subsumption—congeals into a representation of society that Tomba has described as "phantasmagoria," without either head or body. As early as *The Eighteenth Brumaire of Louis Bonaparte*, Marx perceived in the appearance of this phantasmagoric representation (which was of a piece with his deployment of gothic metaphors like vampires, ghosts, and specters) the imaginary scene of shadows no longer inhabited by bodies but only phantoms terrorizing the proletarian masses in the name of a farcical existing order that possessed no more substantiality. In *The Eighteenth Brumaire* it described the Second Empire, but in *Capital* this idea would be enlarged to become the specific form of the social totality, proclaiming the formation of a new "phenotype" resulting in a new kind of human produced by the capitalist inversion of use-value into exchange-value, the expansion of the domain of needs, and the accelerated production of a world of commodities that led to the domination of "consumerism." This became the dominion of the abstract, of value over the concrete, and the appearance of the individual, who creates its own nature and is without history, first revealed in the silhouette of the Robinsonades, what Marx momentarily called "social man" (*gesellschaftlicher Mensch*).[4] This is a familiar story in cultural studies, a staple of current accounts among Marxists and non-Marxists alike that has become a classic cultural cliché. But it is important because it signifies a change in perspective that has become indistinguishable from what we have come to know as Western Marxism, that presumed to stand-in for Marxism itself.

For Marxism, it was the particular circumstances of the Cold War conjuncture that not only eclipsed the claims associated with its long history in Russia and the Soviet Union but also overlooked and even excluded Marxian readings that occurred in the colonial and semicolonial world of Euro-America's periphery before World War II and throughout what came to be named the Third World in the postwar years. It was as if colonialism was an effect of capitalist modernity rather than an interactive relationship, as Marx proposed in his chapter on "settler colonialism" and Edward Wakefield's theory in volume I of *Capital*. Constraints of space and lack of expertise prevent me from detailing the fate of the former—Soviet Marxism—and permit only a brief profiling of the latter, the diversity of Marxisms in the former Third World. Marxian thinking in the interwar period in the Soviet Union was largely subsumed under Stalinist modernization, whereas the peripheral world beyond Euro-America—the colonial world—was consigned to the classification of backwardness and underdevelopment—temporally retrograde, belonging to modernity's past even though paradoxically immanent with modern society—that could be overcome through the helping hand of Western developmentalist assistance. While the Marxism in the industrial periphery during the interwar period was temporarily yoked to the Comintern and its internationalist aspirations, this putative unity quickly splintered into fragmentary constituencies, primarily because of the war. During the Cold War interim, Western Marxism, itself, sacrificed a rich and heterogeneous genealogy for the figure of a homogenous interpretative strategy, founded on the presupposition of a unity based on geographical contiguity that had long given up on the anticipated "withering of the state" or indeed the prospect of an imminent worldwide social revolution[5] for critical cultural analysis of capitalism's domination of the social formation. Much of this was undeniably a response to the perception, made explicit by Walter Benjamin, that historical materialism itself was literally infected by the idea of progressive developmentalism introduced by the Second and Third Internationalist revisions (even though Benjamin showed little interest in the world outside Europe apart from the Soviet Union). This meant taking onboard comparative trajectories that classified societies according to a ranking system that situated them along a developmental arc from advanced to backward. Benjamin's powerful intervention aimed to rescue historical materialism from this fatal affliction, which had made Marxian historical practice resemble bourgeois historiography, joining both at the hip of social history. Maurice Merleau-Ponty used the term "Western Marxism" in the early postwar years to differentiate Lukács's earlier intervention (*History and Class Consciousness*) from the Soviet readings of Marx, beginning with Lenin's *Materialism and Empiriocriticism*. According to Karl Korsch, Lukács's Soviet critics described his now classic text as Western Marxism.[6] For Merleau-Ponty, the postwar moment and the violence he identified with Soviet Communism and the party, which he described as hiding in the "shadow of Marx," provided the occasion to retread the Marxian path to determine where the immense departures and distortions took place. In a sense, this return to Marx in the postwar era, which is usually attributed to Louis Althusser, was, in effect, inaugurated by Merleau-Ponty a decade earlier, despite its chosen path to resuscitate a more humanistic vision.

With this move to cultural critique, the inadvertent effect of promoting the figure of Western Marxism was to reinforce the realization of capitalism's claim to "real subsumption" and the completion of the commodity relation, which often seemed to trumpet the triumph of capitalism. In fact, this presumption accompanied a turn to the "autonomous" status of the commodity form as an all-encompassing structuring force of the social formation, whereby value supplants use-value, presenting itself as self-determining, and the individual misrecognizes the latter for the former. Once capital finally appears as an "automaton," signaling the moment it produces its own presuppositions, singularly personified as money making, it occludes value's source in living labor and the perspective has changed to circulation.[7] This image of an achieved capitalist society in the West dramatized further the contrast between advanced development—modernization, as it was named—and backwardness, resulting in a further abandonment of a meticulous historical materialism founded on a close investigation of specific and often singular contexts sensitive to identifying real differences in the experiences of capitalist development. Yet we must note the Cold War provenance of this particular emphasis on the West as a successful modular example of advancement and progress in a contest of competing theories of modernization. Parochializing Marx thus resulted in adhering to a rigid conception of a Marxian historical trajectory constrained to upholding a particular progressive narrative all societies must pass through, on the template of a geographically (and culturally) specific location exemplified by England as Marx sketched its genesis of capitalism in volume 1 of *Capital*. This scenario was subsequently reproduced in the imaginary of the nation-form to become its principal historical vocation. It is ironic that the proponents of Western Marxism in the Cold War struggle to win the hearts and minds of newly decolonized unaligned nations were more preoccupied with philosophy, as such, than history, whose movement remained bonded to the promise of development leading to capitalism's present or to the identification of a time lag—a discordant temporality announcing its difference from normative social time—that nations beyond Euro-America had yet to cover in their effort to "catch up." What apparently had been forfeited was a perspective capable of recognizing the very unevenness lived by all societies, both the putatively advanced and the backward, as a condition of fulfilling capital's law of accumulation. Yet, in the new Cold War alignment, Western Marxism's progressive distancing from the economic for the cultural, especially in the domain of aesthetic production, art and literature, which contributed to valorizing a specific (and provincial) cultural endowment as unique, superior, and universal, regardless of its critical intent, constituted a modality of thinking more reminiscent of Max Weber than a critical undermining of capitalism's "superstructural" strongholds. Specifically, the principal casualty resulting from the preoccupation with a matured capitalism—the relations of the immediate process of production—risked sacrificing historical capitalism, if not the historical itself, as a subject of inquiry. The consequence of this neglect meant overlooking both the depth and complexity of its multiple precapitalist formations, what Marx called "historical presuppositions" and which functioned to show both the historicity of modes of production and how capitalism had naturalized historic social relationships into a new individuality. But it also signaled a failure to take notice of the "distinct configurations, forms of the accumulation process, implying other combinations" for a commitment to one "unique configuration."[8] What this closing down of such historical complexity demanded is an evolutionary pathway based on a universal model requiring replication everywhere. An example of this compulsion traditionally articulated in Marxian historiography is the insistence on identifying and accounting for the figure of the classic transition from feudalism to capitalism, when no such agenda ever appeared in mature texts like *Grundrisse* (feudalism is rarely mentioned and only to explain how the archaic Germanic communities evolved into this form), while in *Capital* Marx appeared more concerned with primitive or original accumulation and its continuation, and feudalism is mentioned for illustrative purposes to explain the process in England, the West, and in an often observed footnote referring to Japan's feudalism. But the centrality accorded to the category of feudalism, simply reflecting a local variant of tribute, reinforced the West's claim to a privileged universalism, providing an unquestioned model of imitation in the development of capitalism in societies outside Europe. The paradox of this presumption is the consensus that has persistently overlooked Marx's own observation concerning the process of original accumulation: "The history of this expropriation (in original accumulation) assumes different aspects in different countries, and runs through its various phases in different orders of succession, and at different historical epochs. Only in England, which we therefore take as our example, has it the classic form."[9] Marx altered the wording of this passage in the French edition to underscore that the portrayal of a particular modality of original accumulation was limited to Western Europe: "but the basis of the whole development is the expropriation of the cultivators. So far, it has been carried out in a radical manner only in England: therefore this country will necessarily play the leading role in our sketch. But all the countries of Western Europe are going through the same development, although in accordance with the particular environment it changes its local color, or confines itself to a narrower sphere, or shows a less pronounced character, or follows a different order of success."[10] The way was opened to envisioning other forms of expropriation outside of Europe.

If Marx envisaged history as embodying distinct and multiple economic forms, especially in Western Europe, and the heterogeneity of such forms, modes of production that differed from each other, it is also true that when he referred to the example of England he denied that his "historical sketch" of the origins of capitalism was anything more than a description that applies to Western Europe and not "a historico-philosophical theory of a general course fatally imposed on all peoples, whatever the historical circumstances in which they find themselves placed. . . . Success," he concluded in his letter to a Russian journal, "will never come with the master-key of a general historico-philosophical theory, whose supreme virtue consists in being supra-historical."[11] By contrast, the political and economic vitality characterizing Western Europe overshadowed the "monotony" and image of static histories of Asia, which became another way of speaking of "nondevelopment."[12] The Asia that figured in the Asiatic mode of production included a vast region from the Middle East to China, as well as Russia (which Lenin early described as an "Asiatic State"), apparently based on the absence of private property and where the ruling class was subsumed in a state dominating a population inhabiting a large number of stagnant and isolated village communities. But Jairus Banaji has rightly called this mode a "default-category." We know that in *Grundrisse* Marx showed a particular interest in the global prevalence of communities founded on the recognition of communally held property, where proprietors also worked the land as cultivators. In this text, Marx distinguished these archaic settlements as "natural communities" and "agricultural communities," a later development, which varied from time and place but eventually signified a persisting tributary system as the preeminent precapitalist form. By the time he got around to reading M. M. Kovalesky's close account of India (1870s), his notes disclose he had abandoned any fidelity to earlier ideas of an all-encompassing Asiatic mode of production, especially one differentiated by the absence of private property and classes between the sovereign and the isolated village communities.[13] But he was, according to his notes, opposed to Kovalesky's categorization of precapitalist India as feudal.

Even before Marx turned to these ethnologies, he had already reformulated his views concerning the "labor process" or "organization of labor" shaped by the received circumstances of certain kinds of production in industry and agriculture.[14] It is with the introduction of the category of formal subsumption (and its corollary real subsumption), appearing in the "Results of the Immediate Process of Production," which had not been available to earlier generations until the early 1930s, that supplied the necessary analytic optic through which to grasp the refractions of specific forms (not stages) informing the "restructuring of the labour processes to generate surplus value."[15] The completed process was called real subsumption, which Marx related to the realization of "relative surplus value" and the role played by the introduction of technology and the factory system. Whether Marx actually believed capital would ultimately realize the completion of the commodity relation (thus eliminating the last traces of unevenness) is hard to say. What seems certain is that he needed such a concept in order to present capitalism as a completed totality, to literally imagine it, which would allow him to submit it to the analysis and critique that characterizes *Capital*. This was particularly evident in his account of accumulation and the process in which surplus value is transformed into capital. Here, Marx acknowledges that in the process of conversion, "we take no account of the export trade, by means of which a nation can change articles of luxury either into means of production or means of subsistence, and vice versa. To examine the object of our investigation in its integrity, free from all disturbing subsidiary circumstances, we must treat the whole world of trade as one nation, and assume that capitalist production is established everywhere and has taken possession of every branch of industry." Here, Marx has posited the achievement of real subsumption as a model, perhaps as a proto-ideal type, that envisions the possible realization and completion of the commodity relation in an as yet unreached future, in a last instance that never comes. For its methodological function has stripped capitalism of "disturbing subsidiary circumstances" and imagined a society constituted only of capital and labor.[16]

But this is not to suggest that forms of subsumption, and especially the vastly overlooked idea of hybrid forms of subsumption Marx mentioned in *Capital*'s chapter on absolute and relative surplus value, are simply substitutes for the overstated category of transition, nor is it to gesture toward some form of historicist stagism in disguise. It is, however, a way to reinvest the historical text with the figure of contingency and the unanticipated appearance of conjunctural or aleatory moments. Marx referred to such specific processes in several texts (apparently first in notebooks and in *Grundrisse*)[17] and emphasized the coexistence of different economic practices in certain moments and the continuing persistence of historical temporal forms, rather than merely "remnants," from earlier modes in new historical environments. It should be recognized that this identification of subsumption was first and foremost expressed as form, with diverse manifestations, which often prefigured a specific content and invariably outlasted its moment. Moreover, this reformulation of the labor process was consistent with views that disavowed a unitary model and welcomed the prospect of different routes to national economic development. More important, an accounting of the specific ways that labor has been subsumed in a formal modality opens the way to considering both the historical or epochal dimensions of the mode of production as it restructured the labor process, as well as its contingent direction, but also widens the angle of vision to include the world beyond Western Europe. It should be remembered that Marx repeated, on a number of occasions, that *"formal subsumption"* "is the general form of every capitalist process of production; at the same time, however, it can be found as a *particular* form alongside the *specifically capitalist mode of production in its developed form*, because although the latter entails the former, converse does not necessarily obtain."[18] This was especially true of how formal subsumption behaved in its inaugural moment, in societies where there was no clear differentiation between the domains of economic practice, culture, politics, and even religion, which often were seen as integral to the performance of work in these persisting modes of production. Yet it is possible to acknowledge how practices from the noneconomic realm have continued to be pressed into service of capitalist production in societies in Asia and Africa and are frequently seen as indistinguishable from the enactment of work. But it is also true that Marx envisaged the operation of formal subsumption as an ongoing process, continuing with and alongside the development of capitalism. This predisposition for appropriating what was useful from older modes of production and those at hand conveyed the copresence of primitive accumulation it embodied in some cellular form, as Lenin suggested when he observed that "the labour-service system passes into the capitalist system and merges with it to the extent that it becomes almost impossible to distinguish one from another" in the Russian countryside.[19] The importance of the copresence of both formal subsumption and primitive accumulation in future presents alongside capitalist accumulation relays the vague profile of prior histories that advanced capitalism is pledged to erasing. Rosa Luxemburg hinted at this copresence early, and it constitutes one of the principal arguments of this book.

If Marx showed less interest in the putative "historicity" of precapitalist formations than in the immediacy of the capitalist present, he nevertheless recognized in contemporary instantiations of persisting communal societies the form of archaic society he had outlined in *Grundrisse* and political and economic resources for later development. Far from shifting his own perspective, Marx in the 1860s and after extended and enlarged it to give further substance to offset the effect of the inversion that "spatialized time" and restore the reality of the "temporalization of space."[20] In this broadened scheme of possibilities, the most appropriate figure for development was unevenness and the temporal disorder it is capable of producing. Each present, then, supplies a multiplicity of possible lines of development, as Marx proposed in his draft letters to Vera Zasulich, when he both began to change his mind on historical progress and envisioned the promise of the Russian commune freeing itself gradually from the fetters of primitiveness to promote production on a national scale. Yet "precisely because it is contemporaneous with capitalist production, the rural commune may appropriate all its positive achievements without undergoing its (terrible) frightful vicissitudes." Hence, "everyone would see the commune as the element in the regeneration of Russian society, and an element of superiority over countries enslaved by the capitalist regime." For Marx, the Russian commune confronted a crisis that will end only "when the social system is eliminated through the return of the modern societies to the 'archaic' type of communal property. . . . We should not, then, be too frightened of the word 'archaic.'"[21] What appeared important for Marx was the status of the contemporary coexistence of archaic and modern forms of economic production—their copresence—and the realization that the relocation of an archaic silhouette in the present redefined the surviving residue by stripping it of cultural and economic associations belonging to the mode of production in which it initially existed and originally functioned. I should also suggest the possibility that because subsumption was presented as a form, it could embrace coexisting cultural, political, institutional, and social contents as material embodiments, no longer part of systems in which they originated and set loose from functions they once might have executed to now play new roles in a different configuration. Finally, we must also take into account the different temporal associations represented by these historical-temporal forms and the new mode of production. Actually, these surviving practices from prior modes of production were not "remnants," as such, but rather appeared as historical temporal forms no longer bound to the moment and context in which they had originated, now acting in a different historical environment serving the pursuit of surplus value. Here, Marx was moving toward envisioning plural possibilities for transformation among societies beyond Europe. In this scenario, such societies no longer needed to depend on the pathway marking the moments of capital's ascent in the West mandated by stage theory, especially the overdetermined category of transition. The category of transition, it should be noted, provided this narrative in Europe with a bridge for maintaining a continuous linear development from past to present—a narrative that came to be situated at the center of national history to explain the exceptional evolution of its modern society, thereby supplying a historical *deus ex machina,* so to speak, to explain a linear continuity from origins to completion, past to present. One of its principal problems was the indeterminacy raised by how feudalism dissolved and capitalism emerged, whether certain agents like monarchical and aristocratic ambition worked directly to bring down feudalism in order to secure what actually replaced it, instead of supposing that feudalism collapsed of its own accord (internal contradictions) and the pieces were reconfigured into a new constellation. Behind it lurked a fateful and unyielding binary that upheld a trajectory that successively ran from the premodern to the modern. As far as the specific controversy is concerned, its most important function has been to keep alive the transition yet to come from capitalism to socialism, which may constitute the true vocation of retaining the model of a historicist transformation that marked the end of the medieval and the beginnings of modernity.

In any event, the excluded societies on the periphery were no longer required to replicate the European mode promoted by the colonial experience, as thinkers from the margins of the capitalist world like Rosa Luxemburg recognized in Africa (and Eastern Europe, no doubt) and José Carlos Mariátegui observed of Peru in the 1920s, and could draw on a number of surviving historical temporal forms from earlier modes of production to create a new register of either "formal" or "hybrid" subsumption or bypass capitalism altogether. In one of his earliest essays, "The British Rule in India" (1853), Marx already raised the question of whether mankind could fulfill its destiny without a fundamental revolution in the social state of Asia. If not, he replied, whatever may have been the crimes the British committed, the nation was the unwitting tool of history in bringing about the revolution. But only if Asia fails to do so on its own and from its resources.[22] In this regard, *Grundrisse* was more hopeful and geographically expansive when Marx remarked that "when the limited bourgeois form is stripped away, what is wealth other than the universality of individual needs, capacities, pleasures, productive forces etc. created through universal exchange? . . . The absolute working out of . . . creative potentialities, with no presupposition other than the previous historical development," whereby mankind "strives not to remain something . . . [it] has become, but in the absolute movement of becoming."[23]

With the move of Western Marxism to cultural critique and progressive distancing from the economic for the status of contemporary culture and the regime of consumption came the risk of sacrificing historical capitalism, if not the historical itself, and overlooking the persisting role played by pre-capitalist formations, what Marx called "historical presuppositions," which would show both the historicity of modes of production and how capitalism naturalized its process to efface its own historical emergence. But it also signaled failure to discern in the process of accumulation the possibility of producing distinct configurations based on singular experiences in specific sites. Under these circumstances, the problem of capitalism's genesis passed unnoticed and reverted back to the model of a singular origin in the West. Even though Marx designated England as the "classic form" in explaining the process of production, the model was limited to Western Europe at most and to the idea that changes occur according to particular and different spatial and temporal environments. At the end of his famous chapter "The Secret of So-Called Primitive Accumulation," he located the "first sporadic traces of capitalist production" in the early fourteenth or fifteenth centuries "in certain towns of the Mediterranean," which already opened up the possibility of multiple different origins of capitalism.[24] What he proposed instead was the "restructuring of the labor processes to generate surplus value," which could be secured through the analytic prism provided by the operation of "formal subsumption." The operation of formal subsumption—referring to the encounter of capitalism and received practices at hand, appeared first in the appropriation of labor practices belonging to a prior mode of production, which invariably meant taking on the baggage of older forms of exploitation and resituating them alongside and within newer capitalist demands to create value. Under such circumstances, the older forms of exploitation manifest in the appropriated modes of labor proved to be more than compatible with capitalism. But it would be wrong, as Jairus Banaji has warned, to identify the form of exploitation with the mode of production or automatically assume the coexistence of different modes of production. The operation of formal subsumption set up the temporal structure of every present, through its mission to appropriate what it found useful in prior practices and procedures. If capitalism seeks to establish the force of the value form and achieve a sameness in the commodity relation, it paradoxically also produces the very difference it is trying to eliminate with its propensity to challenge every present with a new content in part derived from the past and the shadowing trace of primitive accumulation. This is what Marx described in *The German Ideology* as the tempo of development that proceeds slowly, "the various stages and interests are never completely overcome, but only subordinated to the prevailing interest," and is retained in the "possession of a traditional power in the illusory community . . . a power which in the last resort can only be broken by a revolution."[25]

In this way, the excluded societies on the periphery were released from the constraint of reproducing the singular narrative attributed to the "classic form" promoted by the colonial experience, even though the colonized could recognize in colonial expropriation a principal agent in the development of capitalism. In fact, the experience of colonial expropriation repeated precisely the initial process by which the nation-form, as a specific territorial unit, was configured and enclosed a specific group and fictionalized into a unified and homogeneous "people" who were now said to belong to it. Moreover, this relationship between the formation of nationhood and colonialism implied the copresence of the latter in the former and the mutual implication of these political forms in the emergence of capitalism. In this regard, "so-called primitive accumulation" was actually coterminous with the construction of the nation-form and colony since they all—primitive accumulation, nation-form, and colony—shared the common impulse of "seizure," "theft," and "capture" that ultimately grounds their kinship and thereby implicates each in the other.[26] The really important feature of Marx's conceptualization of formal subsumption as the principal logic of capitalist development was its capacious aptitude for appropriating what it found near at hand, thus designating a division between what was outside of it, what was seen as "different," and what was inside, and incorporating and combining it with the capitalist production process as if it naturally belonged there, literally metabolizing it in such a way that it was retrojected back and seen as an "always-already" presupposition of capital's claim to a natural history. The actual process of what Marx described as capital's "becoming" consistently required absorbing these outside, noncapitalist elements and making them part of its metabolic system, which, in every phase of development, would present itself as completed and identical with its origins. I shall say more about this process when I turn to the way Marx envisioned this process, but it should be said here that I will also be interested in following this particular trajectory in diverse thinkers like V. I. Lenin, Rosa Luxemburg, Antonio Gramsci, José Carlos Mariátegui, Wang Yanan, Uno Kōzō, and, down to our present, Jairus Banaji and a number of others from South Asia and Africa, who shared a ground based on seeing through the logic of capitalist development in the process of production that brought together received practices from different pasts at different times with the new forces of capitalism in the establishment of the wage labor form and the inversion of use-value into exchange-value. For when Marx advised a fusion of the archaic Russian commune and capital, or when Lenin acknowledged the capitalist nature of medieval village handcraft production in Russia, followed by Luxemburg's call for combining noncapitalism with capitalist accumulation, her insistence on the necessity of capital to rely on noncapitalism to achieve expanded reproduction, Gramsci's recommendation to join Italy's northern industry and the South's semifeudal agriculture, Mariátegui's identification of Inca communalism, Spanish feudalism, and modern capitalist elements as coexisting in Peru, and more, we have, I believe, instances of how these historical temporal forms retained from prior modes of production behaved in the new temporal environment once they encountered capitalism, how the logic of development was virtually thought through and made manifest in different ways and circumstances, incorporated as if they naturally belonged to capital's internal mechanism and its operations. I should also add in this connection that all those present-day declarations attesting to an exceptionalist capitalism, such as "Japanese-style" capitalism, "Confucian capitalism," and "Indian capitalism," self-promoting and overstated, reveal the trace of this process whereby the development of capitalist production encounters and appropriates what it finds nearest at hand. Moreover, we must not forget that in the development of capitalism in diverse regions of the world, capitalism itself, with the nation-state form serving as its placeholder, often "re-created" these surviving residues.

It should be pointed out at this juncture that most of our social theory, dedicated to defining the modern or modernity, has been cast into opposing polarities and thus based on making a clean separation between two competing representations of the social. Starting with Ferdinand Tönnies's classic division of the dyad of "community" (*Gemeinschaft*) and "society" (*Gesellschaft*), there have been Emile Durkheim's "mechanical" and "organic" solidarity, Max Weber's formulation of a relationship of a means/end rationality grounded in a singular (as against other) religio-cultural endowment, Gabriel Tarde's conception of a socialization founded on lower-class imitation of the upper classes, Georg Simmel's belief in the central importance of interaction, Talcott Parsons's privileging of greater differentiation, and especially the coupling of modernity and tradition as the foundation of a theory of modernization he formulated with Edward Shils. What these and other theorists of the social aimed to accomplish was an intellectual and research agenda that would make society work better by devising forms of socialization to secure greater coherence among populations as a hedge against the recurrence of conflict and disruption. All these theories of the social and more were thus designed to separate the modern—actually the capitalist present—from precapitalism, the premodern, implying a progressive linear trajectory from one less developed and founded on different principles to a more advanced stage of achievement which even Marxists of a certain stripe have shared in their charting of the "transition" from feudalism to capitalism. Yet the emphasis on the transition to capitalism implied that once the trajectory had completed its course, capitalism and its social formation had been achieved and the state of "real subsumption" realized. The consequences of this strategy have been overlooked and have thus resulted in displacing any real consideration of the kind of society that supposedly was produced once the transition had ended. Ever since Luxemburg put into question the completion of real subsumption by suggesting it was nothing more than a heuristic device Marx employed to totalize capitalism, thinkers outside of Euro-America have, in one way or another, underscored a conception of the social that embodied an uneven mix of practices of prior modes of production alongside the newer innovations of capitalism, even though they occupied a subordinate position in this new society. This was surely the meaning of Uno Kōzō's conceptualization of "late development," as we shall see, Gramsci's political recoding of formal subsumption into the concept of "passive revolution," and Mariátegui's original formulation of contemporaneous noncontemporaneity (expressing synchronous nonsynchronicity) into a palimpsest-like paradigm for both Peru and the whole of Latin America, to name the more obvious examples of this intellectual direction. But Marx, it is well to repeat, with his meditations on formal subsumption as the general rule of all capitalist development, provided a glimpse of a conception of the social that embraced both the forms of the past and the present, precapitalist residues—what he named "historical presuppositions"—and capitalism at the same moment in a continuing dialectical encounter with forms and temporalities that have reached down to our present. In this sense, the conception of the social implied has always been open, incomplete, and exempt from the constraints imposed by binary polarities and its fixed boundaries. Why this orientation appeared more pronounced in societies outside of Euro-America than in the "heartland of capitalism," and why the latter cleaved to the promise offered by a clean separation from the "enchantments" of the precapitalist past for the uninterrupted rewards of a progressive modernity, are the central questions that need to be addressed. This tectonic shift was accompanied by the surety offered by a one-way transitional bridge and the promise of undisturbed and unwanted intrusions and reminders from beyond the modern present, reinforced by the conceits of affirming conceptions of social science. Part of the problem derived from the impulses of modernist and modernization ideologies and the trompe l'oeil imaginary of a progressive future, what Marx earlier called the "illusory community," projected on the present to displace the immense unevenness capitalism was ceaselessly dedicated to producing everywhere it established its dominion. It is the argument of this book that the production of unevenness, like capitalism's organization of the workday, was empowered to act as an agent disposing people into disciplined routines, creating the occasions for animating political events and action. Beyond that, it might additionally

be suggested that the experience of the interaction of "lateness" and necessity of living through more intensely and consciously the spectacle of unevenness early persuaded societies like Japan to recognize that they were
being forced to live comparatively. Marx's description of the results of this
logic of development was closer to what Etienne Balibar much later described
as permanent transition.

There are several reason behind this reading to see a completed capitalism, which, again, Marxists have also reflected in their impatient desire for
the accomplishment of real subsumption. What this dialectic produced has
been great unevenness not always observed by the enthusiasts of a completed
modernity and capitalism. Yet we must recognize in Marx's observations on
the general form of capitalist development, whereby "capital proper does
nothing but bring together the mass of hands and instruments which it
finds on hand" and "agglomerates them under its command,"[27] that its practical application outlined the silhouette of a conception of the social founded
on the ceaseless dialectical interaction of capitalism's appropriation of what
it was able to utilize from the received past by incorporating it as the constant demonstration of the past acting in the present. This image of a social
constituted of the interaction of pasts and presents stands in marked contrast to a good deal of subsequent social theory that has sought to deliber-
ately separate the present from the past. Much of this theorizing on the social, with its implications for implementing an instrumental social science,
was also a response to the combined emergence of capitalism in the nineteenth century and Marx's own critique of it. In fact, much of it, in one way
or another, valorized capitalism and its social formation and sought to en-
visage a countercritique against the Marxian alternative, especially the role
it apparently accorded to a conflict theory of change leading to revolutionary
transformation. At the same time this modernist theory of the social relied
on Marx's privileging of the present as the principal object of analysis. However, it sought to free itself from this reliance over its attempt to dismiss the
past and, by implication, the position of history. Marx and Engels, as early as
The German Ideology, had already proposed that the past, as such, does not
necessarily lead to the present or constitute its cause; at the same time, this
new historical perspective opened the path to the past that is constantly
seen as mingling with the present, depositing in every present its residual
traces that embodied untimely temporalities announcing their unevenness

and difference. This is the juncture from which a good deal of social theory has made its point of departure in the quest to chart a course capable of circumventing the past itself as the source of enduring problems. In this effort, the aim has been to liberate the capitalist present from suffering any longer from the encumbrances of the dead. In this sense, social theory converged with the formation of the modern nation-form in its distrust of history and the challenging spectacle of unscheduled untimeliness.

Modern social theory has not only desired to separate present from the contaminations of the historical past by definitively delinking them in good modernist fashion, inasmuch as the capitalist present was recognized as having already absorbed its antecedents. Appealing to a binary logic of oppositions like modern and premodern, advanced and backward, rational and unrational, even geographical differentiations between West and East, the constraint of this dyadic organization made it obligatory to consider the past as a historical continent that the modern present was now required to sever itself from and eliminate since there could be no adulterated mixing or lingering signs of a surviving past. The reminder of such remainders would immediately be seen as an interference of (or a retrograde contradiction to) the modern or capitalism. One way to prevent the "contagion'" of history from creeping into the modern present was to see it—the present—and its nonmodern other—the past—as belonging to different temporal registers, even though they might paradoxically be immanent to each other or simply chronologically copresent. In this regard, modern social theory and its translation into an operational social science seemed excessively eager to keep the present remote and immune from the historical contamination posed by the past.

Marx's conception of capitalism's general form of development—the logic of formal subsumption—had no trouble supplying capital with its true but forgotten history, which dramatized the constant interaction of coexisting times and practices in a ceaseless process that might lead to the final realization of capital but probably not everywhere. Rather, it projected an idealized vision where the modern social exceeds its antecedent historical other in such a way as to make the capitalist present appear timeless, eternal. Even Max Weber, whose conception of social science appeared to be steeped in history and the primacy of historical development, proposed that the "ideal type," his leading methodological organizing principle, was a heuristic device *of* history but not necessarily found *in* history, as a way of purifying the historical and thus acting as a form of phenomenological bracketing. Social theorists like Durkheim and Tarde through Parsons and Alfred Schütz had no interest in history, as such, nor did Simmel in his sociological work, concerned increasingly with lasting cultural form, on the one hand, and microcosmic sociological interactions and differentiation that signaled "sociation" (*Vergesellschaftung*), on the other, while Tönnies's paradigmatic division of "community" and "society" constituted merely the imaginary of an idealized typology. Freud was perhaps one of the very few theorists who conceived of the social based on the constant intrusion of a personal past in the present. But in most cases, modern social theory and its subsequent transmutation into an operational social science appeared inimical to the historical, if not outright hostile to the past, as well as to any conception that saw the modern present as a heterogeneous and uneven mixture of pasts and presents. It is interesting to note that even among Marxists, a theory of the social that comprised an intricate and changing mixture of past and presents at any given moment in the capitalist epoch still remains as a recessive but unattended vocation of historical materialism.

What the appeal to Marx's conceptualization of formal subsumption offers is a way out of both the vulgate Marxian and modernizing bourgeois historical narratives constrained to fulfilling teleologically determined agendas of capitalism that have claimed the unfolding of a singular trajectory everywhere. Such a perspective requires us to take into account the accompanying demand in seeing the "effectivity" of practices and institutions and the role played by uneven temporalities produced by incorporating and metabolizing pasts in the present. In this regard, the plural instances of how the logic of development was thought through and mediated by close considerations of received historical circumstances and contemporary local conditions disclosed the possible shape of a world history Marx had earlier announced that was yet to be written. The very unevenness shared by different presents put into question the illusory claim of capitalism's inevitable completion everywhere and its claims to sameness and supplied inducements to consider instances attesting to successful resistances to the prevailing forms of capitalism beyond Euro-America. Attention to the different ways capitalism developed in singular and specific sites and times affirms Marx's decision to privilege the global theater reflected in the formation of the world market as the principal organizing principle in envisioning any possible world history. Examining the differences denoted by different histories, as Kyoto philosophers proposed before World War II, and the uneven combinations of capitalist and precapitalist remainders demanded taking into account their singular and specific stories, whose meanings escaped the contaminations of "history's reason" to restore contingency back to the historical text. If capitalism failed to completely control the uneven mix, the practices and institutions embodying the different historical temporalities it retained from the past to serve the pursuit of value, it was because it needed to produce unevenness as a condition of its own continuing condition.

In this study I am concerned with examining only selected individual texts of thinkers and authors instead of trying to provide comprehensive accounts of their collected works. I make no claim for archival authority and the ambition to provide in this account a definitive comprehensiveness encompassing the lives and thinking of the people I have chosen. My purpose has been to show how each, working within the "constraints" and historical necessity of their time and place, produced analyses of their current situation as they sought to chart the prospect of capitalist development as it was specifically mediated by received historical circumstances. Each case discloses a similar but different relationship between the molar and molecular, which invariably reveals how the individual work was able to play the double role of text and context, background and foreground. Yet, at the same time, the collectivity of cases constitutes a possible intimation of the kind of world history Marx imagined when he repudiated Hegel's universalistic philosophy of history: "this transformation of history into world history is by no means an abstract act on the part of 'self-consciousness,' the world-spirit, or of any other metaphysical spectre, but a quite material empirically verifiable act . . . the proof of which every individual furnishes as he comes and goes, eats, drinks and clothes himself."[28] At all times, the individual cases examined reveal the extent to which each individual operated at a local level of being that provided the perspective to realize the "being" of an empirical "world historical existence."[29]

1

MARX, TIME, HISTORY

An often acknowledged paradox of historical practice, whose knowledge has been organized according to categories denoting time and its passage from a "before" to an "after," is how little interest it has shown in actually addressing the question of time and temporality itself and its status in constructing the "historical field." Fernand Braudel's conceptual panorama was an obvious exception, with his successive three-tiered levels of time denoting long durations resembling the glacial movement of geological formations, an "unaltering history," a history of "gentle rhythms," another name for the broader conception of conjuncture, and, lastly, the history of events, whose movement followed a progressive narrowing. Another historian is Reinhart Koselleck, who proposed "temporal levels" (*Zeitschichten*) that followed the stratifications of geologic epochs, which he wanted to differentiate from nature, lying on top of one another to constitute the figure of a palimpsest, inasmuch as the layers signified different durations that remain visible and contemporary to each other that escape the succession of a simple, singular, linear trajectory.[1] Koselleck's "levels" resembled the philosopher Watsuji Tetsurō's "stadialized" pasts (*jūsōsei*), stratigraphic layers imposed on each other representing a vertically organized inventory of past epochal traces, even though their direction appears progressive.[2] While Braudel's temporalities were graded according to scale, from the historical movements resembling large and slow-moving geological structures down to the singular event, Koselleck's temporal levels opened the possibility of nonsynchronous synchronicities, different times coexisting with one another in the same present, rather than a pyramidal hierarchy of levels. Be that as it may, sensitivity expressed by historians toward the temporal dimensions of history rarely exceeds the abstract measuring of time and its quantification in chronology, the marking of calendar time and the passage from one day to the next, contrasting dramatically with the commitment of philosophy, which, since Henri Bergson's and Martin Heidegger's project promising a "reckoning with time," had already embarked on a search for the forms of qualitative time. While this philosophical intervention has rarely assessed the relationship between time and capitalism (and thus history), more recent signs of interest have sought to make philosophy answerable to history and vice versa. This has entailed confronting the central role occupied by capitalism as the temporal dominant of modern society and thereby the need to address the effects of its structuring of time on history and politics. Such efforts invariably have converged on the incontrovertible observation that capitalism itself is, among other things, an immense conceptual organization of time that seeks to regulate and thus dominate a system of "social metabolic" control capable of penetrating every aspect of society.[3] In fact, this view matches precisely the contemporary experience of capitalism as an all-encompassing temporal rhythmology dedicated to ordering the differing tempos of time with an unrelenting and inescapable circularity, which, accordingly, has truncated history itself, if not bracketing it altogether, and appears now to constitute "the exclusive material of the construction of life."[4] Capital's logic thus points to "annihilating" history because it is posited on the eternality of the present, as Marx himself had observed regarding the "religion" of bourgeois political economy and its claims to have no history.

The historian's indifference toward the problem of time, especially its agental aptitude, validates Jacques Rancière's observation that judgments like charges of anachronism reflect a misrecognition because the question of historical time is a philosophic one and cannot be resolved as if it were reducible to the methodology or epistemology of history. Moreover, the charge of anachronism constitutes a political dismissal of any expression of time that does not correspond to the order of a linear chronology since it belongs to another time to represent time out of joint. The identification of anachronism itself may well signal the fear of coexisting temporalities in a present pledged to obeying the rhythms of social normative time. For Rancière, the knotted question posed between the present of historical enunciation and the past it seeks to rescue concerns not a Rankean fidelity to the idea of reality that conformed to the "way things were" but rather the status of the present's priority as the locus of history's representation. In a sense, this move resembles Gilles Deleuze's earlier proposal that both past and future are dimensions of the present tense. Yet even before, Georg Simmel had already perceived how the present under capitalism had virtually been "ontologized," while Marx saw in it the housing of a vast, heterogeneous inventory and "conjuncture" of temporalities no longer stigmatized for having been cast out of time but rather as expressions of contretemps, simultaneous nonsimultaneities (*Gleichzeitigkeit und Ungleichzeitigkeit*), contemporaneous noncontemporaneities or uneven times, and *zeitwidrig*, time's turmoil, times out of joint, multiple temporalities, in other words, instances of *multiversum* testifying to untimeliness itself fully immanent to what constitutes normative social time. The supposed unity of time projected by capital and nation-state is a masquerade that invariably fails to conceal the ceaseless confrontation of different times. For Marx, these were instances of how time, or temporality, temporalized itself in the present, beginning with the process of production and reproduction where the colliding patterns of unevenness generated untimeliness and political struggle.[5] In his own histories like *The Class Struggles in France* and *The Eighteenth Brumaire of Louis Bonaparte*, Marx saw not only that the immediate present was the locus of history, one that, according to Engels, appeared to be unfolding before his eyes, but that political disruptions invariably introduced associations of prior pasts in the contemporary context to jar the presumed stability and "tranquility" of normative social time. In this connection, it became evident that the past could not lay claim to the identity of being historical in itself but rather acquires this status through the mediation of the present. Nor is it, as a result of this bonding to the present, a horizontal perspective, moving from a point of departure (origin) to its place of arrival (completion), since the location of the present is never fixed. Instead, a history derived from the present inclines toward verticality and its appearance is always changeable, brought to the surface by excavating and digging into the layered depths of different historical times, which are never completely lost. Marx was, I believe, the first to see and record the experience of the past as constantly intruding in the lived present, thus persuading him of the necessity of negotiating the multiple temporalities of non-contemporaneity individuals must always confront in their daily lives. This is, in effect, the point of his announcement in the preface to the first volume of *Capital* that "we suffer not only from the development of capitalist production, but also from the incompleteness of that development. Alongside the modern evils, we are oppressed by a whole series of inherited evils, arising from the passive survival of archaic and outmoded modes of production, with their accompanying train of anachronistic social and political relations. We suffer not only from the living, but from the dead. *Le mort saisit le vif!*"[6] This collision of times was dismissed as a vast jumble by Claude Lévi-Strauss but valorized by Louis Althusser as instantiating how different temporalities of semiautonomous domains of what he called the social formation momentarily coagulate into a conjunctural unity, thus providing the nation, driven by the necessity to standardize time by synchronizing it to eliminate the scandal of plural temporalities, with its principal vocation to singularize time into a coherent narrative or story line that was both completed and timeless.[7] It is an interesting paradox that while most history is uneven and unequal, according to Samir Amin, the historical narratives of diverse nations have rarely, if ever, recognized this disparity within their own historiographical borders.

In *Capital*, especially, Marx showed that changing the world required grasping the nature of the temporal dominant ushering in the new, modern era everywhere—the circumstances of the transformative force of capitalism that established the permanence and the primacy of the present as a temporal tense and with it the hegemony of a vast conceptual organization of time deposited and embodied in forms empowered to act as agents capable of reconfiguring the historical field. This reconfiguration resulted in an active erasure of capitalism's own prehistory by accelerating the process of forgetting itself through enacting the task of normalization demanded by the new mode of production that followed a rhythm of repetition. As for the act of forgetting an earlier history of violence, incorporating it within capitalism, Marx reported that it presumably attended the emergence of the capitalist mode of production. Eventually, this history was realized by homologizing the categorial structure of capitalism with Hegel's logic and its preoccupa-

tion with the primacy of forms, bracketing empirical history and presenting the order of categories synchronically. Consequently, this operation underscored the privilege accorded to the present without a past, as such, and
projected a virtual history of and by itself, all reflecting a logic of inversion
that proceeded from abstraction to the concrete, consciousness and reason's
self-activity to history. Yet the history it projected is "virtual" and is one that
must be written according to capitalism's viewpoint, "as a *given* totality retro-
jecting its interior moments in the past." Such a history, moreover, "is both
logically implicit and historically ungrounded and is evident from the hy-
pothetical nature of the language Marx used in discussing it."[8]

Marx's *Capital* is still the most detailed accounting of capital's structure
of abstract temporality, presenting itself as a natural, ordinary time, world
time, whose notice has even escaped the practice of historical materialism
at risk of "dilut[ing]" its conception of history.[9] Georgio Agamben was
referring to how this neglect forced a vulgate version of historical materialism to adopt a linear and homogeneous conception of time alongside a revolutionary concept of history, constraining events to a development along
infinite time progressing toward some distant future. In *Capital*, time is
divided among production, circulation, and reproduction: the time of production, abstract, measureable, divisible, is linear; circulation relates to the
rotation of value, is circular or cyclical; and reproduction consists of an organic union of production and circulation, reproducing them repetitively
but always with a difference.[10] While these temporalities of capitalism constitute different moments in capitalism's operations, they are necessarily
synchronized—a process that is ultimately guaranteed by the state. Despite
the synchronisms linking them into a homogeneous unity, collision and crisis are always possible and punctually probable. In this scheme, there is no
apparent separation between the immanent abstract logic and economic
rationality at work in capitalism and history, ensuring the outcome of a
reciprocal relationship and a shared narrative. If history were subordinated
to capital logic and its temporality designated to serve as a placeholder for
unilinear time, then the meaning of history could not be separated from
capitalism. The abstract logic and economic rationality is realized in concrete historical forms, economic and political institutions, which periodically enter into crisis that exceed all bounds, syncopating history and directing it. By the same token, history is not a predetermined destiny in such

instances since the great crises constitute interruptions of its homogeneous accountancy of (clock) time to produce moments of probability and even possibility.[11] When such critical episodes interrupt the homogeneity of normal social time, historical time is released, in the form of political change, and appears as a distinct temporality. "Capital," according to Massimiliano Tomba, "marks the rhythm of history in structural and tendential terms. But this temporality is abstract until it encounters the historical counter temporalities of the class-struggle. The historical time that results from it is flowing and contingent."[12] In this regard, it often assumes the form of a figure from the past now activated in the present that confers historical status on it but also announces the "presence" of the past in the present.[13]

What lies at the core of this relationship between capital's abstract logic and history is the bonding supplied by formal subsumption—capitalism's rule of development—and its inexhaustible capacity to make history by joining what it takes over or appropriates for use and combining with it the new. Above all else, it should be stated at the outset that the rule of formal subsumption was a temporal category that performed as a form bound to neither a specific time nor place, which, through its protean capacity to appropriate from the past what it found useful to capitalism, constantly introduced practices that embodied past times in every present. It was capital's logic that made possible history, as we know it, and defined the relationship between itself and the past. It occurred at the point when capitalism's abstract logic entered a received history and began altering and directing it on a new course, which produced uneven temporalities along every step of the way but sought to conceal it by implanting homogeneous time as the measure of capital's progressive vocation. This process, constituting the central thematic of this book, results in combining presents with past, fusing a capitalist system of production with what has been appropriated from prior practices that are at hand. But what is often overlooked in such considerations that call attention to the contemporizing of pasts is the temporal incommensurability such a maneuver frequently entails and the tension and discordance it is capable of producing that is difficult to overcome. It seems to me that this was a crucial but unnoticed problem in all those earlier Marxist tactical controversies that sought to align peasants, living under semifeudal conditions belonging more to medieval agricultural life than modernity, to industrial workers, without considering the different temporal regimes characterizing and separating each. It was even truer of the encounter of industrial capitalism and the victims of colonial seizure.

In view of this relationship among capitalism, history, and time, there are, for our purposes, two related and mutually intertwined aspects of this temporal dominant of the present that we need to look at more closely: the separation or differentiation of history from capital logic and its temporal demands and, conversely, the problem of historical time in capitalism. I will be concerned with the role Marx assigned to the historicity of precapitalist formations and the appearance of capitalism as a conceptual organization of time, an active rationality, the idea of the immediate and what Marx often described as "abstraction in *actu*," whereby capital becomes the logic of its own history.[14] As for the former, the production of historical time that remained external to capitalism, Marx described it as a process "lying behind the system," behind its "becoming" that also coexisted alongside of it and is external to it. What seems important is how history, before the emergence of capitalism, is externalized, positioned behind the system and, in some cases, alongside it, which was the way it functioned in late developing and colonial societies. In *Theories of Surplus Value*, Marx explained this history that lies behind and remained external to capitalism, and how *antecedents* from past practices are taken over and subjected to capital. "In the course of its evolution, industrial capital must . . . subjugate these [older] forms and transform them into derived or special functions of itself. It encounters these older forms in the epoch of its formation and development, it encounters them as *antecedents*, but not as antecedents established by itself, not as forms of its own life process."[15] As early as *The German Ideology* (1845), he and Engels were already on record for having proposed that "the various stages (of history) and interests are never completely overcome, but only subordinated to the prevailing interest." While these practices of the past functioned as antecedents, Marx insisted they were not antecedents to capital's life process. They were antecedents belonging to another history and social process. In *Grundrisse*, these antecedents were interchangeable with what Marx called suspended historical presuppositions to capital. The history of such presuppositions could not have been prior to the development of capitalism but were produced by it, which only meant that they became historical presuppositions from the perspective of a later capitalism. Marx, in his accounting of both precapitalist formations and primitive accumulation, shows how the order of history follows the order of the present and its determination of historical necessity, where structure precedes history and event. This particular decision undoubtedly stemmed from the conviction that if the past could be known at all, access to it yielded only a partial knowledge that was secured through the mediation of the capitalist present. What Marx implied was the existence of a wide cleft separating the capitalist present from its prior past, which, for the most part, was not immediately accessible. Capitalism, and the great separation leading from communal ownership to the sale of labor power, stood as the barrier that blocked access to a past that could only be refracted through the prism provided by capitalism. Marx's writing ceaselessly asserted the primacy of the present and privileged perspective it supplies from which to understand the past. Just as the categories of bourgeois society express the relations and the comprehension of its structure, thereby allowing "insights unto the structure and the relations of production of all the vanished social formations out of whose ruins and elements it built itself up, whose partly still unconquered remnants are carried along within it, whose mere nuances have developed significance within it, etc.," so too "human anatomy contains the key to the anatomy of the apes." But the higher development among subordinate animal species can be known only after the higher development is understood. "The bourgeois economy thus supplies the key to the ancient etc."[16] In this sense, the antecedents and historical presuppositions Marx identified as lying behind the system and outside of it were fixed or seen from the standpoint of capitalism, not from its putative prior past. This procedure permitted Marx to avoid and even bypass the presumption of a causal relationship between a before and an after.

In the scenario of capitalism, what happened historically before actually came after. Much of this reversal derived from the conceit of political economy to posit the eternality and natural character of capitalism, its ahistoricity. By arguing that capitalism and its temporal regime both blocked access to the past yet provided a perspective for rescuing some portion of it, Marx was putting forth a new conception of historical construction, where following the "path of abstract thought, rising from the simple to the combined, would correspond to the real historical progress."[17] Hence only the present was in a position to determine its necessary historical presuppositions and antecedents, to define the historical before capitalism as lying behind it at some distance, external to it, and antecedent to the moment when it began to make history. Through the operation of the logic of formal subsumption, the past was constantly chosen and history constructed.

In the process of subjugating older practices and institutions to capitalism, it was not always the case that it was free from tensions produced by attempts to efface their historical identity and incorporate them. There was always the possibility that practices taken over from prior forms of production would manage, in one way or another, to retain their historical identities, even as they were synchronized according to capitalism's system of time accountancy and put into the service of its process of production. This was especially true since the process of combining invariably generated forms of temporal unevenness where older practices appeared alongside newer ones, signifying the difference between what represented the "becoming" from the "being" of capitalism. In this book I will be principally concerned with how the formal logic of appropriation acted as the connecting hinge between every present and past it chose to use, a process that resulted in generating a constantly changing historical landscape. This was the route of capital's historical "becoming," disclosing how the interaction between the appropriation of what was at hand with capital's logic produced the "being" of everyday life as a repository that would continue to embody these unwanted and uneven temporalities. In itself this, too, was a historical event of enormous and lasting consequences that apparently started simply: *"Capital proper does nothing but bring together the mass of hands and instruments which it finds on hand. It agglomerates them under its command,"* Marx wrote in *Grundrisse*, and this "bringing together" constitutes nothing more than a *"stockpiling"* of workers and instruments.[18] While this encounter—the bringing together and stockpiling— may have resulted in a momentary synchronism, it was ultimately an appropriation driven by dialectical interaction, producing a history of forms of unevenness, since what was being taken over belonged to and embodied the historicity of another time and experience. In one sense the old was invariably overcome but reappeared in new relationships and configurations. These appropriated remnants are brought into a new present without any apparent obligation to satisfy the scheduled requirements of the "inevitable" transition from a noncommodity society to capitalism, the dream of orthodox Marxists, who were never able to leave Europe, and the target of rejection by later postcolonialists who wished to account for the presence of precapitalist elements in capitalism by according to it the permanence reserved for culture itself, from which it was indistinguishable.

The process of producing history that led to the formation of new capitalist everydayness as a principal temporal unit was hinted at by Marx in *The Eighteenth Brumaire of Louis Bonaparte*. It was in this contemporary history where he inaugurated a practice of historical materialism that was bonded less to the promotion of another narrative than to "breaking with the form of its representation"[19] and intervening in a particular present by rewriting the past and releasing its revolutionary potential for the current class struggle. Even though this perspective on history sought to reflect the formation of a new present mediated by capitalism's own presuppositions and produced by it, it was probably a premature expectation. As Marx reminds us in this text, it was still marked by the presence of unevenness, as such, rather than with the struggle over the everyday as a primary temporal unit of the capitalist social. Apart from the anticipated repetition of "farce" represented by the nephew, what else was Marx pointing to when he declared in the opening passages: "The tradition of all the dead generations weighs like a nightmare on the brains of the living. And just as they seem to be occupied with revolutionizing themselves, creating something that did not exist before precisely in such epochs of revolutionary crisis, they anxiously conjure up the spirits of the past to their service, borrowing from their names battle slogans and costumes in order to present this new scene in world history in time honored disguise and borrowed language." The manifestation of such uncertainty, relying on exemplars recruited from the past now fitted to function in a new present yet disguising its newness, signaled a pervasive unevenness disturbing the calm surface of everyday life to stir up the spectacle of unscheduled disruptions, interruptions, discordance, contretemps—the world of "time's turmoil," symptomizing the fractious heterogeneity of the capitalist social that would constitute the source of history. Marx explained how recalling the past in the present worked: "Thus the awakening of the dead in those revolutions served the purpose of glorifying the new struggle, not of parodying the old, of magnifying the given task in imagination, not of fleeing from its solution in reality; of finding once more the spirit of revolution, not of making its ghost walk about again."[20] The "ghost of the old evolutions" was the lasting legacy left to Louis Bonaparte.

Since the everyday was reconfigured as the remainder left over by the formation and establishment of the workday, offering what Marx identified as "disposable time" to be used for the general improvement of the worker, the resulting clashes were driven by attempts to determine the length of the workday. In time, the everyday, which contained both workday and the time of nonwork, would provide a challenging alternative source of historical experience to a narrative dedicated to bonding nation and capitalism and the macro structures of modernity and its institutions stubbornly dedicated to subsuming individual identities. The difference came down to a collision between it and a fundamentally temporal everyday—the daily struggles and negotiations of life and work to get through the hours of the day marking the time of individual lives, still mediated by the past and what Pierre Macherey has called the "small nothings,"[21] and the overbearingly and towering nation-state form, which claimed for itself a timeless spatial countenance and sought to cast an eclipse over what lay below it from its distance and height.

This brings us back to taking into account the conditions explaining how Marx envisioned the historical process involved in capitalism's "becoming" and why historical time embodied in antecedents was deposited "behind" the system, occupying both a spatial and temporal registers to form a new chronotope. In fact, we must recognize that Marx had already proposed at least two different conceptions of history in the organization of volume 1 of *Capital* when he began with an examination of the completed commodity form, the result of a process as the starting point of capital that appeared to have no history and then later turned to an accounting of "primitive" or "so-called original accumulation" and the supposed history taking place during the circulation or merchant phase of capital marking the dissolution of feudalism that announced the beginnings of capitalism.[22]

But starting from the commodity rather than its concept meant also that one must start from the present rather than the past. Such a tactic might induce closer attention to those attempts that insist on emphasizing the philosophical over the historical, even after Marx had settled accounts with Young Hegelians and abandoned philosophy. Such a move would turn to the concrete, signifying use-value to disclose how the sensuous acts as the bearer of the supersensuous, that is, of abstract exchange-value. And it is precisely this "tension" between capital's abstract categories and the materiality of contemporary history unfolding in government reports concerning workers' conditions conveyed in *Capital*'s great chapter "The Working Day" and their attendant struggles Marx recounted in his theoretical elaborations. The tension shows that the structure of capitalism is not reducible to a "categorical beginning" but instead constitutes a constant mixing of the historical material and the conceptual expositions from the start, which points to incommensurate temporalities.[23]

The commodity form constituted the condensed abstraction of the developed system, the "cell-form," that would structure the subsequent operation of capitalism up to the realization of surplus value, totalized in "real subsumption" or capital's completion. Just as there was an apparent absence of a visible history recounting the development of the commodity form, so it is important to notice the nonattendance of history in his accounting of this production process. This discussion appears to have no visible history, yet we must assume that such a history was implied by the fact of its own completed achievement and its capacity to bracket empirical facticity for the appearance of its form. The force of abstract form capable of excluding traces of precapitalist formations enables the commodity to appear as *"the necessary universal social form* of the product" and the value form of the commodity to become "a concretely universal determination."[24] Toward the end of volume I, Marx thus embarks on the task of providing a history or, recalling *Grundrisse*, laying down the "historical presuppositions" of the processes by which capital was made possible, even though they would play no role in its later contemporary manifestation. This presupposition was the accessibility of wealth produced not by capitalism but by the precapitalist formation, such as feudalism or other tributary forms of political domination.

Jason Read has provocatively proposed that the first starting point—the commodity form—"assumes what the second (the history of original accumulation) puts into question by historicizing the commodification of labor itself."[25] If the commodity form is presented in its abstract completion devoid of a history, original accumulation is supposed to make fully visible the history of violence, bloodshed, and massive displacement of the population from their means of subsistence that ultimately accounts for capitalism's appearance. While sixteenth-century England surely qualifies as having a monarchical politics embedded in violence and bloodshed, it is not certain whether this constituted the dissolution of feudalism, as such, and/or the origins of capitalism, primarily because these periodizing markers are simply not known. With the commodity form, we have the itinerary of its logical progression to surplus value and the process whereby labor power's commodification is quantitatively bonded to its realization.[26] But this image of the commodity form already reveals not its completion, as supposed by later proponents who believed in the achievement of real subsumption, but only the depth of Marx's need to see it in the image of a completed totality as the means of grasping the whole of capitalism itself. What appears absent here is the history that constituted labor as a commodity in the first place, what Uno Kōzō described as "contingency" (*muri*, literally, "without reason," "unrational"), whereas Marx's accounting of the "bloody legislation" and massive dislocations and punishments in the epochal transformation (the "separation," as described in *Grundrisse*) inflicted by the state on the population discloses the historical circumstances implicated in transmuting peasants into "free laborers" who now had nothing more than their labor power to sell for wages in order to manage their own subsistence.[27] It is interesting to note that Marx seems to have abandoned the order of normal causality to show first the "invisible real structures" that put into place the social formation, which, accordingly, would open the way to envisioning both "genesis" and "evolution." What appeared to be at the center of Marx's theory is the distinction between a developed object—its "being"—and one that is still developing—its "becoming"—which means that the developed structure is really distant from the history out of which it apparently evolved. Hence the act of reconstituting an ideal form was immensely different from the real history it supposedly authorized. In this theoretical scenario, Marx's imaging of an "ideal genesis" allowed a division of origins into the concepts of structure and history, whereby the former presupposes the latter.[28] "The inversion of the relation between the logical order and historical order" becomes manifest when commercial capital, which originally fixes prices and is the sphere of circulation that mediates production in which "the falling rate of profit is . . . formed" and constitutes the starting point (presupposition) of the genesis of capitalism, is made a historical function of capital once it has developed. "It thus appears as a "historical form" of capital before capital actualized production.[29] "In the course of scientific analysis, the formation of the general rate of profit appears to proceed from industrial capitals. . . .

In the course of historical development, the situation is exactly the reverse." Moreover, Marx continued, "in the course of our investigation, we shall find that both merchants' capital and interest-bearing capital are derivative forms, and at the same time it will be clear why, historically, these two forms appear before the modern primary form of capital."[30] Here, Marx explicitly proposes how historically derivative forms are utilized by capital and how the appropriation reassigns them a function according to capital's logic rather than history. While this may represent an effort to dehistoricize these derivatives or displace their historical associations by providing them a logical identity, they still remain historical temporal forms capable of retaining traces of their originating moment. This was especially true of those derivatives appropriated from the noneconomic spheres.

Yet once the inversion takes place, the logical order of capital automatically takes precedence and circulation is stripped of its claims to historical genesis. By concentrating on the ideal form, fixing the precedent of the completed abstract form as the distant product of a prior historical moment filled with violence and trauma, the latter passes into invisibility through a long process of forgetting resulting from the normalization (abstracting) of productive relationships. Indeed, Marx wrote, "by the nineteenth century, the very memory of the connection between the agricultural labourer and communal property had . . . vanished."[31] This is what Massimiliano Tomba named as the ultimate effect of capitalism's "phantasmagoric" process that privileges value over the labor process that produces it. The importance of this forgetfulness is that it made the English example paradigmatic to latecomers who, excepting Uno Kōzō, perceived in Japan's late development a trajectory that had no need to follow the English precedent, which was already three hundred years in the past and historically no longer relevant. Regardless, that history appears nowhere inscribed on the abstract commodity form and cannot be seen as a simple causal agent. Moreover, the reversal infers a simultaneity between the commodity and its forgotten history, since capital eventually produces its own presuppositions as against the historical suppositions of the precapitalist formations. History has no place in the sequence of categories that constitute the totality and remains exterior to it, even though it may have initially jump-started it.[32] In this regard, it seems, the history of original accumulation is apparently one of those remote historical presuppositions Marx referred to in *Grundrisse*, or antecedents that belong not to capitalism's life process but to precapitalism, which lay behind later developments but are no longer present in contemporary formations. But what is important about these historical presuppositions and antecedents is that they aggregated into a history external to capitalism, materialized in precapitalist formations that, in turn, they accumulated into the stockpiling that provided the source of capitalism's eventual appropriation under the logic of formal subsumption. In this way, an external history became the condition for producing history within capitalism. What Marx extracted from this external history and found in the precapitalist formations was first an empirical content of communalism and then the utility of its form for the present.

As a result, history was left behind, lost even, forgotten, as Marx accused bourgeois economists, as was much of the memory of the events that produced so much violence and uncertainty in so many lives. It has often been remarked that national narratives invariably conceal and forget that the origins of the nation were forged in bloody violence, often reaching genocidal proportions, and that few nation-states have managed to escape employing this model of selective amnesia provided by capitalism as a necessary accompaniment to constructing the historical representation of its development from origin to the present. Marx's account of the violence unleashed during the moment of original accumulation and its memory that subsequent normalization, read as abstraction, of the new productive order extinguished exemplifies not only the origins of capitalism but the foundation of the English state that emerged on the ruins of the old mode of production and the beginnings of the new. The putative ruins did not necessarily vanish but gained a new lease on life in a different present and configuration of production. In this respect, the template of memory loss remains at the basis of the emplotment of most national narratives, even when the introduction of capitalism plays a recessive role, if that is imaginable. In this revised scenario, history, as such, as a record of time-bound change disappears for a "natural economic order" for which bourgeois proponents claimed both its eternality and its naturalness, inverting the historical order to "naturalize" denatured historical relationships.[33] Here, it seems, the presumed natural history of capital was succeeded by national history, which concentrated on the exteriority of political events and wars since the economy was seen as inherently and naturally given. In this regard, the nation served as capital's factotum. The coupling of a "natural economy" and the nation appeared appropriate since the state had been so intimately involved in promoting its instruments of violence and coercion—behind the "law"—both to push along the dissolution of the feudal tributary mode and to accelerate the rise of the new capitalist mode of production. To the extent that the nation-state incorporated the necessity of capitalism's "immanent laws" of production, the path was open to both its own "objectification" and naturalization of historical fate, which was recoded as destiny.[34] In this way, *national* history performed merely to mask a more fundamental *natural* history, whereby the nation-form unsurprisingly managed to reveal a close kinship with the commodity form itself. Nation-form and commodity-form shared both the character of a "mystical thing" and a complicity to eliminate the historical, as such, contingency itself, in the making of history, the latter through a repression of its conditions of development (the process of production), the former through its suppression of time, as Hegel proposed in his appeal to the allegory of state formation and the annihilation of time in Greek mythology.[35]

If Marx designated the commodity form as a "mysterious thing," his judgment applied equally to the nation-form, which displaced historical time by the mystifications of a timeless, naturally self-originating national spirit. What national history as a stand-in for natural history forfeited for the promise of eternality (capital's permanent present) was a regard for the record of change in time and memory, in fact a recognition of the very forces of unevenness that powered the nation's historical formation, which Marx's accounting of the horrors of original accumulation—the "slaughter of the innocents" he described so graphically—had sought to restore to understanding the hidden history of the commodity form. Here is the meaning of Ernst Bloch's observation that there is no time in national history, only space. "Thus 'nationhood' drives time, indeed history out of history: it is space and organic fate, nothing else; it is that 'true collective' whose underground elements are supposed to swallow the uncomfortable class struggle of the present." The nation, for Bloch writing in the 1930s, was nothing more than a "state of blood."[36]

While Marx may have been driven by a desire to envision the completed totality of capitalism in order to subject it to analysis, this tactic explains in large measure the "historical" reasons why he started with the completed commodity form before proceeding to account for the processes that it structured, as well as the history—original accumulation—that produced it. In this regard, his now famous appendix, "The Results of the Immediate Process of Production," essentially expanded on what he wrote in the preceding chapters about the capitalist system and elaborated on the role played by science and technology in creating greater relative surplus value by further rationalizing the production process and thus defining in greater detail the contours of the world of real subsumption. Even though the goal of relative surplus value was to introduce new technologies to shorten the working day, Marx had no illusions concerning its role in actually prolonging the workday. Machinery was, in fact, "the most powerful means of lengthening the working day beyond all natural limits in those industries first directly seized on by it."[37] In time, the relationship between absolute surplus value and the impulse to continue lengthening the workday became interchangeable with and indistinguishable from relative surplus value, despite the introduction of new technological forces of production. But the problem raised by starting with the commodity form necessitates considering the mediations produced by its subsequent history. Marx, it should be recalled, was writing in the mid-nineteenth century, which was a moment when the commodity form *still* related to wage labor and its consequential social relationships, not to the later world of mass consumption and the commodification of pleasure. With the intervention of Georg Lukács in the 1920s followed later by the so-called Frankfurt School, the trajectory of the commodity form's career revealed not only that its role had been transformed into one of a central performer in structuring modern social life but that it had become more complex, inasmuch as it now frequently was made to exceed the form of wage labor and the objectification of social relationships. It now involved culture in the broadest sense. However, the most consequential effect of expansion and growing complexity was that any attempt to begin with the commodity form risked ending with it, with little possibility of history making itself visible. But with formal subsumption there is the simultaneous combining of commodified labor power and an explanation of how the capitalist production process was carried out since it embodied the general logic of all capitalist development. However, it needs to be recognized here that Lukács, as will be discussed later, was particularly sensitive to the primacy of the production process and labor and fully acknowledged how older practices were still being utilized with more advanced ones to configure an uneven context that permitted the worker-proletariat, unlike the bureaucrat, to escape from the "prison house" of full-scale commodification. For that reason alone, it is necessary to start with formal subsumption rather than the commodity, capitalism's logic of development, as such, especially if we are intent on gaining access to the historically concrete.

But starting with formal subsumption as a continuing form producing historical unevenness means also seeing the unfolding of original accumulation as an ongoing, accompanying process rather than capitalism's one-time jump-start that enlarged Marx's conceptualization of the present by staging it in the world at large. If, as suggested, *The Eighteenth Brumaire of Louis Bonaparte* marked the moment of a critical historiographical shift that liberated the present from the dead hand of the past, his subsequent turn to "original accumulation" and the broader consequences of an emergent world market and expansion of capitalism introduced the virtual globalization of the time and space of the present. More important, it disclosed the possibility of envisaging other routes to capitalist modernization no longer reliant on a singular national model based on the English experience. I will follow Marx's sense of temporal order in order to avoid the causal argument, which means I will consider the character of formal subsumption and how it overlapped with Marx's preoccupation with precapitalist formations and stockpiling of the presuppositions and antecedents capitalism would appropriate and then return to a present and its relationship with real subsumption and the claims made for it.

II

Marx believed that formal subsumption "is the general form of every capitalist process of production," which meant the general basis of all capitalist development.[38] I would further propose that this recognition means beginning with history, and especially one marked by the encounter of older historical productive practices and the inauguration of wage labor and thus the production of continuing unevenness manifest first in a process whereby capital appropriated what it found to coexist with, and under the subordination of, the new (capitalism in the form of wage labor). In other words, capital posited what it now considered belonged to its outside, practices deriving from a different and earlier mode of production, and sought, through appropriation, to incorporate and metabolize them into its inside to serve the creation of value.[39] But at the same time, this resituating of capitalism's outside to its inside did not result in the disappearance of the identity of the older practice, which continued to mark its difference in unevenness. As far as the formation and appearance of money wealth was concerned, this belongs to the prehistory of the bourgeois economy. But it had to shed its premodern status as the source of objective wealth, locating wealth in an object, for "subjective activity" in commerce and manufacturing; the same could be said of labor.[40] It was not capital that "stockpiled" these residues in order to *create the objective conditions of production . . . and then offered them to the worker.*"[41] Usury, trade, and hoarding played the principal role in the development of this precapitalist fund of wealth, raw materials, and instruments. Orthodox Marxists often referred to these retentions as remnants and residues that were supposed to be ultimately eliminated by capitalism, but in Marx's scattered reflections they continued to coexist in one form or another within and alongside the capitalist mode of production. In many cases they were appropriations that were reconfigured for new use, whereas in other instances, they were reinvented by capitalism itself to assist the pursuit of value. At its inception, Marx asserted, wage laborers form only a small part of the population: "masters and artisans were not separated by any great social distance. . . . The subordination of labour to capital was only formal, i.e., the mode of production itself had as yet no specifically capitalist character."[42] But once peasant cultivators of flax are set "free" and driven from land that has been expropriated, he explained, those who remain are converted into the "day-labourers of large-scale farmers." Under these circumstances, large establishments for producing flax spinning appear, "and these men who have been 'set free' now work for wages." "The flax looks exactly as it did before. Not a fibre of it is changed, but a new social soul has entered into its body."[43] Here, in fact, was precisely the form of colonial appropriation undertaken in the late nineteenth century, as described by Rosa Luxemburg. It was this initial experience of history that subsequently would be repressed in capital's account of itself. It was particularly true of thinkers outside of Euro-America, who were far less concerned with the implications of the completed expanded commodity relation imposing cultural sameness everywhere than with the introduction of wage labor (variable capital) and the organization of the labor process in specific regions and at different times, as well as the cohabitation of older practices capitalism found in its path and suborned alongside and within its own practices. Not surprisingly, it was Lenin, in his critique of the *narodniki*/populists, who perceived in their defense of Russia's irreducible culture the threat of sameness provoked by the introduction of capitalism. By contrast, this perspective kept open the prospect of a mixed and uneven historical beginning, whereby shafts of history—what Walter Benjamin later described as "splinters shot through" the present—continued to interact with capitalist production.

Beginning with formal subsumption is to start at the moment when the commodity form begins to congeal into the wage labor form, introducing abstraction in the form of exchange value, to change the nature of the production process, without changing the received practices involved in the capitalist mode of mode of production itself. [44] It is the worker who acts as the "carrier" of the economic character of labor, which departs from the craftsmen and members of guilds, who personify the "specificity" of their labor and relationship to a master.[45] The history this arrangement inaugurates is thus mixed and uneven, an "agglomeration," as Marx described it,[46] and remained in this state because of capitalism's propensity both to take what it finds and to abstract newer productive social relationships as the means of creating greater relative surplus value.[47] Marx recognized in this arrangement the "necessary *form of appearance* of the value of labour capacity" that was already embodied in the term wage labor. It is the form that signifies that the wage of labor equals the price of labor, which in turn equals the value of labor. "In this *inverted* and derived form, the form in which the labour capacity presents itself on the surface of bourgeois society" as a commonplace, the difference between paid and unpaid labor has been extinguished since the wage is "payment for the working day."[48] From the beginning, the term's capacity to conceal the difference between paid and unpaid labor, as well as the similarity between serf and worker, "forms a *Delusion of the worker himself.*" Yet, because formal subsumption behaved like the value form at the same time, enabling the retention of residues from older practices, the commodifying process was always limited and partial. Despite Marx's desire to envision the completed totality, his insistence on the continued presence and reproduction of forms of subsumption like formal, "hybrid" (*Zwitterformen*), and even "transitional" (to be discussed later) necessitated the continuing appropriation of heterogeneous noncapitalist temporalities and spaces. It is this capacious hybridity that empowers the logic of formal subsumption with such enduring adaptability.

"Since bourgeois society is itself a contradictory form of development, relations derived from other forms will often be found within it in an entirely stunted form or even travestied." Marx was persuaded that the categories bourgeois society employs to express both its relations and an understanding of its structure offered valuable glimpses into the "the vanished formations out of whose ruins and elements it built itself up." Marx added that the "partly unconquered remnants" continue to be carried within the newer social formation. Here was, of course, a prefiguration of the logic of formal subsumption. But even more, Marx was registering a complaint against the way bourgeois economists "smudge over all historical differences and see bourgeois relations in all forms of society."[49] "The so-called historical presentation of development is founded . . . on the fact that the latest form regards the previous ones as steps leading up to itself and . . . it always conceives them one sidedly." Primitive accumulation opened the way for capital to establish the primacy of a dynamic logic of development that necessitated the appropriation of what was at hand, harnessing it for the creation of surplus labor as a continual process. "In Western Europe, the homeland of political economy," he claimed, "the process of primitive accumulation has more or less been accomplished. Here the capitalist regime either directly subordinated to itself the whole of the nation's production, or, where economic relations are less developed, it has at least indirect control of those social layers which, although they belong to the antiquated mode of production, still continue to exist side by side with it in a state of decay."[50] Yet he may have overshot the mark when he presumed that primitive accumulation was more or less realized since earlier in *Capital* he pointed to the evolution of "national debt" as simply constitutive of another register or phase of primitive accumulation and recognized in it "one of the most powerful levers of primitive accumulation."[51] Moreover, the relationship between primitive accumulation and the logic of formal subsumption, deriving from the inaugural overlap and mutually reciprocal dependence, guaranteed that both continue to persist in every future present.[52]

What Marx appeared to be putting forward when he suggested the figure of "still unconquered remnants" was a warning against assimilating older residues to bourgeois practices, identifying them as similar and connected, instead of seeing in them distinct survivals from different pasts and modes of production. They should not be perceived as antecedents or presuppositions originating with capitalism. Here, Marx disclosed how ideology worked to prompt people to misrecognize the old as the new. In a passage that prefigured Lukács's later intervention, he observed: "We have seen how merchant's capital and interest-bearing capital are the oldest forms of capital. But it lies in the very nature of the matter that interest-bearing capital should appear to the popular mind as the form of capital *par excellence*."[53] In his consideration of the Russian scene, Marx referred to these survivals as manifest in the archaic or primal community that "contains a series of layers from various ages, the one superimposed on the other."[54] Their presence called attention to the persistence of past remnants—actually historical temporal forms—derived from other modes of production in a different present that still embody untimely temporalities capable of interrupting the environment of a new time.[55] In the "Notabene" of *Grundrisse*, one of the eight points cited for a new way of writing history, Marx introduces the idea of "uneven development of material production," or the uneven relationship between spheres of social activity such as art, law, and education.[56] In a single stroke, he underscored a critical approach to the abstract notion of progress and the identification of a problematic relationship between historical contingency and necessity. Hereafter, the relationship between real history and written history could no longer be reduced to the narrative that is supposed to impose order on the jumble of facts.[57] "In order to develop the laws of political economy . . . it is not necessary to write the *real history of the relations of production*."[58] Since he had already dismissed the idea that "later history is made the goal of earlier history,"[59] he was convinced it would be "unfeasible" and plain wrong to "let the economic categories follow one another in the same sequence as that in which they were historically decisive. Their sequence is determined . . . by their relation to one another in modern bourgeois society, which is precisely the opposite of that which seems to be their natural order or which corresponds to historical development."[60] The relationship of the categories is determined by capital's logic, by abstraction, in a later present when the system is completed, and not by the actual order of their historical genesis. All this suggests a reordering that ultimately dehistoricizes the concepts by presenting them as "natural" and ultimately as a natural history that banishes their aptitude for making history to externality.[61]

But even before Marx developed a new conception of the historical founded on the time of the present, he and Engels, in earlier works from the 1840s like *The Holy Family* and *The German Ideology*, turned to disassembling the family and history and the claims of historical transcendence.[62] These critiques originated in the period when Marx and Engels were still preoccupied with "settling accounts" with Young Hegelians like Ludwig Feuerbach, Bruno Bauer, David Strauss, and Max Stirner. It was also during this crucial period that they targeted Hegel's conception of a universal history and its replacement by the historical materialism that was beginning to take shape in these texts. Hence the objective of this project was the philosophical history embraced by the German petite bourgeoisie. In Stirner, Marx and Engels charged, history had been turned into the mere history of philosophy driven by abstractions and phantoms, the history of an illusory idea, a history of spirits and ghosts.[63] This history was the "domination of the hold over the empirical, descending down from heaven when it should have ascended upward from the earth. It was something 'extraterrestrial,' separated from ordinary life."[64] As for the favored claim of continuity, "history is nothing but the succession of the separate generations, each of which uses materials, capital funds, the productive forces handed down to by all preceding generations and . . .continues the traditional activity in completely changed circumstances and . . . modifies the old circumstances with a completely changed activity. This can be speculatively distorted so that later history is made the goal of earlier history." Speculative artifices like "goals," "ideas," "destiny," etc. are nothing but abstract alibis drawn from earlier history, reflecting only the "active influence which earlier history exercises on later history."[65] Marx accused Stirner, especially, of resacralizing history instead of secularizing it. The importance of the critique in *The German Ideology* is its explicit recognition of the uneven history Germans have lived, inasmuch as they have lived their revolution in philosophy but not in politics, as France and England have, which makes them both contemporary and noncontemporary to these countries: "We [Germans] are the *philosophical* contemporaries of the present, without being its *historical* contemporaries."[66] This identification of unevenness was carried over to, and amplified in, the later *Grundrisse*.

The theme of "settling accounts" with the prevailing "philosophical consciousness" from the standpoint of the new materialism and its critique of political economy was turned against speculative philosophy of history itself. Here, Marx imagined a "profane history" competent to overcome the illusion of lost "paradises and promised lands" dreamed up by Stirner. A profane history meant fastening onto the present, actively thinking it, rather than a future anterior and a barely known past no more substantial than a "ghost story," as attested by the definition given to communism: "communism for us is not a state of affairs which is to be established, and ideal to which reality (will) have to adjust itself. We call communism the real movement which abolishes the present state of things. The conditions of this movement result from the now existing premise."[67] it is an ongoing practice (praxis) of an existing reality, that is to say, a temporal movement. Even later texts like *The Eighteenth Brumaire* remained faithful to both the critique of philosophical history, recognizing the vast unevenness littering the historical environment of French society in the 1840s, and the privilege accorded to thinking in and of the present.

Once Marx had completed the task of settling accounts and renounced the idea of a "heavenly history," speculative philosophy of history was no longer on his intellectual agenda, and the profane history he heralded receded into his meditations on precapitalist formations in *Grundrisse* and in rare but sporadic performances staged in *Capital*.[68] "Hegelian philosophy," he concluded, "is the last consequence . . . of all German historiography for which it is not a question of real or even political interests, but of pure thought . . . swallowed up in 'self-consciousness,'" and a "course of history therefore appears . . . as a mere tale of knights, robbers and ghosts." Under the circumstance that history is replaced by abstraction—capital's logic—it becomes universal, not simply because it "aims at the fulfillment of its idea, or aspires to the goal from which it derives. But rather history becomes universal only when it performs" as a process of real universalization, only if the "actual empirical existence of men "unfolds on a "world historical level," and when both "world historical individuals replace local ones."[69] This accomplishment requires the development of productive forces, pointing to at the same time "the actual empirical existence of men in their world historical, instead of local being." Marx detected in the world market the globalization of the economy, greater "intercourse" and communications among regions, and the new form of universalization that thereby provided the occasion for history to escape the "detached abstraction of individuals" to become the habitat of "world historical existence of individuals." This goal is no more a foretold destiny than the present causally follows the past. Each present supplies opportunities for realizing the idea of universal history, producing plural possibilities unleashing temporal shifts, discordances, stoppages, and recombinations released by the rhythms of unevenness, which point to new agendas, questions, and answers demanding their own response. History, in this register, could no longer move along a "one-way street," endowing it with singular meaning. Appearing from the ruins of universal history, a temporalizing rhythmology of capital comes into sight, empowering time accountancy and periodic crises that transform the historical environment of the present into a scene where "politics attains primacy."[70] For Marx, once having liberated history from philosophy, time or temporality is left to temporalize itself in the present, from the process of production and reproduction where uneven political and economic intensities surface and generate unscheduled struggle.[71] Thereafter, the history Marx became preoccupied with was the historical presuppositions lying behind the capitalist present, like "primary equations," or antecedents and the means by which they are ultimately taken over by capital. Convinced there was no other time than the present, he professed that the self-temporalization of daily life is the secularization of everyday time, the time of labor and effort, punctuated by the presence of a clashing heterological mixture of differing historical temporalities deposited by capitalism's ceaseless appropriating of what it found at hand sounding out their atonal unevenness. This was a history dominated by constant struggles in the present rather than one driven by a desire coming from the future.

For Marx it was important to determine "where historical investigation must enter or where bourgeois economy as a merely historical form of the production process points beyond itself to earlier modes of production."[72] Cognizant of the copresence of these "residues," often dramatized historically by such historical episodes as the mass migrations transporting precapitalist beliefs, sentiments, customs, and practices from the countryside into the centers of capitalism, he was convinced that historical laws thus led to "primary equations—like the empirical numbers in natural sciences," for example, "which point[ed] to a past lying behind this system," inasmuch as "such indications (*Andeutung*), together with a correct grasp of the present,

then . . . offer the key to the understanding of the past." Yet Marx also suggested in this passage that this model of historiography would reveal the way
productive limits "lead to points which indicate the transcendence of the present form of production relations (capitalism), the movement coming into being, thus foreshadowing the future." Moreover, prebourgeois "phases" appear
as *"merely historical,"* "suspended presuppositions," which, accordingly, are
"gone and past" and "belong to the history of its (capital's) formation" but "in
no way to its contemporary history." It is a history that has been bracketed, to
be sure, but one that has not entirely disappeared from view.[73] These historical presuppositions do not belong to the reality of, say, developed cities in a
later present but remain as their past presuppositions and are "suspended in
their *being*." They constitute capital's becoming, as given, distant external
presuppositions for the "arising of capital," after which capital creates its
own presuppositions. These conditions that precede the creation of capital
belong not to the capitalist mode of production but rather to "preludes of its
becoming, they lie behind it." But as finished forms they still manage to persist beyond the moment of their own production though always in a transformed shape now serving capital.[74] "The formation process of capital," Marx
reasoned, "—when capital, i.e., not any particular capital, but capital in general, only evolves—is the *dissolution process*, the *particular product* of the social
mode of production preceding it. It is thus a *historical process*, a process which
belongs to a definite historical period. This is the period of historical genesis." Its existence becomes a "permanent pre-condition . . . [and] capital is the
sediment resulting from the process of dissolution of a different social formation. It is the *product* of a different [formation], not the product of its own
reproduction."[75]

Hence the capitalist present is still tainted by the retention of faint traces,
remote but still available, from the past, remnants figured from prior modes
(embodied also in thought, custom, and sentiment, as well as economic
activity) within a different time now being tamed for capital. And the appearance and forms of "original accumulation" not only would occur at different times but would also undergo significant mutations. By limiting Marx's
account of primitive accumulation to Western Europe, it became possible to
uncover the existence of multiple different routes of development elsewhere.[76]
In this regard, Japanese were able to utilize and retain the "medieval village"
and its "small producers" in Japan's early development of capitalism in the

nineteenth century. This observation conformed to Marx's own recommendations to Russian progressives and underscored the possibility of realizing
different routes that, instead of signaling temporal lag, no longer depended
on a capacity to replicate the European model supplied by colonialism. Even
Lenin, in his critique of Peter Struve, recognized that capitalism had entered
the Russian village community and considered it an important element in
the further development of a domestic market. Leon Trotsky's formulation
of "permanent revolution" (1906) openly acknowledged the unfolding of
uneven development everywhere and the possibility of historically combined
development on a worldwide scale, and Georg Lukács recognized in the
canonical text of "Western Marxism" (*History and Class Consciousness*) that
capitalism had not been completed and was still suffused with elements and
practices from prior pasts. I will deal with Trotsky and Lukács briefly in
the next chapter.

Marx showed in *Grundrisse* the historic shape of precapitalist formations
as communal and clan-based typifications that might have existed before the
fateful separation of worker from the land and the conditions of subsistence that marked the momentous beginnings of primitive accumulation
and the installation of the wage labor form. Reflecting on the uncertainty
relating to the accessibility of knowledge on ancient societies, in one of his
draft letters to Vera Zasulich, he confessed how little is known of the archaic
communities and suggested that what *is* known from available sources represents the formation in its "*final term*." This was a little like saying that the
knowledge of archaic societies resembles the tip of an iceberg, the final
manifestations of a mostly submerged social formation. This acknowledgment
disclosed that his interest in the history of precapitalist formations was secondary to the importance he assigned to the present since he was convinced
that a practice like ground rent cannot be understood without capital. "But
capital can certainly be understood without ground rent."[77] This formulation prefigured his later description of how formal subsumption could be
understood without referring to real subsumption, but real subsumption
could not be grasped without formal subsumption. Marx's historical perspective was concerned with presuppositions that clearly were important
to later development but in a way to its *contemporary* history, "not to the real
system of the mode of production." It is important to recognize two considerations that governed Marx's own historical rethinking of what constituted

history and its movement. First, he ultimately rejected any linear causality that envisaged a singularly progressive movement from one period or mode of production to the next, as if it were a chain of connected links, but rather saw the multilinear movements as taking place in different regions and among diverse peoples, particularly put forth in his late *Ethnological Notebooks*.[78] Second, *Grundrisse* made it abundantly clear that where the Asiatic mode departed from the capitalist mode lay in the relations of social labor: the former was constituted of unfree labor while the latter was distinguished by free labor. By the same measure, Marx forcefully articulated the view that capitalism "stands opposed to the other, prior modes of production principally because of its departure from nature."[79] On this differentiation Marx wrote that "in all forms in which landed property rules, the natural relation still predominates. In those where capital rules, the social, historically created element."[80] What informed this distinction was the conviction that once human appropriation of land began, there was also the beginning of production that marked the origins of history. "At the beginning these [determinants and preconditions of production] may appear as spontaneous and natural. But by the process of production itself, they were its historic product for another."[81] This proposition clearly pointed to how the archaic world of precapitalist formations remained locked in nature, as such, and had not yet reached true historicity, which came with the inauguration of capitalism and the formation of free labor, which established the conditions that made possible life in society, and the historical, as against the community, and its seemingly endless cycle of repetition. "The positing of the individual as a *worker*," Marx wrote, "in this nakedness, is itself a product of *history*."[82]

Since much of *Grundrisse* is devoted to showing how wage labor developed from the separation of workers from the land and their subsequent fall into a state of dependence based solely on selling the only thing they owned, their labor, it is not surprising that Marx's description would incline toward the opposite of what previously prevailed as the condition of social labor, which was the absence of commodified labor power to create surplus value. The interesting paradox here is that in the archaic village communities, the workers did not own the land they cultivated, which belonged to the community of which they were members. Surplus value in the form of taxes or tribute were skimmed off by those who represented the "higher unity." In contrast to the unfree worker who made up the communities of ancient imperial states, the worker separated from the means of subsistence and instruments of work was a free worker. Here, the presupposition of capital was the free worker before being released from the land as his "natural workshop," which entailed the "dissolution of small, free landed property" under clan-based communal ownership "resting on the basis of the 'oriental commune.'" These communal organizations functioned like chronotopic variations of an earlier precapitalist mode of production. What seemed to characterize the "Asiatic" forms—what Marx eventually called the "Asiatic mode of production," which replaced his earlier name for it, "Oriental despotisms"—was the "commonality of labor" and the extraction of surplus product. According to Lawrence Krader, once these "primitive" modes of production "transformed themselves," they were able to transmute the several differences among the different forms into a commonality.[83] This referred to the process whereby society was constituted and the implementation of the preeminent role played by the production of surplus value became manifest principally in the collection of rent:

> Whatever the specific form of the rent may be, what all its types have in common is the fact that the appropriation of the rent is the economic form in which landed property is realized, and that ground rent in turn presupposes landed property, the ownership of particular bits and pieces of the globe by certain individuals—whether the owner is a person representing the community as in Asia and Egypt, etc.; whether this landed property is simply an accidental accompaniment of the property certain persons have in the persons of the immediate producers, as in the system of serfdom and slavery; whether it is pure private property that non-producers have in nature, a simple ownership title to land; or finally, whether it is a relationship to the land which, as with colonists and small peasant proprietors, appears as directly implied, given their isolation and not socially developed labour, in the appropriation of the products of particular bits of land by the direct producers.[84]

Here, Marx added, "all ground-rent is surplus value, the product of surplus value."[85]

Kevin Anderson has offered the idea that Marx took a "more evenhanded position" toward these archaic communities from the views he expressed in the articles on India written in 1853.[86] But it is important that in *Grundrisse* and *Capital*, Marx includes areas outside of Asia, emphasizing the centrality of the commonality of labor and the appropriation of rent—a proto–surplus value—throughout diverse regions of the archaic world, hinting at a universal disposition, which stands in contrast to what replaced it after the "separation" from conditions of living labor and the means of existence in England and Western Europe. Wherever "free day laborers were found, either in the 'Oriental community' (*Gemeinwesen*) or the 'western commune' (*Gemeinde*)," Marx noted in *Grundrisse*, they "dissolve[ed] into individual elements" through the loss of conditions of self-sustaining labor.[87] Here, he asserted that a "presupposition of wage labor" historically is "free labor." The result of this inversion was the disappearance of the free workers as proprietors—"members of the community" "who at the same time work."[88] In this connection, it seems, Marx resorted to the tactic of inverting the inversion (echoing the negation of the negation), whereby the naturalness attributed to capitalism by classical political economy already constituted an inversion of the historical real, which he now tried to restore with a second inversion. Communal landowners, in any case, worked not to create value but to maintain the individual proprietor and his family, not to forget the "total community" itself.[89] While Marx emphasized this form's relationship to the "property of the community," whereby each individual constitutes a link as both member and proprietor, he was convinced that the form could be realized in different ways—in the Asiatic, Slavonic, Peruvian, and Romanian communes, if not the Russian mir. The diverse forms presented variations of a primary historic presupposition, not evolving in progressive sequences in some inevitable march of time, punctually unfolding as stages of a unilinear chronology, but rather moving according to different temporalities contingent on their received historical circumstances. The form of the commune, wherever encountered, appeared as a "coming-together" (*Vereingung*)—a "unification" made up of independent subjects, landed proprietors, not as a "unity."[90] Their aim was continued survival through reproduction,[91] and the eventual collapse of these archaic communities followed a rhythm determined by their respective historical circumstances. The Asiatic, Marx observed, held out the longest, owing to its

presuppositions that constrained the individual from becoming independent vis-à-vis the community—displaying their difference from what
appeared as a universalist norm of "communal labor" and "naturally arisen,
spontaneous communal property."[92] Accordingly, this form of appropriation occurs through labor under *"presuppositions* that are not themselves the
product of labor, but appear as its natural or *divine* presuppositions."[93] Marx
saw no contradiction between the "comprehensive unity" standing over the
multitude of semiautonomous village communities because it appeared as
either the "higher proprietor" or even the "sole proprietor." And because the
unity is the real owner and thus "the real presupposition of communal property," it appears as a particular unity hovering over many real particular
communities—semiautonomous villages, isolated, autarkic, where individual
cultivators are "propertyless," or, as he put it, "the *natural* conditions of labour
and reproduction belonging to him . . . appears mediated for him through a
cession by the total unity . . . to the individual, through the mediation of a
particular community," one realized in the form of a despot, patriarch, the
father of many communities.[94] Hence the surplus product automatically
belongs to the highest unity. This arrangement marked the conduct of "Oriental despotism" and its claim to propertylessness and the prevalence of communal property as the basis of clan property, "created . . . by a combination
of manufactures and agriculture within the small commune." Such communities were self-sustaining and possessed all the conditions of their continuing self-reproduction and surplus production. A part of the surplus product
was given in the form of tribute. Within this sociopolitical template, Marx believed there was room for the development of a variety of different practices,
whereby the small communal property can appear in the form of "vegetat[ing]
independently alongside one another," as in the Slavonic and Romanian
communes, or the unity might be extended to encompass the "communality
of labour" itself, as in Mexico, Peru, the early Celts, and some clans in India.
Moreover this communality can appear within the clan system, inasmuch
as the particular sense of unity is represented in a chief of the clan-family, and
so on, which would determine either a "more despotic or a more democratic
form of this community system."[95] Finally, the realization of communal
labor in large-scale projects like aqueducts was particularly prominent in
Asia and surely siphoned off large quantities of workers from agricultural
cultivation, organized by an overarching centralized state.

Marx envisioned a second form that resembled the first because it assumed the community as its principal presupposition but differed as a result of essential "modification[s]" produced by history. In this new incarnation, the clan community, the putative natural community, is no longer seen as the outcome of the presupposition for the communal appropriation and utilization of land, but rather its existence has become its own working presupposition. In this phase, Marx proposed that individuals are no longer considered as "mere accidents," and the countryside is replaced by the town that owns cultivated fields as the base and center of rural population. The more the clan is removed from its original setting and "occupies *alien* ground," it becomes possible for the individual to exploit the conditions for acquiring the status of private proprietors, becoming "small land owning peasants," whose independence relies on relations as commune member and the protection of state or public land for "communal needs and communal glory etc."[96]

By the 1860s, Marx began to alter earlier views and interests and widen his perspective. In his later writings, especially, there is a lessening of concern for the content of the historicity of these earlier modes than the form they signified. There are even instances where Marx's own considerations are diminished because the empirical content apparently fails to justify his enthusiasm for the associations identified with forms. This is particularly the case with his draft letters to Zasulich, where his approval of the archaic communal form is disregarded because of either its inconstancies or the paucity of evidence.[97] Yet if the perspective is shifted from the emphasis on mere empirical content to the appearance of form, especially in "its final term," as he put it, which is precisely the interpretative optic Marx employs with great consistency, it is plausible, I believe, to see the logic of his analysis rather than the disappointment produced by its evident "failure." Because, as he explained, the "final term" came at the end of a long, virtually unknown historical process that provided accessibility to what could be known about the archaic commune, and because these remote formations were invariably seen through the lens of a capitalist society organized on the basis of its time accountancy, Marx was clearly pointing to "abstract[ing]" the form of the rural commune from its historical and degraded practices to "consider its constitutive form and historical context" to signify commonality and communalism culminating in the form of commonness.[98] When he appealed to the priority of the surviving commune in Russia as the most modern form of the archaic type because of its practice of "communist property," he was proposing that it was its "final term," and therefore it was not necessary to destroy the commune in order to make way for capitalism since the "death of communal property did not give birth to capitalist production."[99] Beyond that, he was convinced that communal property constituted "a higher form" of the archaic type of property, pointing to (collective) communist property that is vastly superior to capitalist private property, which in the West will become no more than a "regressive form." As a form signifying communalism, the agrarian commune was capable of avoiding meanings tied to fixed themes or specific historical content for more general and flexible associations capable of being adapted and applied in any future present. For Marx the "constitutive form" of "rural commune" was separated from its known "evils that have weighed upon it" and "has preserved itself not as scattered debris . . . but as the more or less dominant form of popular life spread over a vast empire."[100] Its constitutive form allows for flexibility because in the last instance "everything depends on historical context" in which the communal form is situated.[101] And it is especially the "contemporaneity of capitalist production" that provides common landownership with the proper historical context, which was the ready-made material conditions for huge-scale labor. In this regard, Marx's recommendations to Zasulich recalled the operation of formal subsumption that always aimed to bring together historical temporal forms from the received past with the historical context of the new required by the contemporaneity of the capitalist present.[102] Much of this became explicitly manifest as he broadened his vision, but the emphasis on form was precisely the strategy by which Marx sought to articulate the precapitalist formations (including the Asiatic mode of production) and its historic presuppositions as a resource for the present. Apart from this privileging of form, Marx also took into consideration the role played by time, especially the different time of the capitalist present—its contemporaneity—which reflected the form's historically unbound capacity to link up to different moments.

In Marx's broadened scheme of possibilities, the most appropriate figure of development was unevenness and the temporal asymmetry and discordance it is capable of producing. As a result, each present then supplies a multiplicity of possible lines of development, as he began to envision the possibility offered by the Russian commune (*obschina*) freeing itself gradually from the fetters of primitiveness to promote production on a national scale. Yet "precisely because it is contemporaneous with capitalist production," Marx advised, "the rural community may appropriate all of its positive achievements" to achieve a fusion of archaic and modern forms. This meant that "everyone would see the commune as the element in the regeneration of Russian society, and its superiority over countries enslaved by the capitalist regime."[103] For Marx, the Russian commune confronted a crisis that will end only when the "social system is eliminated through the return of the modern societies to the 'archaic' of communal property." It is, in fact, the contemporaneity of the archaic commune and its combining with the advances introduced by capitalism that spares it from being reduced to simple romantic nostalgia and organic nativist fantasies, especially when it is joined with the temporality summoned by new technological practices. What he seemed to be driving toward was the conviction that "archaic" or "primary formation" was itself as a "series of layers from various ages, the one superimposed on the other." "Similarly, the archaic formation of society exhibits a series of different types (which together form an ascending series), which mark a progression of epochs."[104] But the progression appeared more vertical than horizontally linear and resembled more the figure of a palimpsest. Its importance lay in the status of the contemporary coexistence of archaic and modern forms of economic production. The realization of an archaic figure in the present thus redefined the surviving historical temporal form by stripping it of cultural and economic associations belonging to a mode of production in which it had originally functioned. Although Marx had cautioned in *Grundrisse* that precapitalist presuppositions were vitally important to later development even when they were no longer visible emanations, the presence of the commune, like that of other survivors, attests to their propensity for realizing a new, visible lease on life under entirely different conditions. Moreover, given the contemporaneity of the Russian commune with capitalist production and its links to a world market, not to forget the nation-state itself, it could be transformed. For archaism, when self-consciously yoked to capitalism, as in Germany, Italy, and Japan during the 1930s, played a role reversal to become the "frightful" foundation for fascist cultural ideology, as both Ernst Bloch and Tōsaka Jun observed. As suggested above, the political effects of this specter of unevenness were already implied by Marx in *The German Ideology*. But Marx may also have understated the political consequences of recognizing and mobilizing these spectral reminders of temporal unevenness, untimeliness, and arrhythmia in producing discordance, consequences such as disturbing the homogenous linearity projected by the nation-state busy promoting the claims of another kind of contemporaneity. For these "ready-mades," taken over and utilized in a different way, released from the role they once played in modes of production that generated them, were not completely emptied of their historicality but still indexed the intimation of a time external to and dissimilar from capitalism, a world where use-value and the nondifferentiation of subject and object still supposedly prevailed, bringing with it possibilities for different forms of political community. However much Tōsaka criticized the archaism in Japan during the 1930s as an empty ideology or Bloch condemned the appeals to medieval German life as a romantic fiction, the forms signifying their respective pasts in the present were not entirely invented or had lost their association with still accessible historical times. They continued to strike deeply rooted resonances in the historical humus of everyday life.

This would lead to Benjamin's later plea to awaken from the dream in order to restore a "primal history." If contemporaneity was the moment that embodied present and past in an uneven mix of temporal asymmetries and possible discordances, it also marked the moment of the modern. Yet this recognition also brings us back to the question of subsumption as the possible form for the making of history in Marx and after.

III

The importance of Marx's scattered reflections on the process that congealed into formal subsumption and its hybrid subsets, whereby workers were "divested" from their conditions of subsistence to constitute labor power as a commodity exchanged for another commodity (money), lies in its capacity to signify the place of historical time, which is the moment when older economic practices attesting to the cultivator's independence gradually give way to the dependent status of wage labor. But, it must be repeated, as a form formal subsumption is not constrained by the history that had generated it. This transformation, which yoked wage labor to the production of surplus labor (and surplus value), pronounced the beginning of the capitalist process of production, even though the mature mode of production evolved over time to lay down the necessary preconditions for the appearance in the later organization of the factory. If it appeared in the sixteenth and seventeenth centuries and subsequently entailed enshrining an experience of confrontation between received economic practices from earlier modes of production and the demands of the new, it also marked capital's penchant for reorganizing the process of labor and commodity production.[105] What Marx named as formal subsumption thus consisted of the process in which the small, more or less independent cultivator was subordinated to capitalism's requirements and was linked to the creation of absolute surplus value. "The existence of absolute surplus value," Marx wrote, "implies nothing more than a . . . productivity of labour *of natural and spontaneous origin,* that not all the (possible) (daily) labour time of a man is required for the maintenance of his own existence or the reproduction of his own labour capacity. The only further requirement is that he should be compelled—that an external compulsion should exist for him—to work more than the necessary labour time, a compulsion to do surplus labour."[106] Moreover, "if the relation of domination and subordination replaces those of slavery, serfdom, vassalage, patriarchal etc., relations of subordination," Marx explained, "there takes place only a *change in their form.* The form becomes freer, because the subordination is now only of an objective nature; it is formerly speaking voluntary, *purely economic.*"[107] It is important to note, here, that in the initial subsumption process, Marx clearly designated subordination as "objective," "purely economic." The creation of absolute surplus value was already implied as a given of the workday's existence, and any change in it meant a change of the "total working day," which would entail its further extension. Real subsumption thus referred to the creation of relative surplus value and rests on the utilization of science and technology to increase the productive capacity of the worker to change both the labor process and the "relation of the worker to his own production and capital."[108] It is evident from Marx's extensive account of the "history" of original accumulation that capitalism at birth relied on noncapitalist presuppositions and practices and would continue to do so into the future. In both *Capital* and "Economic Manuscripts of 1861–5," he proposed the necessity of creating absolute surplus value as prior to production for relative surplus value. But what seems important is that the two forms of surplus value should be considered separately, as coexisting practices, which "corresponded to two separate *forms of subsumption of labour under capital*, or *two separate forms of capitalist production*," whereby the latter appeals to the earlier form as the basis for the introduction in new branches of production.[109] But the differentiation also implied the possibility of coexistence. Hence the form of formal subsumption "differs from previous modes of production, in which the active producers provide surplus," meaning a level of surplus value that invariably demands working more than the required or necessary labor time, now for others rather than themselves.

With this early formulation, Marx stages the confrontation of capitalist, owner of money, and laborer, who "as proprietor of his labour capacity" is positioned to sell its "temporary use." Both meet initially as equals, as commodity owners, seller and buyer. No other relation intervened apart from buyer and seller, which meant no politically or socially "fixed relation of domination and subordination." Implied in this negotiation is the shadowed presence of an uneven relation between buyer and seller that requires the worker to sell labor capacity and to recognize that the "objective conditions of labour," such as the raw materials, instruments of labor, and means of subsistence now belonged to the buyer of labor power. "The more completely these *conditions of labor* confront him as the property of another, the more completely is the relation of capital and wage labour present formally, hence the more complete the formal subsumption of labour under capital."[110] The mode of production has not yet changed, the received practices remain intact, alongside newer relationships. "The labour process continues as it did before," but now subordinated to capital, which already suggests a political relationship. *Grundrisse* pointed out how, after the initial exchange, the force of law entered the equation to protect the buyer who owned the means of labor, the "objective conditions," instruments and raw materials, as property that immediately changed the nature of the relationship into one of inequality and domination.[111] Where the new form differs from the older practice is in introducing the mediation of abstraction initially realized in the exchange between commodity owners and laborers who forfeited their labor capacity for the wage form. By the same token, the continuity of labor the new relation engenders points to a production process whereby money is constantly being converted into capital.[112] But it is important to acknowledge that the introduction of abstraction—value—in the production process at the same time means bringing into it commodities whose content will induce nondifferentiation between the wage workers. Both the quality of abstraction and the worker's indifference to the commodity's content that the selling of labor power for wages establishes must be related to the status of formal subsumption as a form, albeit a historically derived one, which has no specific stakes in the content being produced under its system of time accountancy that determines the wages for the workday. This is in part the "secret of the commodity form itself," and the reason that "work assumed the form of value of a commodity" is thus committed to "affirm[ing] its social character only in the commodity form of its product."[113]

For Marx, the category of formal subsumption was first and foremost a form rather than a singular event, a one-time content or theme reflecting a historical moment or a stage in a developmental and evolutionary chronology, since it was "the general form of every capitalist process," insofar as it implicated the ceaseless "compulsion" to extract surplus value and the agency of capital as the "immediate owner" of the production process.[114] The form, in this regard, is external to whatever its immediate content. Hence the worker's own indifference to the content of what was being produced was paralleled by the indifference demanded by formal subsumption itself, which, far from being content driven and attached to embracing traditional practices, was enacted by a form produced from the encounter of different production systems whose traces would be inscribed in it and thereafter utilized what it found useful for the sole extraction of surplus value. In *Grundrisse*, Marx has already observed labor's indifference to "its particular specificity, but capable of all specifications," even though "the particularity of labour must correspond to the particular substance of which a given capital consists."[115] The interesting thing about this form is that it embodied the inscription of experience of the encounter between capitalism and what it found from previous modes of production but was no longer bound by it; and its conduct disclosed that its hidden meaning was its generality and particularity, sanctioning a perspective that permitted both comparability and singularity and thereby a capacity to generate forms in both registers. In this way the logic of formal subsumption acted to interrupt the temporal continuum of the very process of capitalist production it also fueled.

Because of its formal nature and its capacious aptitude, indeed compulsion, for combining past and present in any and all presents, it implied both a conception of repetitive historical time, always occurring in different registers, and comparability reaching across different social formations. At one level, its function mimicked the value form, especially in its abstracting propensities, but it also left open, at another level, the retention of concrete remnants and residues, what I have instead called historical temporal forms, in the figure of practices and "living labor"—the chards of use-value— from prior modes of production that made possible the identification of that absent historical experience of unevenness that Benjamin named as the "primal history" disavowed by capitalism's temporal rhythms. The logic of this form would not only affect the economic domain but conceivably spill over into other realms and relationships associated with it in the social formation, notably those concerning politics and culture. Its status as form thus bespeaks its indifference toward the commodity's content, if not manifesting its propensity for abstraction, and supplied the surety of a continuous process of labor into the future. Yet at the same time that formal subsumption occupies the status of the general form of every capitalist process, meaning "it can be found as a *particular* form alongside the *specifically capitalist mode of production in its developed form*" (realized real subsumption),[116] we must recognize in it the form of history itself, inasmuch as it constituted the depository of coexisting different modes of production and practices and their temporal tenses, despite the eventual domination of capitalism, to define the site where contemporary difference and thus contradiction is constantly produced.[117] Finally, it is important to suggest that formal subsumption constituted the sign of capitalism's contingent development, imprinted in an inaugural impulse to utilize whatever received practices from the past were near at hand or "present-at-hand." With this inaugural gesture to stockpile and appropriate what was available or found, capital logic reordered the categories into the temporal figure of a circular and repetitive sequence that would satisfy the requirements of its productive process. The effect of this sequential reordering was not only to motor the productive process for endless capital accumulation into the future but, equally important, to remove even the hint of contingency—history—that had accompanied capitalism's own accidental appearance in the scene of history. Yet the reproduction of a contradiction in a category that mimicked the commodity while it invited the possibility of retaining older historical practices by appropriating and reconfiguring their purpose in a new productive process under different social circumstances worked against the completion of full commodification and the imposition of total social control to supply entry into a history that capital logic struggled to repress and forget. Under capitalism's subordination, these older, appropriated practices were usually synchronized to its production process but not always or fully.[118] Synchronization included both appropriated practices now made to conform to capitalism's productive agenda and living labor, which was exchanged for wages calculated according to the constraints and the magnitude of time it took to make a commodity. In both instances, synchronization prefigured a new context marked by the imperatives of abstraction in the form of objectification, averaging, and quantification. With the worker, there was the possibility of making use of the collision produced by a double temporality between new use-values relating to free time, devoted to the worker's reproduction and consumption, what Marx named as disposable time, with nonwork and the qualitative time of workers' reproduction and consumption and a time dedicated to fulfilling the abstract requirements of labor as a commodity.[119] Whatever the extent of synchronization, the temporal identities were not always lost and completely erased; that is, synchronization did not always successfully transmute the appropriated practice and make it appear as a result of capitalism's own presuppositions. Marx pointed to this problem in both *Grundrisse* and *Theories of Surplus Value*, where he seemed more concerned with showing the extent to which certain practices and economic procedures retained their identity with "antecedents" that belonged to precapitalist historical presuppositions rather than to capitalism. My argument is that this process of naturalizing past practices is accomplished through the attempt to synchronize them to the production agenda, reorganizing their position and resituating them according to capital logic, literally seeking to recontextualize them by situating them in a new present. But this still does not prevent them from appearing as remnants or showing traces of a prior historical identity, or, as in societies like Japan, surviving in the form of a feudal unconscious in thought, conduct, and custom long after the institution of feudalism has disappeared; nor does it occlude the fact that one is living in a capitalist society that is visibly filled with daily reminders that constantly announce the past's still persisting presence. The problem of "naturalizing"

MARX, TIME, HISTORY 61

these residues to make them appear as results of a mature capitalism was the task assigned to ideology and reification, which Georg Lukács explained in *History and Class Consciousness*. For Lukács, synchronization simply represented another instance of rational "calculability." His task was to show that many of the practices taken over and used by capital logic had derived from historic presuppositions prior to capital and were not produced by capitalism's life process, even though they appeared to the "bourgeois mind" to be products of the latter. I will turn to this problem in greater detail in the next chapter.

Referring to formal subsumption as one of two ways the transition from feudalism might take place, Marx (and Engels) proposed it could not "bring about the overthrow of the old mode of production by itself" since it functioned to preserve and retain its "own preconditions." The method stood in the way of the genuine capitalist mode of production.[120] If capital logic thus dehistoricized the categories of capitalism in such a way as to rob them of their historicity, it also left open a narrow corridor through which to secure access to the lost historical and the identity played by the role of contingency in producing it. Moreover, this sense of contingency explaining the reception of capitalism marks virtually every colonial seizure from the late nineteenth century on. A close look at the results of these historical developments will reveal the operation of the various forms of formal subsumption put into play and the refiguration of older practices and institutions into hybrid combinations. In this regard, the appearance of contingency accompanied the logic of formal subsumption from the beginning and undoubtedly explains the "fortuitous" coming together of so-called primitive accumulation and wage labor.

With the introduction of wage labor, we should recall, Marx was convinced it was possible to assume the organized existence of some sort of workday. The remainder, which came to constitute the everyday, the domain of "disposable time," containing the pool of practices received from past modes of production, provided a reservoir of what is ready at hand from which capitalism was able to draw on once it recognized a need. We must reflect on the importance of this event and scene of utilization, which invariably is prompted by what Marx recommended as an accounting of the current situation. The act of utilizing in any present meant taking over tools and related labor practices from older modes of production, as well as their

entailing customs, beliefs, mores, pleasures, and so forth from daily life recruited from the domain of nonwork that were not always directly involved
in production but were still not sufficiently differentiated from work, as such,
to appear separate and independent. Even in early capitalism, there was still
no sharp differentiation between domains of work, as such, and nonwork,
since the economic was hardly distinguished from other realms of social activity and comprised a miscellany of customs, mores, habits, and beliefs that
would inevitably accompany the appropriation of methods of work. This
would occur in time and with greater specialization and differentiation in
the production process into relative surplus value, along with the greater expansion of the wage form. In this way, the new everyday configured by the
introduction of wage labor came to encompass a vast container for making
select contingent choices demanded by an analysis of the immediate present. As for the subject who decided what might be utilized—surely it was the
owner of capital in collaboration with workers, and the decision must have
been based on a complex assessment of production requirements involved
in the experience of working in agriculture, recognizing what was useful,
available, even necessary, and how it might supplement new productive goals.
In such circumstances, workers who left the farm for wage labor, expropriation for exploitation, still retained the undisturbed memory of who they had
been and what they had done before. Moreover, the logic of formal subsumption was undoubtedly formed in the process of expropriation as the ground
basis for subsequent modes of exploitation that developed with the expansion of wage labor. In a sense, it is possible to argue that the undisturbed
accompaniment of older modes of work and tools, along with customs and
religious beliefs that were seen as vital to or indistinguishable from work,
may very well have blunted the direct consequences of both expropriation
and exploitation or masked their harshness and contributed to delaying the
realization of real subsumption. A good deal of agricultural practices in Japan carried associations of work and Shinto beliefs well into the Meiji period and probably beyond, and it is reasonable to assume that this kind of
identification persisted throughout colonized and semicolonized areas. And
we know that even in postwar Japan, firms and companies recruited Zen Bud-
dhism to inculcate a sense of "spiritual" discipline into employees designed
to reinforce their work performance.

Hence formal subsumption was the categorical logic delegated to express the sensible materiality of historical change and the form of intelligibility by which it grasped what might be called the historical. It was a form that marked the making of history the moment capitalism encountered older economic practices. Emerging from a mutation of forms of experience founded on what Jacques Rancière has widely described as the "material sensibility in the perceptual field," it consequently managed to formulate a mode of intelligibility from these reconfigurations of experience by reshaping them. In *Grundrisse*, Marx's perception of the historical called attention to this process; consider his discussion of the transformation of money into capital and the separation of agricultural workers from their previous conditions of labor and means of subsistence:

> It is at the same time the effect of capital and of its process . . . to conquer all of production and to develop and complete the divorce between labour and property . . . everywhere. It will be seen in the course of further development how capital destroys craft and artisan labour, working small-landownership etc. together with itself in forms in which it does not appear in opposition to labour—in small capital and in the *intermediate species between the old modes of production (or their renewal on the foundation of capital) and the classical, adequate mode of production of capital itself.*[121]

The preface of *Capital's* first edition acknowledges the "incompleteness of development" throughout Western Europe as a result of the "passive survival of archaic and outmoded modes of production."[122] It was precisely this sense of "passiveness" that informed Antonio Gramsci's refiguration of the form of formal subsumption into its political equivalent called a "passive revolution."

Yet the question remains as to what constituted completeness. In *Capital*, moreover, Marx elaborated further on these forms and their conduct. He identified formal subsumption as the first moment when the "capitalist intervenes in the process" of production. Even though the form might develop further into a realized capitalism, the latter always entailed the pre-existence of the former. The converse does not necessarily occur, and formal subforms of subsumption can be found in the absence of a specifically capitalist mode of production.[123] Marx called these "transitional" and "hybrid" forms. "The distinctive character of the formal subsumption of labour appears as its sharpest if we compare it to situations in which capital is to be found in certain specific, subordinated functions . . . where it has not yet succeeded in becoming the dominant force, capable of determining the form of society as a whole." Here, he cited the example of colonial India and the usurer's advance of "raw material or tools" and the "exorbitant interest" that he demanded, another name for surplus value.[124] Formal subsumption thus *"thrives* on the withering away of this [archaic] mode of production. With the advent of merchant capital, which commissions a number of immediate producers, then collects the produce and sells it . . . it is the *form that provides the soil from which capitalism has grown"* (italics added). It should be injected here that formal subsumption also *lives off* the archaic mode of production, as Marx's recommendations to Russian progressives demonstrated. "These forms," he added, " . . . survive and reproduce themselves as transitional subforms within the framework of capitalist reproduction."[125] Here was the example of formal subsumption as the general form of capitalist production at the same time it also performed as a "particular form alongside" capitalism in its developed form.[126] Here, too, it disclosed its principal difference from real subsumption, which was its capacity to situate practices from earlier modes alongside newer ones under the command of capital to constitute the force of temporal interruption, unevenness, fracturing, and heterogeneity. Real subsumption simply affirmed capitalism's homogenous, unitary, and linear trajectory of time, appearing more as an aspiration than its realization. Capital speaks through these forms, much as a ventriloquist speaks through its dummy. In fact, those who live this contradiction of forms through which they are compelled to transact and negotiate the everyday life of capitalist society are scarcely aware of them. The reason for this is that

> these irrational forms in which certain economic relationships appear and are grasped in practice do not bother the practical bearers of these relationships in their everyday dealings; since they are accustomed to operating within these forms, it does not strike them as anything worth thinking about. A complete contradiction holds nothing at all mysterious for them. In forms of appearance that are estranged from their inner connection and, taken in isolation, are absurd, they feel as much

at home as a fish in water. What Hegel says about certain mathematical formulae applies here too, namely that what the common human understanding finds irrational is in fact rational, and what it finds rational is irrational.[127]

Along with this form of exploiting labor, Marx identified a subset of "transitional" and "hybrid" forms of subsumption, which referred to performing certain kinds of service "work, from the formal point of view, [that] are hardly subsumed formally under capital. They belong rather among transitional forms."[128] In other words, there was a class of transitional forms that actually remained outside of capital, as such, yet continued and were reproduced alongside it. In *Capital*, he explained that "hybrid" subsumption embraced a practice in which surplus labor is not "extorted by direct compulsion from the producers" even though the producer has not been subjected to formal subsumption and capital has not yet captured direct control over the labor process. "Alongside the independent producers, who carry on their handicrafts or their agriculture in the inherited, traditional way, there steps the usurer's capital or merchant's capital, which feeds on them like a parasite." Such a form of exploitation excludes capitalist production but may form a transition to capitalism. "Finally," he continued, "as in the case of modern 'domestic industry,' certain hybrid forms are reproduced here and there against the background of large scale industry, though their physiognomy is totally changed."[129] Marx, in short, was speaking of forms related to circumstances in which the capital relation had not formerly appeared but where labor is already being exploited by capital before the latter has developed into the form of productive labor. Such forms appear in "social formations which antedate the bourgeois mode of production" and which "constantly reproduce themselves with the latter and *are in part reproduced by the latter itself.*"[130] We know from modern and contemporary instances of nation-state formation and the inauguration of capitalist political economies that newer states have, on numerous occasions, reproduced such older forms and practices as supplements to modern economic development. These transitional forms will exist "where the relation of buyer and seller . . . prevails formally between the real producer and the exploiter" and thereby wherever the "content of the transaction" is not mediated by relations of servitude and domination." The forms capital takes in such circumstances are "trading capital" and usurers' capital (interest-bearing capital). Both forms appear within capitalist production as special and derivative, but in "previous forms of production as the sole and original forms of capital." In this connection, Marx drew from the example of the Indian usurer, as already suggested, who advances to the peasant (*ryot*) money he will require for planting his cotton. In return, the peasant pays back to the usurer 40 to 50 percent per year in interest on the debt (not forgetting the principal). At the same time, the peasant is his own employer, his mode of producing is traditional, independent, and self-sustaining, and he is not yet "subsumed" by wages.[131] But the usurer still appropriates both the whole of the surplus labor (and surplus value it creates) and much of what would be used for his reproduction. And what describes the actual immiseration produced by the usurer's capital will be even truer for merchants' capital, especially where the merchant assumes the role of the manufacturer.

With regard to formal subsumption, Jason Read has observed that it has produced a contradiction: at the core of its impulse to destroy previous modes and their practices to pave the way for the completion of the capitalist production process lies its simultaneous habit of perpetuating prior practices or archaic modes by situating itself within, or coexisting alongside, elements of other modes of production. Read argues that "if formal subsumption can be an element of capitalism against a non-capitalist environment" at the same time as it seeks to retain traces and residues from earlier practices in the future and actively reproduce them, some sort of concept is needed to explain the "differential articulations of the social" and resolve the contradiction.[132] While he's correct to recruit Louis Althusser's conception of a social formation capable of embodying multiple, coexisting, and contradictory modes of production or even a conjunctural gathering that brings together such fractured heterogeneity into a momentary unity, this is precisely the function the nation-state has delegated to itself. If capitalism could tolerate no alternatives to its claims, especially the spectacle of different but coexisting temporalities disturbing the untroubled succession of homogenous time, neither could the nation-state, once it aligned with capital to become its placeholder. In time, as we can observe today, we can see how the state became solely dedicated to saving capitalism from itself. It was, as I have already proposed, the state's principal vocation to synchronize all signs of temporal discordance, to smooth out capitalism's own asymmetrical temporal accounting that reflected the different moments in the production process. This was no less true of temporalities that challenged normative time. The nation-state's efforts to homogenize time into an empty seriality did not always succeed; more often than not it failed to conceal the contradictions that periodically have surfaced to tear the social fabric into shreds. This has been especially true when the nation was confronted by global conjunctures and the threat that time would overtake space. Concealing persisting unevenness and contradiction occupying the center of modern society, particularly when faced with unscheduled interruptions from both capital and the everyday, proved difficult and provided dramatic witness to both the unresolved contradictions between capital and the remains from earlier modes of production. Within capitalism it signified how the binary composition of the social was always in peril of being exceeded. In fact, unevenness was omnipresent everywhere capital prevailed, constantly reminding every present of the vast contradictions that people in modern society lived daily and that lay at its heart. But it was precisely this reminder that reinforced the state's desire to impose an image of a smooth and undisturbed social countenance, the evenness of an eternal present. Moreover, this failure to find an adequate conception of the social to resolve and even contain the contradictions capitalism has injected into modern society points to the messiness that actually defines what we have named modernity.

If the nation-state was dedicated to preserving capitalism, it was also committed to ideologizing an image of homogenous empty time signifying its untroubled completion, as Benjamin observed and what Marx called "real subsumption." Whether Marx actually believed capital would ultimately realize the completion of the commodity relation (thus eliminating the last traces of unevenness) is hard to say. I have already stated that he needed such a concept in order to present capitalism as a completed totality, which would allow him to submit it to the analysis and critique that characterizes *Capital*. This was particularly evident in his account of accumulation and the process in which surplus value is transformed into capital. Here, Marx acknowledges that in the process of conversion, "we take no account of the export trade, by means of which a nation can change articles of luxury either into means of production or means of subsistence, and vice versa. In order to examine the object of our investigation in its integrity, free from all disturbing subsidiary circumstances, we must treat the whole world of trade

as one nation, and assume that capitalist production is established everywhere and has taken possession of every branch of industry." It is just likely
that Marx, in this regard, has posited the achievement of real subsumption
as a model, perhaps as a proto-ideal type, which envisions the possible realization and completion of the commodity relation in an as yet unrealized
future, in a last instance that never comes. For its methodological function
has stripped capitalism of "disturbing subsidiary circumstances," and thus
bracketed the messy reality of contemporary history, to imagine an "ideal"
society constituted only of capital and labor.[133] It is plausible to suggest that
he was driven as much by an analytic desire to totalize capitalism as he was
by a conviction that capitalism had reached real subsumption. Elsewhere he
suggested that such a totalization of the bourgeois system conformed to an
organism. "This organic system itself," he explained, "as a totality, has its
presuppositions, and its development to its totality consists precisely in subordinating all elements of society to itself, *or creating out of it organs which it
still lacks. This is historically how it becomes a totality.*"[134] The prompting of a
projection of an imaginary social completely captured by the actualization
of real subsumption must surely derive from the eagerness to see the system's
completion and the elimination of its regressive elements. This desire is
undoubtedly driven by a further preoccupation with the scheduling of a socialist revolution and the final transition yet to come, which, according to
some, depends on the completion of capitalism and the commodity relation.
Yet it must be wondered what world or register of reality such interpreters
inhabit who fail to see what clearly is around and before them, everywhere:
the persisting traces of historical-temporal forms from the past, the shadowed silhouette of "living labor," and the ever present signals they emit of
continuing unevenness. In this regard, it may be that among the strong recent readings of Marx, like those of Antonio Negri, Hans-Georg Backhaus,
and Moishe Postone, not to mention Frankfurt culturalism with its insistence
on the commodification of life at the level of mass consumption and culture, an
older version of stagism still manages to squeeze through the cracks to continually haunt historical materialism, inasmuch as the presumption of real
subsumption discloses a desire to speed up the process in order to accelerate
the path to the crucial and final transition to socialism. An equally compelling explanation for this penchant to secure guarantees supplied by the reliance on stagism is the impulse of political quietism it encourages that

defers the right moment until the last instance, which has yet to come. Many
contemporary interpreters of Marx have strongly argued from both a contemporary perspective that sees the immediate results of production completed and the conviction that it is capital's aim to complete the process of
subsumption in order to set the stage for its ultimate overcoming. What this
tendency reveals is the power of stagism to act as a political unconscious
that posits the ironclad necessity of a completed capitalism as the condition
for realizing socialism. But in this mind-set there are only two stages, as
such, capitalism and socialism, and Marxism is made to appear like an older
modernism that demanded the disavowal of all its historical antecedents.
More important, it denies the presence of both traces of pasts in the present
and the uneven temporalities that point to deeper, material contradictions
and asymmetries. Put another way, it is somewhat similar to viewing the
presence of ruins from different pasts, randomly strewn and silently standing in a landscape, or the visible layering of cultures occupying the same
space in a cityscape. However, the difference is that these material reminders now belong to a landscape (Georg Simmel's "ruins") and are
visually projected into the background and distanced to rarely, if ever,
intervene in the immediacy of the present, whereas the uneven results produced by formal subsumption are always in a foreground (even though
capital seeks to displace them to a forgotten background) that must be
daily lived to be negotiated precisely because they put into question the claim
of unmediated immediacy and put in permanent question the assumption of
completion.

If there is disagreement among Marxists over the analysis of the current
situation and the scheduling of the transition to socialism, it is far more a
historically necessary and realistic assessment than the contemporary discovery of global "inequality" and the solutions offered to ameliorate the run-
away income disparity between the very rich and the rest of us. Marx and
the subsequent tradition of Marxism had always recognized the presence of
inequality as one of the principal consequences of the contradiction between
capital and labor. While it is undoubtedly helpful to now have available precise
quantitative corroboration and breakdown of the actual number and character of the great divide amid us, it is important to acknowledge that this
gathering and organizing of great quantities of comparative data that now
provide a fuller picture of the historical development of inequality was

prompted by the desire to find a solution to capitalism by moderating its excesses through redistribution. For Marxists, the figure of persistent inequality has always constituted a symptom of a deeper and more fundamental problem, which has been capitalism's compulsion to produce unevenness as an unyielding condition of its law of accumulation and guarantee of its continuing existence. In other words, the elaborate methodological exercise to validate the extent of inequality in contemporary life was pegged to maintaining the viability of the capitalist system by determining how to lessen the growing gap between the few very rich and the majority through the implementation of a program aimed at redistributing wealth more equitably. But this move would run counter to capitalism's logic of accumulation founded on sacrificing some people and regions for the development of others. To ignore the relationship between the putative growth of the economy and the returns on capital that exceed it overlooks all that is now known about the relationship of economic growth to development. What has ordinarily been called economic growth is harnessed to the fiction of economic development that has provided the official sanctions to mobilize and make sure that the interests of increasing the returns on capital are continually fulfilled. In this regard, in any case, there appears a curious, if not ironic, commonness shared by Marxists eager to see the final realization of real subsumption and bourgeois economists convinced that capitalism dominates every sphere of global society: with the completion of the commodity relation, Marxists see the promise of the contours of the next stage to socialism, while bourgeois economists envision the possibility of achieving greater equality and fulfilling the fantasy of all "boats rising to the same level."

What Marx thus aimed to realize with his early identification of historic presuppositions that lie behind and alongside of capital's becoming but never really vanish is that (1) bourgeois economy is disclosed merely as a historical form of the processes of production, which itself "points beyond itself to earlier historical modes of production,"[135] and (2) these prior modal historical emanations continue some form of existence under and alongside the domination of capitalism. This was the role ascribed to the form of formal subsumption. But it is important to recognize the trajectory of capitalism's process of "becoming" and how the route was paved for it before it developed its own presuppositions. When Marx turned to assessing the significance of precapitalist formations, he dropped any further commitment to a stagist trajectory enacted by the succession of one form (mode) after another, appearing on the plane of an evolving history and then disappearing after their role had been played out, in imitation of Hegel's charting of Spirit's itinerary to the present. In the account of precapitalist formations, Marx was less preoccupied with any linear unfolding that ultimately led to the realization of capitalism and with privileging the feudal mode as the sovereign carrier of transition. Rather, he envisaged the precapitalist world as an archaic space/time characterized everywhere by tributary relations inflecting local circumstances. In this regard, Samir Amin, in a perspective he shares with Jairus Banaji, is correct to have proposed that even Western feudalism represented merely a weak form of the tributary mode of production that could not have been empowered to provide the sturdy and sole bridge of the "transition" to capitalism's world historical ascendance. The perspective in *Grundrisse* juxtaposes only differing forms of an archaic tributary mode of production to the beginnings and development of the capitalist production process, with the reservoir of historical presuppositions put behind the "becoming" and its virtual disappearance in the "being." Yet, as Marx observed, once the "becoming" of capital had reached the status of its "being," the inversion altered the sequence to situate the logic before the history that lay behind it, an act that István Mészáros has described as the "annihilation of history."

I have already suggested that this recovery of a narrative authorized by the logic of formal subsumption encouraged many Marxist analyses to turn to assessing commodity reification in a modern society presumed to be totally integrated into capitalism: the world of real subsumption. This was the project of "Western Marxism" as envisioned by the Frankfurt School and their fellow travelers. But among Marxists in the periphery, attention turned back to the development of the production process itself, especially the organization of wage labor in specific world regions and times. For one reason or another, these societies came to capitalism chronologically after England and thus confronted circumstances (local histories and political mediations) that departed from the "modular" patterns supplied by earlier developers. What seems striking about the conduct of formal subsumption in these remote regions was an experience of the appearance of a temporal figure composed of mixed times embodied in the survival of practices and remnants of the past now suborned to capitalist domination. When thinkers like Uno Kōzō recorded the persistence of a "feudal mentality" and customs in Japan in capitalist Japan and José Carlos Mariátegui recognized the survival of Inca land arrangements and agricultural practices in 1920s Peru, they were not directly visualizing the coexistence of different temporalities in their present but pointing to the ambiguous silhouette of temporal discordance such a coexistence signified. But it was not until the German philosopher Ernst Bloch dramatized this phenomenon as "synchronous nonsynchronisms" (*ungleichzeitigkeit*), in the effort to grasp the wider psychological consequences of people who occupied the same present but lived in a different time, a different now, that the world figured by the form of formal subsumption acquired a visible temporal identity. The significance of Bloch's timely intervention and figuration of nonsynchronic synchronisms of contemporaneity lay in the expansion of the objective conditions of capitalism and mode of production to include the more subjective dimensions of intellectual, emotional, and cultural experience, which invariably highlight the role performed by the everyday in the merging configuration of world history. What Bloch demonstrated with this move is that capitalism had not yet integrated the whole of society "into the contemporaneity of modern society."[136] In what follows, I will trace the interpretative trajectories of a number of thinkers on the periphery of Euro-America, whose analyses of capitalist development in their immediate circumstances either prefigured the form or actually employed its logic.

2

MARXISM'S
EASTWARD MIGRATION

We know from the doxa of "Western Marxism" that while Marxism turned toward philosophy and privileged the role occupied by the commodity form in structuring the social formation wherein capital had presumably completed its trajectory, historiography at about the same time in the interwar period became preoccupied with the path of linear development, following a plotline that continued to promise the realization of progress into the Cold War. Both perspectives remained within the shadow cast by the Second International's commitment to historical stagism and to the achieved completion of bourgeois revolution as a necessary condition in the final transition to proletarian socialism. It should be noted that the turn to philosophy also meant an abandonment of the expected withering of the state and the realization of a revolutionary transformation. During the Cold War, this viewpoint became enmeshed in a larger comparative strategy that sought to set the agenda for a developmental schedule for newer, nonaligned nations by showing them how they would be able to "catch up" with societies in the West that had completed the course. For its part, the Soviet Union promoted a Stalinist version of the bourgeois modernization scheme but recommended pursuing the route leading to revolutionary conflict to compete with the evolutionary change sponsored by bourgeois modernization. It was, I should add, precisely this obsession with linear progress that Walter Benjamin had earlier warned against in his call for a new vocation for historical materialism.[1]

Undoubtedly it was the appreciation of capitalism's relentless synchronic system, whereby value repetitively valorizes itself to reproduce contemporaneity and brackets its historical antecedents, that commanded Marx's own analytic attention and encouraged later followers to follow in his path. This would explain why he appeared less concerned with the precapitalist formations, as such, and seemed somewhat skeptical toward the possibility of knowing them, even though he considered their putative history in *Grundrisse* and subsequently revisited the scenes of these earlier formations in his ethnologic notebooks, which widely surveyed literatures concerned with regions like Algeria, India, and that of the North American Iroquois. It may be that, for Marx, categorizing certain societies as precapitalist reinforced the figure of the primitive, undeveloped, and nonmodern in societies that had not yet turned to capitalism. I mention this here because bourgeois historians and social scientists promoted evolutionary development among new, decolonized societies during the Cold War years as a preventative against revolutionary transformation, usually calling for complete makeovers that corresponded to a "standard" model, persuaded that the world was divided between the advanced modernities (capitalist) and the backward (noncapitalist). Embossed in this developmental impulse was the conceit that "backward" and "underdevelopment" were the primitives and the colonized identified by an earlier generation of social scientists. It is difficult not to assume that Marxian historiography, especially, with its preoccupation with progressive schemes and commitment to what might be called the "bridge of dreams" promising to link past to present—the "classic" transition from feudalism to capitalism representing the historical development of Western Europe—constituted an encouragement to share this perspective with its bourgeois contemporaries. Be that has it may, *Grundrisse* is where Marx began to foresee a new understanding of history, as I have already suggested, moving beyond his reflections in *The German Ideology* at the moment he was driven to construct a critique of the world of contemporary bourgeois political economy. The urgency of this mandate came from the conviction that because bourgeois economy remained the most "developed historic organization of production," it now required a new understanding of history.

This impulse was particularly compelling in view of political economy's convention to posit the natural development of capitalism—David Ricardo's belief in the economic "laws of nature"—and thus its claims to transhistoricality. Here, also, Marx had observed that bourgeois society itself was a panoply of coexisting, contradictory forms that attested to its mixed historical composition. In this reckoning, the familiar horizontal trajectory associated with historical reconstruction and its reliance on a linear chronology—the before and after—receded from the foreground to be replaced by the recognition of verticality and the necessity of digging and excavating the depths of the present for the traces and resonances of pasts that continue with and within it or behind it, as Marx asserted, "always with an essential difference."[2] This presentism and the thrust of its critical intervention was already visible in his early histories like *The Class Struggles in France* and *The Eighteenth Brumaire of Louis Bonaparte*, which, according to Engels, presented the succession of events in the speech of direct discourse. But the difference came when Marx situated the old being under a new mode of production, which allowed the retention of both temporal associations from an earlier time and its shape in a new context, however "stunted" and "caricatured." Here, as suggested, he disclosed the possibility of a new configuration of the historical field, which relied on implementing a metonymic strategy of substitution and displacement that invariably transposed elements of a prior context into the environs of new one, the present, a movement from absence to presence.[3]

For Marx, then, the historical profile of precapitalist formations came into view in the capitalist present as the polar opposite of capitalism's present, as communal and clan-based typifications that might have existed before the momentous separation from land and means of subsistence that signaled the beginnings of original accumulation and inauguration of wage labor. Marx's historical perspective was concerned with identifying presuppositions, as suggested earlier, what he named as "suspended presuppositions," the "merely historical," "past and gone," that were no longer always visible or evident but clearly important to later development. In this respect, the world of precapitalist social formations would always remain captive to the capitalist present, always mediated by the unstated force of its time-saturated sense of accountancy. It was one thing to put oneself in an ongoing process and another to look out at a past long passed from a perspective wrought by a complex of contemporary mediations. The mediations worked to recode the past in such a way as to allow seeing that it possessed genuine difference that required not the quest for meaning, as such, but a way to analyze and understand it and, as Eelco Runia advised, "transfer presence." If this precapitalist past was no longer visible, its "suspended" state nevertheless suggests its capacity for action had not altogether disappeared and would remain a distinct possibility In the future. With the epoch of capitalism, its vestiges would appear with the exercises that actively enlisted past practices to make of every present an uneven mix of "then" and "now," what I call presents' pasts. But it is important to add that this form, empowered to serve as the basis of all capitalist development, was reinforced by an insight Marx supplied in his recommendations to Vera Zasulich: "In order to expropriate the agricultural producers," he wrote, explaining how to circumvent the "conspiracy of powerful interests" threatening the existence of the Russian commune, "it is not necessary to drive them from the land, as happened in England and elsewhere; not to abolish communal property by some *ukase*."[4] Not only was this a clear repudiation of a standardized model that must be emulated at every step in the development of capitalism, it demonstrated how time itself intervened to short-circuit the process and that the chronology of one historical experience differed from that of others. Japanese economist Uno Kōzō presciently worked this out in the 1940s and after in his meditations on capitalism in Japan, but it is implanted in a number of other textual responses as Marxism migrated from the center and Western Europe and was progressively deprovincialized. It seems natural, then, that in order to escape the aura of exceptionalism that has settled around the figure of Western Marxism and restore its historical place by providing it with a critical supplement it may have often forgotten or ignored and even on some occasions foreclosed, we must turn to precisely those Marxists on the periphery of Euro-America who were not conscripted by a subsequent provincialization, veiled as universal, but convinced they were involved in an undivided global effort in confronting an ongoing process.

The temporal unevenness accompanying the dissolution of the ancient forms was at the core of Marx's new view of history. In fact, what separates Marx's conception of the archaic world of premodern formations from its capitalist successor was the introduction of time and temporality beginning with the introduction of wage labor form, the quantitative calculation of the magnitude of labor power involved in producing a commodity differentiated from the required socially necessary labor, and the implied existence of a workday devoted to creating surplus value. With this temporal transformation and the creation of the workday, along with a new conceptualization of the everyday, we can note a fundamental change from the earlier chronotopic relation by which space dissolved time to a new arrangement whereby time now works to dissolve space.

"Thus, while capital must on the one hand strive to tear down every spatial barrier," Marx wrote in *Grundrisse*,

> to conquer the whole earth for its market, it strives on the other side to annihilate this space with time, i.e., to reduce to a minimum the time spent in motion from one place to another. The more developed the capital, therefore, the more extensive the market over which it circulates, which forms the spatial orbit of its circulation, the more does it strive simultaneously for an even greater extension of the market and for greater annihilation of space by time. (If labour is regarded not as the working day of the individual workers, but as the indefinite working day of an indefinite number of workers, then all relations of population come in here.)[5]

In *Capital*, it was made clear that the history of the appropriation of agricultural producers "assumes different aspects in different countries, and runs throughout various phases in different orders of succession, and different epochs."[6] While original accumulation referred only to countries already embarked on the capitalist route, there is no reason to exclude colonized regions like India, China, and parts of Southeast Asia in the nineteenth century, where forms of wage labor had already begun to appear in the production of commodities and their price calibration and distribution by the world market. This suggests that differential temporal rates, if not histories, marked each society's development along a capitalist trajectory that reflected the uneven development of material production that was especially evident between different spheres of social activity and among a diversity of societies. While older temporalities accompanying labor practices may have prevailed in the production of goods in various regions, once they reached the world market they were submitted to the leveling "command" of standardization.

When both nation and its representation of history were designated as the political form for entry into the world market, the imperative to extinguish spectral reminders of unevenness and untimeliness became even more compelling. At this juncture, the category of the time lag appeared to become identified with backwardness and was exported to regions outside of Euro-America as the sign of their collective underdevelopment, even though it functioned to conceal both its instance within advanced capitalist societies and capitalism's own law of uneven development and unscheduled cycles, waves, irregular rhythms.

We can infer from all this that Marx had moved toward envisaging multiple possibilities for transformation among the world's societies. As contemporary Russia showed, different societies could utilize the remnants and residues of prior modes of production inherited from their own pasts to either create a new register of formal subsumption or bypass capitalism altogether. In pursuit of this trajectory, I follow Marxism's migration to the east and turn first to V. I. Lenin (1870–1924), whose observation of Russia as an "Asiatic state" and analysis of the importance of the domestic market in the development of capitalism in Russia opened the way to appraising the effects of the "invasion" of capitalism within the context of medieval commodity production—that is, how the utilization of older practices under the direction of capitalism was carried out. I turn then to Rosa Luxemburg (1871–1919), whose theorization of accumulation ultimately led to the world outside Euro-America and the importance of noncapitalism for capitalist accumulation. With Luxemburg, we get more than a fleeting glimpse of the formation of what Marx had early named as world history, whereby "universal competition . . . made all civilized nations and every individual member of them dependent for their satisfaction of their wants on the whole world, thus destroying the former natural exclusiveness of separate nations." It is necessary to point out that both Lenin and Luxemburg were able to think through the logic of subsumption and often presented its presence without naming it as such, without having accessible the texts in which its description was detailed that appeared in later editions of *Capital.* The chapter will conclude with a brief consideration of Leon Trotsky's contribution to this discourse and, paradoxically, Georg Lukács, who despite laying the foundations for Western Marxism, perceived in contemporary capitalism's unrealized state the persistence of older "feudal" practices alongside the new.

II

The importance of Lenin's early economic work is reflected in his concerted attempt to construct a critique against cultural reductionism and the defense of exceptionalism articulated by *narodniki*[8] as an explanation of Russia's economic development. There appeared to be a historical urgency to overcoming the problem of delayed development. "In Russia," he charged in an early text,

> the relics of medieval, semi-feudal institutions are still so enormously strong (as compared with Western Europe), they are such an oppressive yoke upon the proletariat and the people generally, retarding growth of political thought in all estates and classes, that one cannot but insist on the tremendous importance which the struggle against all feudal institutions and the bureaucracy has for the workers. . . . The workers must be shown what degrading pressure [it] exerts . . . , how they keep capital in its medieval forms, which, while not falling short of the modern, industrial forms in respect of the exploitation labour, add to this exploitation by placing terrible difficulties in the way of the fight for emancipation.[9]

In this regard, Lenin turned his attention to and aimed at dissembling an argument promoted by what he called bourgeois populists, represented by Peter Struve, who condemned the appearance of capitalism in Russia as an unnatural accidental and "temporary deviation" of Russia's "right path" that urgently needed to be eliminated because it was inflicting damage on the country's "natural economy."[10] Lenin's critical purpose was to demonstrate that the idea of a "natural economy" in Russia was a culturalist fantasy that had resulted from a romanticized hermeneutics, which further claimed an irreducibly exceptionalist identity between Russia and nature. The effect of this populist exceptionalism was to move discourse away from the reality of economics (political economy) and the world at large—the world market—because it departed from "ancient principles" and the "age-old basis" of peasant labor.[11]

At a more general level, it should be stated that the stakes Lenin and Struve shared were determining the nature of Russian society and its subsequent "modern" course in view of the penetration of capitalism into the country-side. For the *narodniks*, the spreading specter of capitalism proclaimed the doom of a traditional way of life that had enjoyed the status of an unques-tioned status quo.[12] Struve's view stretched back to the early nineteenth century (and beyond) and was premised on the challenge posed by Western-ization to Russia's spiritual uniqueness. Much of this explicit antimodernism was directed at capitalism and its broader social consequences for moderniza-tion and vocalized by a Slavophil ideology that valorized Russian Ortho-doxy, autocracy, and its unique spiritual mission to stand as a protective bulwark against the non-Christians hordes. These constituted the principles embodied in Russia's "exceptionalist" cultural endowment and supplied the foundation for the formation of an incipient cultural nationalism.[13] Embed-ded in this cultural nationalism was a virulent distrust of the figure of modern civilization in which capitalism undoubtedly occupied a prominent position. Specifically, it was opposed to instrumental reason, rationality, technology, the scientific method, and a host of political philosophies that privileged the importance of the individual and the adoption of ascription based on ability rather than heredity. By the time Lenin began to imagine his critique, a good deal of this antimodern nationalism had been absorbed by the *narodniks* and their idealization of a natural economy. The merit of Lenin's critique was to show how these populists, "naïve bourgeois roman-tics," as he variously called them, had identified Russia with a natural econ-omy, dominated by agriculture and peasant labor. At the core of the *narodnik* ideology was the figure of the "people," who, in Struve's description, com-prised the village community, possessed little land, and were burdened by taxation. In Lenin's view, "the meaning of the word 'people's' . . . rules out the exploitation of one who works—so that by definition . . . the author actu-ally conceals the undoubted fact that in our peasant economy there is the very same appropriation of surplus value."[14] Like workers in a factory, peas-ants lacked independence; if the factory represented a progressive capital-ism, the village community differed only to the degree that its capitalism was more recessive and the forms of exploitation were applied "singly, by semi-feudal methods."[15] In other words, the term "people" was already a disguised category of capitalism rather than the embodiment of Russia's long, con-tinuous historical culture. In the ensuing exchange, Lenin represented the forces of modern rationality, and his magisterial text *The Development of Capitalism in Russia* (1900), filled with exhaustive empirical and quantitative evidence, deployed his own defense of capitalism's development as a self-evidently inexorable process, whereas Struve articulated an argument that tried to clarify the rootedness of Russian life in a timeless natural economy.

In *The Development of Capitalism in Russia*, one of his earliest economic works, Lenin concentrated on plotting the course of Russia's evolving capitalist development and especially the central role performed by the expansion of the domestic market. His earlier critical assault on the *narodniki* theorist Struve (1894) had already brought to light the question of the disintegration of the old system. In the later work on development, he supplied both coverage (surveying all regions) and an exhaustive mining of data to demonstrate the expansion of capitalist production and practices in the countryside to uphold its significance for stimulating the growth of the domestic market. Where the *narodniks* saw in the appearance of capitalist practices a slow but steady invasion of the countryside and the gradual decline of the peasantry, denoting both economic and moral disintegration, Lenin detected in the same landscape, especially in signs indicating the formation of contradictions forged by a fusion of the old and new, precapitalism and capitalism, the promise of transformation that ultimately would bring the establishment of industrial capitalism and its mode of production to transport Russia into the modern world. The *narodniks*, he charged, had misrecognized the handicraft industry as precapitalist, when, in fact, its organization had already begun to reflect capitalist principles.

In this early critique directed at Struve, the principal issue of contention seemed to be over the populist's notion of the "natural economy." This view was favored by proponents of an agriculturally based economy close to nature, and dramatized by the call urging all "to go to the people" that resonated throughout the country in the late nineteenth century. This premise also contributed to the preservation of large landowning rural estates (*kulaks*), even though earlier radical populist platforms had called for their dissolution as a condition of redistributing the land among the peasantry. The signs of capitalism in the countryside signaled the intrusion of contamination, an "accident," "an artificial hothouse plant" imported from Europe's history that would seek to undermine the natural economy.[16] It is interesting

to note the populists' inability to see in political economy the same claims
to nature they attributed to the natural economy. Even more, the *narodniki*
populists were not simply agrarianists, as such, but also nativists, who feared
the damaging effects introduced into Russian life by the penetration of a
foreign—European—system of economic exchange and everything else it implied for social and political modernization. In this, their fears were nour-
ished not simply by the presence of a different mode of economic activity but
also as much by the threatened cultural destruction it would surely bring in
its wake. The apparent accident of capitalism's appearance constituted a departure from "ancient principles" founded on peasant labor, from archaism
itself.[17] Lenin's critique pointed to the importance of commodity economics
precisely because it represented a "money economy" that would lead Russia
to capitalism. For this reason, he was prepared to defend the spread of capitalism, especially as it was embodied in rural handicraft manufacturing, as
a prescient prefiguration of capitalist organization rather than as an augury
of the disintegration of the precapitalist socioeconomic order, as Struve
had supposed. The presence of "buyership," or "buyers-up, "Lenin asserted,
"is the all prevailing fact of the actual organization of our handicraft industries," which not only yields "high profits" and "low wages" but proves how
"this form of organization is not only capitalist" but has "prevailed" in the
midst of what *narodnik* economics assumed had been precapitalist and simply a function of a natural economy.[18] In other words, the populist defense
of "small-scale" handicrafts and "hand-held" manufacturing had blinded
theorists like Struve from grasping the actual coexistence of capitalist forms
of organization and older practices of agricultural cultivation belonging
to the precapitalist medieval village community. Lenin was keenly aware
of how the older practices derived from medieval precapitalism were harnessed to newer capitalist conventions like the wage form and surplus value.
What the *narodniks* overlooked with their intention to preserve the fiction of
a "natural economy" was the development of capitalism that already was
beginning to appropriate what it found useful for its purpose. "Narodism," he
wrote, "which stands for leveling out the peasants (. . . before the *kulak*), is
'regressive' because it desires to keep capital within . . . medieval forms that
combine exploitation with scattered, technically backward production with
personal pressure on the producer."[19] One of his earlier texts on narodism
pointed to how the "friends of the people" will never grasp the simple fact

that "despite its general wretchedness, its comparatively tiny establishments and extremely low productivity of labour and small number of wage workers, peasant industry is *capitalism*."[20] What they failed to comprehend was that capital was a social relation between people, and it made no difference whether the level of development was high or low.

Lenin wrote *The Development of Capitalism in Russia* before the 1905 Revolution, during the brief hiatus after the occurrence of the large labor strikes of 1895 and 1897. In this lull, the working class withdrew, expanded its numbers, deepened its grip on Russian society, and "pav[ed] the way for the beginning in 1901 of the demonstration movement."[21] While the principal purpose of the book was to show the importance of the domestic market in the expansion of capitalism in Russia, its analysis concentrated on critically analyzing class structure in Russia on the basis of economic investigation that would subsequently be confirmed by the revolution. Lenin's study disclosed both the disproportionate political significance of the numerically small industrial proletariat and the "dual position and dual role of the peasantry," which, on the one hand, referred to the survivals of corvée labor, economy, and serfdom, and, on the other hand, "the inherently contradictory class structure of this mass."[22] For Lenin, this revolutionary arrangement in Russia constituted the economic basis of what he believed would be a bourgeois revolution. Such a Russian revolution could have two possible outcomes: the old, landlord economy, "bound by the thousand threads of serfdom," would prevail and slowly evolve into a capitalist "Junker economy," or the landlord economy would be dissolved by the revolution, destroying also the residues of serfdom and large landowners, paving the way for the free development of small peasant farming. If the former occurred, the agrarian system controlled by the state would become capitalist and continue to retain feudal features; if the latter succeeded, the whole agrarian system would become capitalist, and the faster older feudal remnants were swept away, the faster the peasantry would be able to differentiate into specialized divisions of labor. The choice came down to either continued landlordism and all it implied or destruction and all its reinforcing structure, which Lenin called the "old superstructure."[23] In the event of the success of this type of bourgeois revolution, conditions would be in place for the "further accomplishment by the working class of the real and fundamental task of social reorganisation." What is interesting and even visionary about this analysis made on the eve of the 1905 Revolution is how it anticipated Gramsci's conceptualization of a passive revolution, which brought together the competing outcomes and anticipated the Japanese division between those who saw in the Meiji Restoration of 1868 a counterrevolution and re-feudalization and those who envisaged it as a genuine bourgeois transformation. In Lenin's scenario, the Meiji Restoration for some would constitute a Junker-type counterrevolution; for others, a genuine bourgeois transformation. In this regard, it should also be pointed out that Lenin was not constrained by his own strategic thinking and readily acknowledged that an "infinitely diverse combinations of elements of this or that type of capitalist evolution are possible, and only hopeless pedants could set about solving the peculiar and complex problems arising merely by quoting this or that opinion of Marx about a different historical epoch."[24]

Lenin detailed the coexistence of the corvée and capitalist systems of economy to demonstrate the compatibility of a combined system consisting of continued labor service ("labor-rent") and capitalism's hired wage workers.[25] In this connection he put into question "Narodnik reasoning: if it is forgotten that the allotment of land to the peasant is one of the conditions of corvée or labor-service economy," then the next step is to "omit" the circumstances that this putative "independent" cultivator must therefore offer labor-rent, either rent in kind or money rent, which retains the fiction of the "pure" idea of "the tie between producer and the means of production." But, he observed, "the actual relation between capitalism and precapitalist forms of exploitation does not change in the least from the fact of simply omitting these [precapitalist] forms."[26] Here was evidence that two different economic modes were in a relationship with each other and that the accompanying forms of exploitation did not necessarily correspond to specific modes of production but rather were often expropriated from prior practice to serve entirely new systems of economic production.

The point of this observation was to demonstrate the extent of *narodnik* misunderstanding. Populists saw the perseverance of precapitalist forms of exploitation as reflections of the energetic prevalence of the older system of natural economy rather than the strength and adaptability of the new.[27] In the critique of Struve, Lenin explained that the populists had failed to grasp the fact that the existence of the natural economy was subject to "influences" of the exchange economy. Accordingly, the natural economy had already become captive to a process of embourgeoisement, inasmuch as Struve's identification of "economic rationalization" with high rents forgot to add that rents regularly presuppose the "bourgeois organization of agriculture" and its subordination to the market. Moreover, they disregarded the fact that the "initial form of *capital* has always been merchant's, money capital, that capital always takes the technical production *as it finds it*, and only subsequently subjects it to technical transformation."[28] Instead, the *narodniks* have clung to upholding "contemporary agriculture" against the capitalist incursion, which bolstered "medieval forms" of capital against the newer bourgeois ones.

For Lenin, paraphrasing Marx's brief remarks on formal subsumption in volume I of *Capital*, it was essential to explain that "feudal relations—in both the economic sphere . . . and still more in the social and juridical-political spheres" coexist alongside agriculture.[29] What seems so extraordinary about the proposition is that it actually worked to extend the scope of formal subsumption to include areas outside the economic domain. The consequence of extending the logic of capital in this way was to reveal the obviously close relationship between economic (agricultural) production and other activities in the social, political, and juridical spheres; it also sanctioned the utilization of such practices that apparently belonged to prior modes of production now pressed into serving capital. There is often a tendency to forget that the sharp differentiation of spheres of activity and its resulting production of specialized knowledge was a recent phenomenon characterizing industrializing societies since the late nineteenth and early twentieth centuries. This extension of the range of formal subsumption beyond the merely economic (labor and production) to the political and juridical realms opened the way for capitalism's subsequent utilization of religion, culture, and custom in late-developing societies. Lenin reminded Struve, in this regard, that despite the "progressive character of change," development, once the "commodity economy" began to fuse with bourgeois capitalism, the "subordination of labor to capital is covered up by thousands of the remnants of medieval relations which prevent the producer from seeing the essence of the matter."[30] In other words, the medieval order was already within the process of change, even though it appeared to remain intact as it had been, which was another of way of describing how formal subsumption worked and recalls Marx's own description of the flax worker who does the same kind of work as a wage laborer as he did before acquiring this new status. Nothing, as Marx added, has changed but his soul.

In spite of Lenin's consistent advocacy of capitalism's "necessary" progressive domination of the economic sphere of relations in Russia, he was equally insistent that it was still characterized by visible traces of received "medieval practices," beginning with the communal village. The Russian village dominated the place of central concern among *narodniki* preoccupations concerned with preserving the sanctity of the "natural economy." In response to their claim that the village was incompatible with capitalism, Lenin argued that no aspect of peasant village life was exempt from the "contradictory form," one that specifically signified the supreme importance of capitalism. Against Struve's valorization of an exceptionalist "people's production," Lenin countered in *The Development of Capitalism in Russia* by explaining that the contradictions revealed that the system of economic relations in the commune and village no longer represented a rural imaginary idealized by populists but instead now pointed to a new reality consisting of a struggle of interests characteristic of capitalism and an ordinary bourgeois order[31] Apart from referring to a process implicated in generating contradictions, there is more than a distant echo of Marx's advice to Zasulich concerning the joining of the archaic and contemporary, whereby the surviving residue of the commune coupled with capitalism. Yet it is likely that Lenin was not nearly as optimistic about the capacity of the village commune's traditional character to fuse with modern capitalism. What he saw was the willingness of the countryside to incorporate the new elements as the means of replacing the "wretchedness," "its domination of the Asiatic way of life," that hobbled peasant life for so long. In Lenin's critique of populist economic theory, it is not certain that he knew about Marx's recommendations to never fear the archaic, even though his reflections suggested a similar sentiment.[32] More to the point, he was trying to make, it was the modern that should never be feared, rather than the archaic. At the center of these aggregate contradictions lived by peasants was a course that differentiated them into carrying out newer work practices Lenin named as "depeasantizing," whereby the peasantry would undergo a more recent kind of socialization.[33] He discerned in the contradictions introduced by the merging of capitalist and older work routines the "deepest and most durable foundations" of the Russian rural community that irrefutably shows its departure from the "artificiality" of influences attributed to it by the *narodniks*. At the same time, Lenin accepted the enduring stamina of traditions inherited from the "distant past," which weighed heavily on the peasant community and continually functioned to retard the transformative process. The "germs" of development depended on the implementation of the "next form of rent, *money rent*," which represented a change from rent in kind (*Produktenrente*). And this changeover undoubtedly accompanied the differentiation of the peasantry into the register of newly socialized wage workers, who increasingly would be forced to remit the rent in money. The differentiation of the peasantry also contributed to the creation and expansion of the domestic market, especially in the appearance of the "middle peasantry."

Lenin's identification of the "transition" from corvée to capitalist economy best exemplified how he fixed on the figure of a "combination," the mixing of the older labor-rent system (payment in kind) with newer forms driven by money that appeared alongside it (after the reforms of the early 1860s). The combination illustrated the difficulty in distinguishing "between such a 'peasant'" and the "West European or Ostee" farm laborers, who receive a plot of land on the understanding that they were obliged to work a definite amount of time as payment. But here, again, Lenin's commitment to rationality as the key to accelerating change in the countryside was curbed by his own acknowledgment that reality is more complex. "Life creates forms," he confessed, "that unite in themselves with remarkable gradualness systems of economy whose basic features constitute opposites. It becomes impossible to say where 'labour service (corvée)' ends and where 'capitalism begins.'"[34] In his view, these quite different and diametrically opposed systems frequently prevented the transition from taking place overnight. The issue of the awaited "transition" was further complicated because labor service appeared in diverse types—peasants working for the landlord for money, peasants using their own tools in the cultivation of fields owned by landowners, and other forms manifest in cultivators who were persuaded to borrow grain or money, on the promise to work off the loan or its interest. In this case, he concluded that the form of labor service plainly dramatized "bondage," the usurious character of hired labor. In still other instances, peasants would work for "trespass" (working off legally established fines they may have incurred) or voluntarily express a willingness to work out of "respect" in order to avoid future unemployment imposed by the land-owner.[35] This complexity resulted in payments for rented land use in these and other varying forms that often combined with rent in kind, accentuating the "imperceptible" passage from one type of rent to another.[36] Lenin believed the system of labor-rent and half-cropping was little more than labor service and bonded hire to frequently throw poorer peasants into the ranks of wage labor. As far as the combination of labor service and work for payment in kind (exploited by usurers) was concerned, capitalism "makes the present system of landlord farming extremely similar in its economic organization to the system that prevailed in our textile industry before the development of large scale machine industry."[37] In those cases, industrial capital combined with merchants capital, and the handicraft worker, apart from carrying the burden of capital he now had to assume, was further fettered to subcontracting, trucking systems, and so forth. This "transitional system," Lenin noted, lasted for centuries, attesting to the "remarkable gradualness" of the process. But he was less concerned with the historically temporal consequences of these combinations of pre- and proto-capitalist procedures and capitalism than in demonstrating how the combination worked to facilitate the transition to capitalism in the countryside. Nor did he, and to a certain extent Luxemburg as well, register any sensitivity to the necessarily complex calculation involved in the reconfiguration of expanded working times demanded by these new forms of combinations.[38]

If Lenin was convinced of the inevitable progress of capitalism in Russia and the certain defeat of a seminatural (feudal) economy, which the *narod-niks* sought to save from the "artificial hothouse plant" of capitalism, this faith in capitalism's eventual victory was actually founded on the deeper conviction in the necessary triumph of socialism. Capitalism, he proposed, was driven by the imperative pressures of a future imperfect in which the antici-pated society would be composed of vast contradictions capable of eventually tearing it apart and that could be overcome only through transformation. Although he paradoxically shared a common ground with the populists over the combined coming together of different and opposing economic systems, he rejected Struve's ideological representations for viewing this arrange-ment as simply one system and not as a constellation of contradictory conse-quences for the development of class differences. Specifically, he pointed to how the *narodnik* vision ignored the consequential effects of differentiation, which were producing different and competing forms of social life that were beginning to compose the basis of interest and ceaseless struggle, drawing in especially the "fully appropriated worker." Where Lenin's analysis clearly departed from the populist representation was in his refusal to accept their claims for a natural economy, free from the contagion of the commodity product, even in its most precapitalist feudal form. For it was precisely these forms that showed first signs of capitalist economic organization on which an incipient bourgeois capitalism could be founded. Yet his differences from the populist perspective were not always as distant as he hoped to dramatize.

In *The Development of Capitalism in Russia*, Lenin inserted a narrative that reported the conditions of a farm managed by a well-known *narodnik*, titled "The Story of Engelhardt's Farm," based on the account written by the farmer Engelhardt, "Letters from the Countryside."[39] But it should be divulged that between the earlier text, "The Heritage We Renounce," and the later text on economic development, he changed his mind. In the former, he condemns Engelhardt for embracing older feudal methods of agricultural production at the same time as he begins to resort to innovative measures clearly derived from capitalist practice and experience, without acknowledging it.[40] On the one hand, he recommends the retention of labor-rent at the same time as he "completely fails to realize that the social form of these improvements in farming methods is the most effective refutation of his own theory that capitalism is impossible in our country."[41]

According to his later portrayal, it seemed that Engelhardt was held in high esteem in populist circles. In Engelhardt's experiences in farm management after the reforms, Lenin uncovered a change in views in his appraisal of labor service and capitalist practices that differed from those traditionally embraced by most *narodniks*. "The evolution of this farm," Lenin commented, "reflects in miniature . . . the main features of the evolution of all privately land owned farming in post-Reform Russia."[42] Charting Engelhardt's history, Lenin took special notice of the fact that when the farmer started supervising the estate it was still within the context of the old system's dependence on labor service and bondage; in short, it still identified with a semifeudal patriarchal order. The farm's reliance on labor service had caused a decline in conditions and productivity, whose effects were particularly detrimental to the raising of cattle, further reflecting inadequate cultivation of the soil and continuous utilization of obsolete methods of field cultivation. Engelhardt, according to his own account, confessed to the impossibility of "farming in the old way." Grain prices were dropping because of increased competition from agricultural regions in the steppe. In a response designed to offset the inevitable decline of the farm's productivity, Engelhardt was aware from the beginning of his administration of the estate that routine dependence on the practice of labor service was being accompanied by the use of wage earners. Impressed by the results of this precedent, he started modestly to simultaneously supplement the utilization of labor-rent service with a capitalist wage system. Even though the presence of wage workers was numerically small compared to workers who provided "rent" through labor service, they were employed when the farm was still operating on the basis of the old system. The low levels of productivity opened the way to raise the wage level of the newly hired, which had been historically low. What caught Lenin's attention in this story is that in spite of the fact that Engelhardt's farm started from procedures familiar to all Russian farms dominated by prevailing forms of bondage, the dramatic change that occurred was the shift from the "bound peasant to the farm labourer." The results of this change in productivity and profitability were measurably great, and Engelhardt "triumphantly report[ed] the success of his innovation, the diligence of the labourers, and quite justly show[ed] that the customary accusations flung at the labourer of being lazy and dishonest are due to the 'brand of serfdom' and to the bonded labourer 'for the lord.'"[43] Lenin was convinced that the new organization of farming implemented by Engelhardt demanded a display of enterprise, knowledge of people, and a capacity to handle them, as well as a familiarity with the technical and commercial aspects of agriculture—qualities, he added, that were never possessed by Ivan Goncharov's famous fictional protagonist, Oblomov. Above all else, Engelhardt was calling attention to a new rationality implicated in capitalist management and ratifying with the various changes the inseparable relationship between agricultural technology and the transformation of the economy. But he also knew that new agricultural technology was intimately bound to the "elimination of labour-service by capitalism."[44]

Personifying the classic model and representative of *narodnik* ideals committed to preserving the values of the natural economy, Engelhardt turned first to making flax cultivation into a commercial crop, which meant recruiting an adequate supply of wage workers. The problem he encountered was how to obtain sufficient numbers. "His success was achieved," Lenin reported, ". . . thanks to the introduction of the *piece-rate system of paying* his workers" and "does not even suspect that substitution of piece rates for time rates is one of the most widespread methods by which a developing capitalist economy heightens the intensification of labour and increases the rate of surplus-value."[45] At the same time, he resorted to utilizing workers based on the older system of labor service in the new commercial endeavor, which failed, inducing him to deploy his hired hands in flax production and hire laborers for other specific jobs. Engelhardt also engaged women to work in certain jobs, all of which resulted in the successful outcome of his plan; and he recruited workers for other agricultural pursuits like threshing, testifying to greater specialization of the workforce, when it previously had been carried out within the older system. In all cases, when operations were withdrawn from the labor service by capitalism and assigned to wage workers, Engelhardt noted an increase in productivity, fewer workers to do the job, a reduction of actual labor time as a result, and an increase in profits.

In this way, Lenin was able to trumpet Engelhardt's own testimony as crowning evidence of the effectiveness of the new system and its rationality against the populist valorization of a seminatural economy, which had overlooked the prevalence of commodity production and the beginnings of a form of protocapitalism in the precapitalist epoch. Populists had viewed the institution of labor service bondage as a direct dictation from nature. Above all, Lenin saw in the populist referral to its claim of eternality simply a fiction masking a historically developed system based on continued bondage and exploitation. Just as the process of combining different systems proceeded at a gradual and almost imperceptible pace, in which capital took what it found useful, so the elimination of the older practices would also take time. Engelhardt's examples already provided proof that capitalism had taken over what it found useful and that production and labor were already being subordinated to its command. Yet it is interesting to notice that Lenin made little or no mention of this new hegemonic relationship between capital and production installed in the countryside. His silence hinted at the resumption of a "natural" process of change leading to the simple replacement of one set of practices by another, as if, in fact, to make the case for the self-evident

superiority of capitalism's natural rationality. The system of farming continued the combining of the old and the new, even though Lenin had been
able to signal a significant shift in "weight" from the former to the latter
that literally redefined the nature of the farm's economic system. But, again,
he failed to consider that the transferring of weight between two systems of
labor would inevitably introduce a temporal unevenness within the same
workspace of the farm's system of production, as implied in Engelhardt's report. While Engelhardt tried to solve this problem by differentiating work
functions, calling attention to the importance of the division of labor and
implying that over time work had become "varied," and even separating their
spatial locations, the problem required systematic calculation, which neither
he nor Lenin reported. Lenin was persuaded that capitalism would eventually remove these older traces as anomalous remnants and that if labor service and bondage were indefinitely retained in a subordinate position, it
would continue to change its character, inasmuch as it involved not only
peasant farmers but additionally regular laborers and agricultural day laborers. Implied in this observation was the certainty of the ongoing process
of socialization that would transmute all work into wage labor.

Lenin's point was clear: the experience of the *narodnik* Engelhardt repudiated his own idealized image of the relationship between natural economy
and agricultural cultivation. Although Engelhardt proceeded to envision a
rational agenda of production by increasing capitalization, he remained a
committed *narodnik* nonetheless. He had been prevented from realizing this
new goal under a social and economic system that unquestioningly had relied on semifeudal labor based on "ancient principles." Instead, he turned
toward both the employing of wage laborers, who proved to be more productive, and raising the level of technical competence of agricultural cultivation
on "all private landowner farms in general in Russia," to which the new wage
workers were making a substantial contribution.[46] But Lenin's own analysis was distinguished by an insistent affirmation of the centrality of wage
labor in supporting older methods of work even as it absorbed and metabolized its procedures to serve its own process of production. The thrust of this
argument was to discount the exceptionalist explanatory claims of culturalism rooted in the soil of the unique cultural endowment of "Holy Russia" for
economics and history. Where Rosa Luxemburg departed from Lenin, as we
shall see, was less in her sensitivity toward the destruction of local cultures

of reference caused by the penetration of capitalism in establishing its production system (even though it was considerable) than in the presumed final
realization of capitalism. It was her criticism of real subsumption that constituted the principal condition for recognizing that capital needed noncapital (and thus newly acquired colonies) to expand accumulation. When
Lenin later emphasized the primary consequence of the growth of finance
capital and how it quickly coupled with imperial expansion and the colonial
seizure, the scene of this emerging finance capital and its spread would alter
the logic of capitalist development once industrial capital was exceeded. This
change was verified in the aptitude of finance capital, as the dominant form
of capital, to bypass the need to eliminate the remnants of older modes of
production, accepting them as they are, since it could easily "accommodate
their differences" by managing the different temporalities they represented
and making use of what they had to offer, which also included taking over
their exploitative practices to now serve the pursuit of value. This was particularly true of newly acquired colonial possessions (see Chinua Achebe,
Arrow of God), but finance capital could just as easily incorporate any
combination of practices as a permanent relationship.[47]

III

While Rosa Luxemburg never used the term "formal subsumption," her
conception of expanded reproduction was based on the necessity of capitalism
to rely on regions characterized by noncapitalism. If she recognized the
devastation capitalism inflicted on such areas, long before Fanon remarked on
how colonialism destroyed "cultures of reference," she also affirmed how
capitalism needed to coexist with noncapitalism, where it would find "buyers," not "consumers," to absorb its surplus product.[48] The distinction referred
to the absence of a capitalist framework in the case of the former, and its
prevalence in the latter, whereby workers would constitute consumers of
much of what they produced. In fact, it was Luxemburg who saw early that
a mature capitalist society, what Marx would call "real subsumption," composed of capitalists and workers, could not possibly expand indefinitely without reaching out to the noncapitalist world. With this insight she indirectly
suggested that a fully matured capitalism was simply a methodological model
allowing Marx to envision the totality of capitalism. Luxemburg's attention

focused on precisely those experiences that either prefigured capitalism, like the organization of archaic communal forms that had managed to exist alongside the development of capitalism, or inevitably necessitated the exactions from colonial expropriation, if it was to reproduce the process of accumulation. In the case of colonial extraction, it meant turning to explaining the reasons that capitalism needed continual involvement with noncapitalist countries. Yet it is crucial to understanding the symmetry between Luxemburg's account of archaic agrarian communal societies and their "natural economies" that would ultimately be undermined by capitalism and the introduction of advanced technology in the countryside and her conviction (contrary to Marx) that capitalism's necessity to realize expanded accumulation required relying on diverse forms of colonized societies that reflected the organization of rural communalism—the world of noncapitalism. This combination of capitalism's necessary penchant for expansion and the acceleration of the forces of production overdetermined both the rapidity of its global extension and the relentless depreciation of native cultures of reference and received practices in domestic societies already committed to capitalist development. In the former instance, capitalism threatened to destroy the residues of precapitalist historical formations, digging them out of the soil of these cultures with the same kind of relentless intensity as the bulldozer that plows under everything in its way and erasing the material remnants of the rich sediments of village histories of precapitalist rural communes; in the latter case, Luxemburg observed how the quickened pace of technological innovation in industrial production and with it the establishment of a domain of relative surplus value were making workers' skills obsolete and driving them into unemployment. But in both cases, Luxemburg discerned the stubborn endurance of older practices in a capitalist present and revealed a grasp of the general logic of capitalist development.

It is possible to detect in Luxemburg's preoccupation with the question of how capitalism and noncapitalism were brought together in a close kinship a delayed continuation of Marx's earlier formulations on accumulation and subsumption that accompanied the genesis of capitalism. Despite the passage of time between the two events (original accumulation and colonialism) and changed geographic locations, it was virtually the same logic at work. "What are the conditions of this universal accumulation," she asked, "to what elements can it be reduced?" Her answer: *"The conditions for the ac-*

cumulation of capital are precisely those which rule its original accumulation and reproduction in general."[49] With Marx, accumulation—especially primitive or originary accumulation (*ursprüngliche Akkumulation*)—comprised the conditions whereupon the capitalist "became possessed of money by some form of primitive accumulation that took place independently of the unpaid labour of other people, and this was therefore how he was able to frequent the market as a buyer of labour power."[50] What began as simple "continuity of the process, by simple reproduction," whereby material wealth was ceaselessly converted into capital thus became the "capitalist's means of enjoyment and . . . valorization." The worker leaves the process as he entered it, "deprived of any means of making that wealth a reality for himself."[51] But Marx maintained that primitive accumulation was the historical base, not the result of capitalist production.[52] The utilization of surplus value as capital and its reconversion back into capital is called accumulation. At the basis of this process is unpaid labor. During the moment of originary or primitive accumulation, Marx claimed that its source lay in money that belonged to a precapitalist mode of production, and Luxemburg, with Marx, agreed that the occurrence of the momentous event in England, especially, came with the "expropriation of the agricultural producer of the peasant from the soil." This became the basis of the whole process.[53] What this meant once labor power was exchanged for wages was that former agricultural workers were thrown onto the labor market as "free workers" engaged in the creation of surplus value that necessitated the operation of formally subsuming workers to now perform tasks either by employing labor practices they had hitherto inherited from a prior precapitalist mode of production or by being slowly recruited to carry out newer productive operations, as Lenin had reported on Engelhardt's Russian farm. In the former case, the immediate result was some form of subsumption or hybrid mix; in the latter case, a slow, developmental process that took a long time, new technologies gradually entered the production process as capitalism differentiated into forms of specialization to become a distinct mode of production. But the kinship between older and newer practices continued to perdure as a partnership, even as Luxemburg observed that once production for surplus value was undertaken, it worked to undermine older skills and practices that aimed at their eventual destruction. Here, it should be recalled that she was far less persuaded by the possibility of realizing a completed state of "real subsumption" in the foreseeable

future and constantly repeated this doubt in her criticism of Marx's conceptualization of enlarged reproduction, which was founded on this premise.[54]
"The decisive fact," she charged, "is that the surplus value cannot be realized by sale either to workers or to capitalists."[55] In fact, she took exception
to Marx's explanation of expanded accumulation that required nothing
more than a society constituted of only capitalists and workers to consume
the surplus product and looked to regions of "noncapitalism" as the solution
to continuously expanding production and as the source for the surplus
labor it necessitated.

Luxemburg's identification of noncapitalist regions outside Euro-America colonized by European imperial powers corresponded closely to her own
experience of socialization in occupied Poland and an Eastern Europe still
haunted by a "second serfdom," perched on the periphery of Western industrial societies.[56] She was intimately aware of colonial domination of economically less developed areas and the role played by forms of "dispossession" in
the process of expanded accumulation. Russia surely saw in Poland and Eastern Europe regions less developed economically that could supply a steady
source of exploitation (raw materials and cheap labor) and fuel its own aspirations for capitalist development. In this regard, Luxemburg disagreed with
Marx's earlier views supporting Polish independence, principally because she
was convinced that the Polish Kingdom depended on "backward 'eastern
markets' (in Russia)" for its own expansion, even though it was probably
the other way around.[57] Poland's economy was already deeply implicated in
Russia's development, and any effort to separate it through national independence was contrary to the historical tendencies of capitalist development,
which meant capitalism's intricate dependence on noncapitalism. In her
subsequent discussions of the effect of capitalism on the process of colonial
expropriation, especially its destruction of received social forms of communalism, customary practices, and culture, Luxemburg was effectively providing a narrative account of primitive accumulation in the origins and
consequent operation of formal subsumption once capitalism got started. In a
sense the originary accumulation, which derived from noncapitalist formations and provided the money for capitalism's jump start and the continuing
reliance on this source of wealth at the beginning of the accumulation process furnished a mirror for reflection and template for later colonial seizure
and expropriation.[58]

As for Luxemburg's explanation of how and why accumulation could expand only on the basis of noncapitalist buyers (not necessarily consumers that suggest the presence of a capitalist context), Luxemburg concretized Marx's own trajectory of emphasizing not the singularity of the nation form and national history but rather the globalizing activities defined by the limits of the world market as the space of contemporary world history. Her accounting appears even more internationalist than Marx's *Capital*, which, despite his own warnings that England simply constituted a "sketch" and "classic form," too often saw the nation as a metonymical stand-in for the world and clearly led to provoking controversy and providing a justification for England's claim to modularity for subsequent capitalist development.[59] By the time Luxemburg wrote *The Accumulation of Capital* (1913), the broader extension of world development exceeded the narrow constraints of the nation, the world market literally encompassed the globe, and even nations were involved in this transformation as the agents personifying capitalism. Luxemburg's concern with the question of expanded reproduction and enlarged accumulation already implied the existence of the broader space of the globe that had become capitalism's new habitat. "From the very beginning," she wrote,

> the forms and laws of capitalist production aim to comprise the entire globe as a store of productive forces. Capital, impelled to appropriate productive forces for purposes of exploitation, ransacks the whole world, it procures its means of production from all corners of the earth, seizing them, if necessary by force, from all levels of civilization and from all forms of society. . . . It becomes necessary for capital progressively to dispose ever more fully of the whole globe, to acquire and unlimited choice of means of production . . . so as to find productive employment for the surplus value it has realized.[60]

Moreover, she added, the process of accumulation demands "free access to new areas of raw materials . . . both when old sources fail; or when social demand suddenly increases."[61] In her unfinished text on political economy, she already identified noncapitalist regions as sources of labor, as well, on which she elaborated in the later work on capital accumulation. Everywhere there is the arrival of European capitalism, there is immiseration, wage slavery, the extermination of native population, and the disappearance of a way of life that had existed for centuries. "The capitalist world economy increasingly means the yoking of humanity to heave labor with countless deprivations and sufferings, with physical and mental degeneration for the purpose of capital accumulation."[62] In addition, she continued, the development of the world economy draws the indigenous peoples first into commodity exchange through the entry of trade and then transforms the received forms of production into commodity production. This move finally results in the "expropriation of these peoples from their land . . . from their means of production."[63]

The problem Luxemburg confronted was Marx's claim that it was possible to enlarge reproduction and progressively expand the process of accumulation by relying on only a social formation composed of capitalists and workers. But as she perceived, this proposition was based on the presupposition of a society of capitalists and workers as the sole agents of capitalist consumption "under the universal and exclusive domination of the capitalist mode of production."[64] There are no other groups in this society, Luxemburg reasoned, no "third persons" who could act as consumers capable of absorbing the surplus product. At stake was her perception that a closed society composed only of capitalists and workers could not possibly realize the surplus value that is to be capitalized.[65] The answer to Luxemburg's question as to how this surplus value was to be consumed and where the additional buyers would be found was provided by the "third person" excluded in Marx's diagrammatic scheme on enlarged reproduction (*Capital*, vol. 2) based on a society made up solely of capitalists and workers. Behind this presumption was the obvious interest in how capital develops, which Marx located in the accumulation process that Luxemburg extended to the global expansion of capitalism to noncapitalist environments as the fundamental propellant of accumulation. "Imperialism," she remarked toward the end of her principal work, "is the political expression of the accumulation of capital in its competitive struggle for what remains still open of the noncapitalist environment."[66] The exercise of political violence is "nothing but a vehicle for the economic process." The conditions of reproduction of capital, she affirmed, tie political power to the economic process to form the principal props of a "historical career" and narrative of capitalism. "Sweating blood and filth with every pore from head to toe" marks both the genesis of capital and its successive progress throughout the world.[67] In its wake, then, it brings incalculable violence and destruction leading to the decline and destruction of noncapitalist societies. What appears important is Luxemburg's belief that Marx based this limitation on conditions that did not "know other consumers than capitalist and workers," which pointed to a model of society rather than its empirical existence that had achieved "real subsumption" and the completion of the commodity relation everywhere and embodied the premise that the capitalist mode of production "represented [a] universal and exclusive foundation," thus constituting the singular "setting of this process."[68] Her capacity to see through this methodological "fiction," as she called it, that misrecognized a model for real existence meant that the introduction and spread of capitalism in the world would inevitably follow a route marked not by imitating a "classic example" of a single nation but by capitalism's local struggles with received "natural" and "peasant economies," which were occurring at the same time that the production process would seek to incorporate prior practices of producing to serve the creation of surplus value and embody the coexistence of the traditionally old and the capitalistic new.

While Marx's model intended to show that capitalists and workers are the sole agents of capitalist consumption, Luxemburg proposed that "real life has never known a self-sufficient society under the exclusive domination of the capitalist mode of production" and the axiom can serve only as a theoretical device to demonstrate the problem but not prevailing conditions that have to be taken into account.[69] Since capitalism in Western Europe developed historically amid a feudal environment, Luxemburg saw its arising in primitive accumulation as a key to grasping the forms of its appearance elsewhere, especially in the non-West. What interested her most was the struggle against the "natural economy" and how capital utilized what it found at hand. Not every environment was in a position to supply what it needed: "non-capitalist social strata as a market for its surplus value, as a source of supply for its means of production and as a reservoir of labour power for its wage system."[70] Under these circumstances, forms of production derived from the environment of a natural economy have little use for capital. But what appears significant for a natural economy is the linking of production of both the means of production and labor power in a single form. These natural economies incarnated in peasant communal orders or even feudalism (corvée labor) are able to maintain their form of economic organization by "subjecting" both labor power and land, the principal means of production, to the "rule of law and custom." Hence, "a natural economy . . . confronts the requirements of capitalism at every turn with rigid barriers. Capitalism must therefore always and everywhere fight a battle of annihilation against the historical form of natural economy that it encounters," usually through force that assumes the form of colonial policy. It is particularly vital, Luxemburg continued, for "capitalism in its relation with colonial countries to appropriate the most important means of production."[71] Luxemburg recognized that this process of capital appropriation of what it found at hand in societies beyond Europe was inevitably accompanied by a policy of "annihilation" of anything that stood to obstruct its development. Passage through this phase of appropriation represented the completion of a process of accumulation, which is still continuing, leading to the introduction of the commodity economy in these regions. Violence is the immediate result of the collision of capitalism and organizations derived from the natural economy, whose very presence would be seen as a restrictive barrier to development.[72] But Luxemburg also discerned how, in the process of primitive accumulation, the operation of capitalism's propensity to appropriate from natural economies was the agent of force and violence. "Accumulation," she observed, "with its spasmodic expansion, can no more wait for, and be content with, the natural increase of the working population."[73]

It was, I believe, for this reason that she turned to the history of precapitalist formations, in imitation of Marx's own trajectory, to track the demise of these communal agrarian communities and noncapitalist societies once they were forced to face the invasion of capitalism. The picture she portrayed of these archaic societies conveyed the prevalence of common ownership of land, despite regional differences, agrarian communities among German tribes, Incas, ancient Greeks, groups in India and Russia. "One cannot imagine anything simpler and more harmonious," she concluded, "than the entire system of the German *mark*.[74] Evidently we have the entire mechanism of social life. . . . Everyone works for everyone else and collectively decides on everything." The source of this system is "nothing other than communism of land and soil," the common possession of the most important means of production on the part of those who work. Moreover, she was certain that the "typicality of communistic economic organization of these societies" would appear more persuasive if they were studied "comparatively on an international scale" capable of illustrating it as a "global mode of organization in all its diversity and flexibility."[75] The Inca Empire of Peru initially disclosed the form of organization found among the Germans. As outsiders, the Inca conquered the Quechua Indians and incorporated their mode of communal organization, refining the system of economic exploitation and political domination. Luxemburg here called attention to a shared characteristic of societies subjected to conquest from the outside: the development of vertical multiple layers, and the subsequent formation of a kind of historical sedimentation, whereby each stratum lay on top of its predecessor, with the latest as dominant, to form a stratified configuration. (It should be recalled that Marx had already foreseen these geological structures in history in his letters to Vera Zasulich.) In this vertical arrangement, the earlier layers did not disappear but remained visible and available in traces whose communal system remained intact. (We will see how this worked in greater detail when dealing with the writings of José Carlos Mariátegui.) The later arrival of and conquest by the Spanish, which introduced colonization, genocide, and systematic theft, added yet another layer to this stadial configuration of hierarchical domination by implanting a noncommunist feudalism (private property) on top of the Inca system. For Luxemburg, what seemed significant about this Inca precapitalist society and its "unique structure" is that it provided a key to grasping a number of other, similar formations in antiquity, particularly the protohistory of archaic Greece.[76] These early historical experiences exemplified a process of how older agrarian communes developed into a "mass of small peasants indebted to an aristocracy" (conquerors) that has managed to appropriate the instruments of power and domination, especially military service and the undivided communal estates and a "determined opposition between the generally free and exploited slaves."[77] The multilayered economic orders prepared the ground for the later development of a rapidly implemented slave trade among the ancient Greeks. With the British in India and the French in North Africa, namely, Algeria, Luxemburg marked the beginning of the end to this vertical historical configuration and the forced entry into an entirely different historical path that eventually organized societies according to their position relative to a horizontal developmental itinerary that would classify them as either advanced or "backward," locked in a "time lag" and the prospect of catching up to a modern present and an allegedly completed capitalism.

In this encounter Luxemburg saw the "tragic" dissolution of the "ancient communist economic organization through contact with European capital."[78] In Russia, she announced, "the varied primitive agrarian communism comes to an end."[79] Moreover, the incomplete proletarian revolution (1905) "had already destroyed the last residues of the organic commune," which she proposed "had been artificially preserved by Tsarism," a view that distinctly departed from Marx's earlier recommendations to Zasulich, which Luxemburg probably could not have known.[80] It also distanced her somewhat from Lenin's earlier response to the Russian commune and the possibility of temporarily linking the temporally archaic to the contemporary present. The enthusiasm Marx showed for possibilities offered by the Russian commune had diminished by the time Luxemburg began writing, whereas Lenin appeared more ambivalent. If his polemics against the populists dramatized impatience with romantic idealizations of the Russian peasantry, masking more fundamental petit-bourgeois economic theory he associated with Jean Charles de Sismondi, and looked forward toward the final dissolution of the traditional communities, he also acknowledged their utility in augmenting the spread of capitalism throughout the countryside and expansion of the home market. It is this advocacy of an arrangement of what might be called combined unevenness that suggests a kinship with Luxemburg and Trotsky, by which I am referring to the act of bringing together labor and other kinds of practices, institutions, and customs from the past to serve a capitalist-oriented present. The operation of combining joins incommensurables in a hierarchic and uneven relationship.[81]

This closing of the circle, as Luxemburg put it, was thus sparked by the end of the Russian commune. The death blow was delivered by capitalism, which, unlike older forms of domination, aimed to alter and vanquish reminders of the old political system it sought to occupy. It should be recognized that this perspective pointing to capitalism's immense capacity to rapidly wipe clean the received political and economic slate seemed unusually urgent in Luxemburg's thinking on the eve of World War I, as well as among Marxists of her generation. It surely must have been driven by anticipation of revolution, since much Marxian discourse at the time centered on determining the proper moment of its beginning. Luxemburg, as is well known, opted for a position that advised proceeding as the only way of knowing with certainty that the instance of revolution had arrived. She was of mixed minds concerning the "maturity" of the capitalist system (as she was later in her decision to throw her support in with the Spartacus League). On the one hand, she had consistently disputed Marx's claims that substituted an idealization of the capitalist totality for "real life" by showing how older modes of production still persisted alongside capitalism; on the other hand, she seemed impatient with the pace of development and often claimed that the speed by which capitalism was dissolving older economic practices was occurring at an unprecedented velocity. While she recognized the force of capitalism in removing the "fetters" of the past in her present, at the same time she provided testimony affirming the perseverance of that past in the present to reinforce and solidify her argument of how much capitalism needed a noncapitalist environment for continued expanding accumulation.

This was precisely what Marx envisioned as the general form of all capitalist development. The classic example of evidence Luxemburg mobilized was the layering of strata from precapitalist formations, where the latest layer on top constituted a politically dominant group that nevertheless allowed each predecessor to retain its traditional associations of identity and integrity. Marx also ratified this view earlier and offered the additional supplement that ancient imperial conquerors usually sought to enhance conquered territories with all kinds of improvements, whereas the British East India Company contributed nothing to India but massive expropriations and theft. But from the moment *The Communist Manifesto* appeared, it was known that he was sensitive to capitalism's relentless aptitude for tearing down all barriers to its development. It should be pointed out that this judgment has to be squared with the conduct of formal subsumption and its continuing capacity for bringing past and present together, a form of layering where older labor practices remained intact even as they were harnessed to a process of capitalist production. Among Marxists of Luxemburg's generation, like Lenin especially, there seemed to prevail an urgent desire to see capitalism rapidly remove the layered vestiges of prior pasts that marked the historical record until the capitalist mode of production appeared on the scene. The reason undoubtedly stemmed from the circumstances of the historical present and the conviction that capitalism itself had reached the necessary state of completion when it would begin to self-destruct. Yet Marx clearly saw in the behavior of formal subsumption and its continuation the form of constant layering, with the same political relationship between the top stratum and those below it.

Although Luxemburg envisaged the appearance of capitalism as a challenge premodern societies could not overcome, she recognized that "primitive society, through its internal development, leads to inequality and despotism."[82] Such societies produced over the long duration the conditions of their own demise. While in the early, unfinished *Introduction to Political Economy*, where she considered the historicity of primitive communism and certified its capacity to persist for centuries, she recognized that this social form invariably "succumb[s]" to foreign conquest that leads to broad-scaled "social reorganization." This kind of transformation marked the "fate" of African society, until it was overtaken by Europeans in the sixteenth and early seventeenth centuries, who impressed native populations into forms of slavery to work mines and plantations in America and Asia. In fact, the "intrusion of European civilization" changed the life world of archaic societies forever, not simply from military subjugation but by introducing a new mode of production that "rip[ped] the land underneath the feet of the native population" and thereby removed the very basis of life and social order.[83] Under these circumstances, such societies were thus destined to collapse everywhere, owing to a new form of economic process, promising developmental progress, allied with political domination that the received communal order could not resist, rendering laborers into slaves or simply exterminating them if they failed to satisfy conditions of work, consigning the economic practices of communal society to obsolescence, assimilating surviving remnants—labor process and means of production—to capitalism. In her *Accumulation of Capital*, however, the process of decline and the disappearance of older vestiges have lost the speed of urgency. As a result, Luxemburg, through the argument that privileged the vital necessity of a noncapitalist environment, was compelled to consider a more complex picture of the relationship between capital and its outside.

When Luxemburg questioned the reality of society constituted solely of capitalists and workers as consumers, and finding it impossible to realize the portion of surplus value it is supposed to capitalize, her response was that consumption could come only from outside capitalist society not identified with the immediate agents, "sold to such social organizations or strata whose own mode is not capitalistic."[84] She pointed to the nineteenth-century practice of supplying cotton textiles to peasants and petit bourgeois of Europe and to peasants of India, America, and Africa. Convinced that there was no good reason "why means of production and goods should be produced by capitalist methods alone," she arrived at a position that now accepted the probability that this constraint did not conform either with daily practice or to the history of capitalism and clearly reflected how older methods might be put into the service of capitalist production and the creation of surplus value. Her example of the extent of capital's dependence on noncapitalist modes of production was the U.S. Civil War, when plantation production was put on hold, or the crisis provoked by the Crimean War when flax for linen could no longer be imported from Russia. In these cases, Luxemburg proposed that "cheap elements of constant capital are essential to the individual capitalist who strives to increase his rate of profit." Moreover, the desire to improve labor productivity continuously *"as the most important method of increasing the rate of surplus value, is unrestricted utilization of all substances and facilities afforded by nature and soil."*[85] It would be clearly inimical to capitalism and capital's "mode of existence" to place before it such restrictions. The utilization of these practices signified the operation of formal subsumption and showed how capital easily reached out to older, noncapitalist methods in the interest of general development. Luxemburg recalled that the capitalist mode of production remains only a "fragment of total production, and even in the 'small continent of Europe,' it has not yet succeeded in dominating the entire branches of production."[86] This claim was also true of North America. And it disclosed the meaning of her assertion that capitalism, from its inception, and its laws of production have ceaselessly sought to encompass the entire world as "a store house of productive forces." Compelled to appropriate the forces of production everywhere, which meant those practices that are "near-at-hand," capitalism "ransacks the whole world, it produces its means of production from all corners of the earth, from all levels of civilization and from all forms of society." She shared with a number of contemporaries, notably Trotsky, the conviction that societies undergo diverse rates of uneven development and experience the coextension and combination of different temporalities within the same social formation.[87] The Italian Antonio Labriola considered Russia to be the reservoir of all phases, a sentiment already put forth by Lenin, even though he, unlike Lenin, foresaw the likelihood of coexisting temporalities but not their mutual interpenetration.[88] With Luxemburg it was even more explicit. In an article on the Ottoman Empire, written in 1896, she argued that while the Turkish Empire in the eighteenth century had been possessed by an oppressive and despotic political regime, it enjoyed a modicum of stability. In the following century, things began to fall apart as a result of conflict with centralized European states and especially Russia. These conditions compelled the empire to resort to a round of domestic reforms that "abolished the feudal government, and in its place it introduced a centralised bureaucracy, a standing army and a new financial system." In a sense Luxemburg was describing an early modernizing program aimed at buttressing the sagging supports of the empire, which were underwritten by taxes and duties imposed on the population. Accordingly, paying the cost of this burdensome and ambitious modernization program produced what Neil Davidson has described as a "hybrid form of state." Luxemburg explained that in "a strange mixture of modern and medieval principles, it consists of an immense number of administrative authorities, courts and assemblies, which are bound to the capital city in an extremely centralized manner in their conduct, but at the same time all public positions are *de facto* venal, and are not paid by the central government, but are mostly financed by revenue from the local population—a kind of bureaucratic benefice." Under these circumstances, the material conditions of the people deteriorated with the introduction of an irregular tax system, leading to uncertain conditions of landownership that produced permanent "insecurity" in everyday life. According to Luxemburg, the principal problem behind this failed modernizing makeover was "above all the money economy as a result of the transformation of tax in kind into tax in money and the development of foreign trade." Superficially, these modern changes resembled Russia after the reform of 1861, but Turkey failed to implement an "economic transformation corresponding to the modern reforms."[89] Unlike the Russia that Lenin described, there was no attempt to make the capitalization of agriculture in the countryside act as a spur to the growth of the domestic market and establish the foundation for the subsequent formation of capitalism and industrialization.[90] Even later, when Turkey and Germany colluded to build railways, the developmental metabolism was still mixed. This time it was between "European capital and Asiatic peasant economy, with the Turkish state reduced to its real role, that of a political machinery for exploiting peasant economy for capitalist purposes—the real function of all Oriental states in the period of capitalist imperialism."[91]

When Luxemburg referred to the "cotton famine' caused by the Civil War in the United States, she demonstrated how its immediate solution prompted the Lancashire textile mills to look elsewhere. New and large cotton plantations appeared in Egypt, virtually overnight, that reflected "Oriental despotism, combined with an ancient system of bondage." But it was only "capital, with its technical resources," that could engender the production of cotton in so short a time and "on only the pre-capitalist soil of more primitive conditions was it possible to develop the necessary ascendency."[92]

Capital also requires new sources of labor, as well as buyers. In the new environment of the colonies, especially, she found the source of new labor from what Marx had designated as an "industrial reserve army of workers." While Marx looked on this reservoir of workers as a result of the population increase enabled by capitalist production and as a "necessary product of accumulation of the development of wealth on a capitalist basis," the existence of a surplus population becomes a condition of the capitalist mode of production. But by the same measure, it "forms a disposable industrial reserve army" and "creates a mass of human material always ready for exploitation in the interests of capital's own changing . . . requirements."[93] In short the demand for labor reflects the pace of accumulation and the relation between employed ("active army") and unemployed reserve army that correspond to the "periodic alternations of the industrial cycle."[94] Marx's reflections on the industrial reserve army was related to a national social formation where capitalism prevailed, and not necessarily to those regions that lay beyond Euro-America and remained noncapitalist. In Luxemburg's reckoning, the reservoir for this army stretched out to include the vast regions existing outside the dominion of capital that are "drawn into the wage proletariat only if the need arises."[95] Only the availability of noncapitalist workers and countries can supply and guarantee needed additional labor power. But it should be acknowledged that Luxemburg reconfigured Marx's original category principally because it had been restricted to older workers who had been displaced by machinery (signaling the appearance of a production regime dedicated to "relative surplus value"), migration of jobless rural workers to the cities because of the capitalization of agriculture, workers who have fallen out of the labor market, and the overpopulation of paupers. In this respect, she was persuaded that Marx had failed to consider the release of superfluous workers created by the disintegration of peasant economies and artisanal handicrafts in Europe, victims of the ceaseless transition from noncapitalist to capitalist conditions, "cast-off by pre-capitalist, not capitalist modes of production." The historical circumstances of Europe's transition from noncapitalist to capitalist means of production became the mirror of the later transformation of non-European colonies.

Capitalism's recruitment of indigenous workers in the colonies and its propensity to "utilize all productive forces of the globe, up to the limits imposed by a system of producing surplus value," meant implicating labor power in traditional organizations of production, requiring first to set such workers "free" and then integrating them into the wage form system. For Luxemburg, this announced "the indispensable historical basis of capitalism."[96] Actually realizing this process of transferring "labour from former social systems to the command of capital" resulted in producing a "peculiar combination between the modern wage system and primitive authority" in the colonies. Explicitly dramatizing the logic of formal subsumption and its relation to a history of uneven and combined development institutionalizing it, Marx foresaw this development in England as an expression of "so-called primitive accumulation," which initiated the genesis of capitalism and the growth of its productive process empowering it. Even though these Marxian reflections on the general logic of capitalist development were not accessible to Luxemburg, she was able to think through the process of production and accumulation to reach both the logic and the "peculiar" way it produced history and thereby express a fidelity to the logic and history Marx had identified. She was determined to reach this position by conceding that even if Marx's picture of a mature capitalism was something more than a mere theoretical "ideal type" of the capitalist totality (and it is doubtful she did), it still required the utilization and exploitation of the noncapitalist stratum and its corresponding social organizations "existing besides it"[97] or below it and subordinated to its pursuit of surplus value. In this regard, the existence and utilization of noncapitalist modes of production constituted a principal historical condition enabling the realization of expanded accumulation, thereby enshrining the presence of uneven history inscribed in the logic of formal subsumption in any present and making the figure of originary accumulation always immanent to it. But Luxemburg attributed the original insight to Marx, who first saw the dialectical interaction capitalism invariably necessitates with noncapitalism and its social organization as the "setting for its development."[98]

It was Leon Trotsky (1879–1940) who gave a name to this developmental strategy that called for merging capitalism with precapitalist elements as the means of economically "leaping" over history and politically suborning the peasant masses to the industrial proletariat, who would lead them and concentrate their energy into the realization of "permanent revolution." Trotsky, perhaps more so than Lenin, was able to dialectically connect the local realities of Russia's social formation to the larger trajectories of capitalism on a global stage and thus cement a concrete yet ongoing relationship between the particular and universal, glossing Marx's earlier advice to link the "local being" to the "universal being" in order to enter world history.[99] This move permitted Trotsky to overcome the purely local and contradictory discourse waged by Russian Marxism and populism for the broader arena of the world that exceeded national intensities yet was able to maintain sufficient concreteness. Like Lenin, he discounted slavophilism as the "messianism of backwardness," whereas the *narodniks*, who replaced them and toned down their more retrograde principles valorizing monarch, orthodoxy, and pan-Slavic racism, suffered from their own "democratic illusions" and a "one-sided" understanding of the "deep peculiarities of Russia's development."[100] What for him spared Marxism from this defect, as Lenin's polemics against the populist revealed, was its capacity to "demonstrate the identity of laws of development for all countries," instead of falling into "dogmatic mechanization" that results in "throwing out the baby with the bathwater."

According to Michael Löwy, Trotsky's pamphlet of 1906—*Results and Prospects*—prefigured these "methodological innovations," for which the later and magisterial *History of the Russian Revolution* (1930) provided a more detailed blueprint. Specifically, his articulation of the concept of combined and uneven development supplied substance to his effort to universalize the theory of permanent revolution, which drew from the political experiences of both China and Russia in the post–World War I period.[101] The idea of combined and uneven development permitted envisaging capitalism as a totality, and the class struggle mirrored this world process by refracting the contradictions produced by the "interpenetration" of capitalism and Russia's social formation. This contradiction was manifest in the "appetite" of a totalizing process propelled by the development of world capitalism to subsume local economies. In Trotsky's view, capitalism, as Marx had observed of the world market, became the space of a totalizing system, setting up the principal contradiction between a concrete totality and forms of development that required the less developed to follow the example of the advanced nations yet not in slavish imitation of the course of its temporal order. What this pointed to was a "law" that compelled the "backward" countries to adopt the latest capitalist advances along with the utilization of precapitalist elements put into the service of creating surplus value—configuring a mixed amalgam of practices in which the parts of the combination remain unequal and uneven. Yet the formulation of a universal law of uneven development was founded on combining mixed temporalities that neither Trotsky nor his later interpreters have addressed. Trotsky's theory fell short of accounting for the temporal disjunction between the parts constituting the specific combination, the apparent time gap between peasant life and work and the industrial worker in the cities, even though he rejected a rigid stagist imperative of realizing the completion of a bourgeois-democratic revolution as a necessary historical stage before the achievement of the next. Specifically, the transformation of agricultural worker into industrial worker did not happen overnight, which meant especially that such workers were able to maintain a foot in both temporal domains. His solution to this problem was to look forward to the time when a democratic revolution would eliminate precapitalist economic residues, forms of exploitation, and Asiatic despotism.[102]

Although Trotsky was convinced that "law of combined and uneven development reveals itself . . . in the historical character of Russian industry," by inserting itself into capitalist development without imitating the model of advanced countries, its success derived from a capacity to skip over epochs.[103] Even more important was the generality of the "law" that invited all those societies that had either lagged behind in their development or were captive to some variant of colonialism to find their own route. In this regard his theory actually configured a global chronotope consisting of differently constituted local spaces with their mixture of times that shaped the form of a world history:

> Capitalism means . . . an overcoming of those conditions [a "repetition of cultural stages"]. It prepares and, in a certain sense, realizes the universality and permanence of man's development. By this, a repetition

of the forms of development by different nations is ruled out. Although compelled to follow advanced countries, a backward country does not take things in the same order. The privilege of historical backwardness . . . permits, or rather compels, the adoption of whatever is ready in advance of any specific date, skipping a whole series of intermediate stages. Savages throw away their bows and arrows for rifles all at once, without traveling the road which lay between those two weapons in the past. . . . The development of historically backward nations leads necessarily to a peculiar combination of different stages in the historical process. Their development as a whole acquires a . . . combined character. . . . Unevenness, the most general law of the historical process, reveals itself most sharply and complexly in the destiny of the backward countries. Under the whip of external necessity, their backward culture is compelled to make leaps. From the universal law of unevenness thus derives another law which, for the lack of a better name, we may call the law of combined development—by which we mean a drawing together, an amalgam of the different stages of the journey, combining the separate steps, an amalgam of archaic with more contemporary forms.[104]

But in the end, Trotsky was merely reaffirming Marx's observation that the logic exemplifying the operation of formal subsumption, what is near at hand, resembling a form of *bricolage*, which constitutes the general form of all capitalist development by combining the archaic with the modern. In short, capitalism combined the mixed elements it stood to appropriate.

With the powerful intervention of Georg Lukács (1885–1971) and the transfer of objectified social relationships into the interiority of subjective consciousness, this earlier route was eventually bypassed by others and ultimately diverted into privileging the commodity form and its domination of culture. As a result of Lukács's turn to Hegel in his reading of Marx, and his philosophy of consciousness, the image of a world of uneven development produced by formal subsumption seemed to disappear, to reappear only on the margins of "Western Marxism" in the process of capital's logic of production and development. Only with Antonio Gramsci and, especially, Ernst Bloch's political intervention and conceptualization of contemporary noncontemporaneity, cultural vestiges of earlier pasts situated in modern German life, was the sense of temporal unevenness retained. Even in Bloch's penetrating analysis of how fascism utilized forms of archaism in a modern society, the unevenness it represented was still confined to the horizon of the West. In fact, this turn constituted a commitment to moving from a perspective of the objective—economic—to subjective—cultural— realms: commodification and consumerism, a world dominated by the primacy of value rather than labor, putting into practice the force of the commodity form to structure consciousness in its entirety rather than only objective social relationships related to labor in the production process. Yet this is not to suggest that Lukács was either indifferent to the production of unevenness in the development of the labor process of capitalist production or saw in reification its displacement by the commodity form. Lukács's interest in the problem of unevenness brought him closer to a thinker like Ernst Bloch, who conceptualized temporal unevenness, than to either Max Horkheimer or Theodor Adorno.

But it should be said that even though Lukács provided the foundation for the subsequent Westernization of Marxism, with its reorientation toward the dominance of the commodity form, his thinking at the same time had grasped the central importance of unevenness as the immediate result of capitalist production.[105] Hence to start with formal subsumption as the motor of the process of capitalist production both permits restoration of the knowledge of historical unevenness it must produce and clears the path to envisaging the diverse regions outside of Europe and the different and multiple routes they were compelled to undertake. "While this process is still incomplete," Lukács reasoned, "the methods used to extract surplus labour are, it is true, more obviously brutal than in the later, more highly developed phase, but the process of reification of work and hence also of consciousness of the worker is much less advanced."[106] Here, Lukács was undoubtedly pointing to Marx's meditations on the primitive small Indian communities that produced for their own use, not for commodity production, with whatever surplus remaining becoming commodities that were sent to the state, still representing an incipient form of extraction of surplus in the course of production. But Lukács further added that even though it is not possible to provide an analysis of the "whole economic structure of capitalism," it is important to remember that "modern capitalism does not content itself with transforming the relations of production in accordance with its own needs. It also integrates into its own system those forms of primitive capitalism that led an isolated existence in pre-capitalist times, divorced from production; it converts them into members of the henceforth unified process of radical capitalism (cf. Merchants capital, the role of money as a hoard or as finance capital, etc.)."[107] In short, he was pointing to *antecedents* that did not belong to capitalism's life process, forms that eventually are "objectively subordinated to the real life process of capitalism." Lukács recognized that these forms would be explained only in terms of the process of industrial production and thus appear in the minds of the bourgeoisie as the "pure, authentic and unaltered forms of capitalism." In them the original relations between men that lie concealed in the commodity, not to forget the relationship between humans and objects that should gratify their needs, have virtually disappeared behind a veiled screen where they can no longer be recognized.[108] Under these circumstances the reified mind come to look upon them as the "true representatives of his societal existence." Since the abstract and quantitative character of the mode calculability is revealed in its purest form, it is grasped as the form in which an "authentic immediacy" is manifest. For Lukács, synchronization of time simply represented another instance of capitalism's capacity for rational calculability. What he seemed to be explaining was the process of naturalizing residues that lingered on in the new capitalist present and make them appear as results of mature capitalism. His task was to show that many of the practices taken over and used by capital logic and recognized as fully capitalistic had derived from historic presuppositions prior to the emergence of capitalism. But, as he conceded, despite this deepening of reification, the proletariat would internalize the outer barrier of immediacy as the means to overcome it, that there persisted a living core lying unseen beneath the overlapping crust of quantification, resembling Marx's historical presuppositions lying behind the process of capitalism's becoming. Such is the power of reification that what is capable of being seen appears only immediately, concealing the very mediations—antecedents and presuppositions—and, in fact, the whole process of becoming that has left its mark of unevenness on capitalism but whose presence remains hidden from view. It is important to recognize in this formulation that Lukács fully acknowledged the existence of a contemporary society filled with pre-capitalist remainders and reminders and that the commodification that prevented workers from seeing the way things are was also shared by the bourgeoisie and was related to and represented a part of the development of capitalism's production process. For him, the course of action leading to such an over-coming of reification, the "pernicious chasm" of the present, involved a "becoming," the recognition of the "present as a becoming." "Only concrete (historical) becoming can perform the function of such a genesis. And consciousness (the practical class consciousness of the proletariat) is a nec-essary, indispensable, integral part of that becoming."[109] Yet this view of rei-fication must be tempered by later recognitions that have proposed that the only social relation in capital that appears in the form of a thing is money and the real power it exercises over humans.[110]

3

OPENING TO THE
GLOBAL SOUTH

In this chapter, I focus principally on situating Antonio Gramsci's (1891–1937) *The Southern Question* and some of the writings of the Peruvian José Carlos Mariátegui (1894–1930), who, like Gramsci (whom he apparently knew), reconfigured the analytic perspective into a larger contextual process that managed to break with more rigid formulations of Marxism to release it for an understanding of the local realities on the ground. In both cases this move led to considerations associated with the "national question" in the interwar period. With Gramsci it steered him to a call to unify the capitalist North and semifeudal agrarian South in Italy, and in Peru the fusion of local realities and Marxian theory became known as "National Marxism," glossed from prior efforts, including those of Gramsci, to resolve the agricultural question. But Mariátegui also expressed the desire to unite coastal mining wage workers with the Peruvian agricultural proletariat who were landless peasants—in short, indigenous day laborers alongside the urban industrial worker. The latter, Mariátegui believed, were capable of injecting into the combinatory the "spirit of class."[1] Moreover, his observations prefigured later accounts reported from Africa, inasmuch as Indians, who spent a good part of the years in mines, regularly returned home to work lands and were thus partially responsible for assuming their self-subsistence and reproduction. Yet it is possible to perceive in both thinkers a grasp of the logic of capitalist development Marx had proposed, especially in capitalism's conduct to appropriate what it found useful at hand, to create a form of unevenness that combined both the general and particular, often in a larger process of deprovincializing Marx that addresses the question of how Marx was read in the interwar period. What appears so significant about both thinkers was their willingness to imagine a present filled with heterogeneous and fractured nonsynchronicities or co-evalities, where the presence of pasts unwillingly and unknowingly mingled with each other and the present to provide them with a habitat that defined capitalist modernity and shaped the ambiguous outline of its unwritten world history.

This figuration of a deprovincialized Marx, as I have already argued, was inaugurated by Lenin in his early work *The Development of Capitalism in Russia* and driven by his conviction that Russia resembled an Asiatic society. But, as we have seen, it was forcefully conceptualized by Rosa Luxemburg, whose thinking emphasized both an opening to the colonial regions of the world, the South, semicolonies and latecomers on the industrial periphery, and the singular importance of concentrating on the process of production and labor in their regions of the world. In this context I will consider Gramsci's *Southern Question* as an inaugural text announcing the appearance of what has become known as the global South, a text that signified an early departure from those more dominant forms of Marxism as they were formulated in the interwar period to later authorize a cultural unity during the Cold War. I am referring especially to Gramsci's capacity to see in Italy a divided and uneven assemblage of regions recently cobbled together into a "unified nation-state" and his effort to repair the division between North and South that had weakened Italian national unity in order to resolve the problem of unevenness it exemplified and complete the work begun with the Risorgimento in the 1860s. This task requires resituating Gramsci's text in a broader context preoccupied with the production process at the same time that the more immediate contemporaneity of Italian history and his reading of its past were intervening to mediate his observations of the political situation. Finally, I consider the historical identity and vocation of the Gramscian conceptualization of what variously has been called "revolution without revolution," "revolution/restoration," and ultimately "passive revolution" in explaining large-scale historical transformations, which grew out of his historical analysis of Italian unification in the nineteenth century and the conditions attending the industrialization of the North.

Gramsci and the Southern Question

Antonio Gramsci's call to combine northern industry, with its proletariat, and the archaic semifeudal rural communities of the South and islands was a project that appeared to merge different historical temporal forms as a solution to persisting unfulfilled national unity. In the envisaged fusion of different regions, it is important to recall that each region embodies a different form of history and time, and their coming together promised to produce a figure of synchronous nonsynchronicity, entailing the presence of presents consisting of times out of joint. How else to describe the joining of the archaic and industrial capitalism? Gramsci's reading of Italian history concentrated on showing a heritage of failure in developing and creating a strong central state; any final unification, in his view, would result in combining residual elements of the political and, I would assume, economic pasts with the desire to achieve a new national unity. At the same time, if his active involvement in the Comintern—the Communist International—turned his attention to the wider world beyond Europe, his reading of Italy's history must have persuaded or provided him with the occasion to break discipline, pulling him back to bend a little in view of the recognition that the Comintern's policies often seemed arbitrary and uninformed by local conditions. In its history, the Comintern's program to impose policies on the world outside Europe frequently bypassed the specific conditions of the region.[3] But what undoubtedly lay at the heart of Gramsci's analysis was the decision to seize on Marx's privileging of the present as the locus of history— as the momentous intersection of present and pasts, significantly glossed by Lenin's promotion of the "current situation" and made into a formal category by Uno Kōzō (*genjō bunseki*). Analysis of the historical transformation announced by the Risorgimento revealed the conditions informing the failure to establish a strong central nation-state: the circumstances that favored and promoted industrial development in the North and the unrealized offer of land to southern peasantry that remained only a "mirage," ultimately displaced to colonial acquisition overseas. It is interesting to note that Gramsci on several occasions situated this split between North and South within the category of the classic division of unevenness between city and countryside as envisaged in *The German Ideology*, and the consequences of this separation once capitalism was introduced. In Japan during the 1920s, for example, critics condemned the state for sacrificing the countryside, which they increasingly identified as a colony to the sprawling urban centers and development of industrialism. Like Marx and Engels in *The German Ideology*, Gramsci was won over to the proposition that since so much of the Italian present was still filled with elements from a more distant past, it was urgently necessary to account for their persistence in any explanation of the current situation. His appeal to history was thus cast within the tensions generated by the city-countryside division, authorized by the more profound division between mental and manual labor that lay behind it, and the deeper economic erosions of unevenness scarring the peninsula, which, accordingly, the Risorgimento had apparently widened and preserved with the spreading domination of Piedmont and northern capital.[4] In effect, the growing hegemonic domination of the North over the South reinforced the territorial relationships between city and countryside, making the South appear as a colony to the North. It should be remembered that by Gramsci's time, the division had become "naturalized," inasmuch as a large mythography had replaced the explanations based on more objective conditions attending the division that held the South responsible for its own backwardness, attributing to it inherent laziness, barbarity, "biological inferiority," and "criminality" that weigh like "a ball and chain" on the nation. Despite performing the labor of bringing about the unification of the Italian peninsula (1861–1870), the Risorgimento fostered the very economic and political unevenness that would continue to confound the modern nation-state and prevent it from fulfilling its initial goal. Paradoxically, the creation of a unified Italian nation-state accelerated the separation of the two regions into semiautarchic spheres marked by differing temporal rhythms of social life. Between the capitalist North and a semifeudal South, there were two distinctly different forms of time accountancy, the former regulated by a workday based on quantitative calculation and averaging of labor time (abstract labor) and its everyday remainder (disposable time), the latter determined more by seasonal constraints and obligations of labor service that made it difficult to separate work from nonwork during certain times of the year. In this connection, Gramsci conceded that the split constituted a vital role in construing a new arrangement of authority that would, in time, elevate the southern question in the near future and raise again the necessity of resolving a past that had become an unyielding nemesis in the present. By the time Gramsci began to address the question, its resolution was even more difficult, especially in view of embracing a strategy that sought to organize the proletarian subaltern classes for political mobilization, one aimed at forging a bloc with southern peasants for whom northern workers had the lowest regard.

It was the history of Italy of the late eighteenth and early nineteenth centuries, especially the expulsion of foreign rule and influence, that both fixed the foundation for the subsequent historical move to unify the country awakened by the "consciousness of national unity" and introduced the reasons that Italy had failed to develop a hegemonic class capable of exercising power. The very ambiguity of the Risorgimento settlement, the "revolution/restoration," and the insufficiency of class leadership would affect the subsequent education and mobilization of the subaltern classes. What the text of *The Southern Question* dramatically stages, therefore, is precisely the sense of urgency needed to make up for the historical deficit left by the uncompleted unification and overcome the oscillating economic and political asymmetries that had become the modern nation-state's unwanted legacy. In this way, *The Southern Question* recalls *The German Ideology*'s perceptive and relentless critique of contemporary German political and economic backwardness, paralleling the contemporaneity and advanced modernity of philosophical reflection. At the same time, it shared its sensitivity to the temporal disjointedness of the lived noncontemporaneous. In each text, the central theme was unevenness, even though separated geographically and by local circumstances and temporally by more than half a century.[5] Gramsci's reckoning of the problem in Italy was to see it as a more complex issue that required attention. To address the economic deprivations inflicted on the South and the peasantry, and to appreciate the reality of the South subjected to conditions of semifeudalism, made it equally necessary to come to an understanding of how an oppressive political and cultural domination had organized life. The real reasons for southern underdevelopment in large part came from the expansion of northern industrial capital, resembling the course of colonial expropriation but reflecting the expansion of urban development at the expense of the countryside. If the predominance of northern capital did not exactly create feudal remnants, as, say, it did in places like Japan, its presence certainly reinforced their durability within a capitalist nation-state. Instead of developing the ground for subaltern participation, the Italian state had been marred by the formation of a ruling class that increasingly extended its reach after 1868. This is what he identified as "liberal politics" and "molecular" private enterprise that pooled their power to defeat any subsequent achievement and expectation of agrarian reform, thereby sacrificing the South to the expansive requirements of northern industrial growth. In fact, he wrote, "the dominant class inaugurated a new policy of class alliances, of political class blocs, a policy of bourgeois democracy." Once confronted with a choice between aligning with the southern peasantry, promising a "free trade policy of universal suffrage," low prices for industrial products, and a decentralized administration or a "capitalist/worker bloc," without universal suffrage, with tariff barriers and the preservation of a highly centralized state, the dominant bourgeoisie unsurprisingly chose the latter.[6] In response, Gramsci advised the formation of an alliance of northern proletarian and southern peasantry as the solution to unevenness and the condition for improving the productive capacities of southern agriculture. The obstacles to this strategy for realizing a new "revolutionary" formation required overcoming the hold of southern intellectuals over the peasant masses and their mixed sympathies for peasant democracy, on the one hand, and the reactionary politics of large landowners and the state, on the other. He was certain that the solution was available in the new political bloc he envisioned that could not only carry through with the incomplete unification and exceed the class-based central authority but work to alleviate the historical conditions that maintained economic unevenness. Gramsci's call for an alliance was possible because he recognized that the present is never identical with and transparent to itself but rather always an ensemble of heterogeneous mixing of encounters between different temporalities, synchronous nonsynchronicities.

Reflecting on the problematic status of the "southern question," Gramsci recalled that the issue had been raised first by the Turin Communists in 1920. (The actual text of *The Southern Question* was written seven years later.) At the time, he had also written a brief statement on the necessity of forging a coalition aligning industrial workers and peasants. The merit of this early gesture toward the possibility of realizing a class alliance was less in its obvious offer to distribute land among the peasantry, utilizing what was called the "magic formula," than in finding a strategy that incorporated it into a genuine "revolutionary action" of allied classes. It had already become evident that the only way to resolve the problem of division and unevenness on which Italian national unity was supposedly founded was through designing a strategy that would bring workers and peasants together to form a mass bloc since combined they represent the major component in the population. Seven years had passed, he reminded his readers, since the Turin Communists had forcibly brought the southern question to the attention of the "worker vanguard," successfully extracting it from its "intellectual phase." Little had been accomplished in the duration to realize its promise. Neither had northern workers been able to separate themselves from antisouthern prejudice nor had the proper organizational structure been put into place for such an ambitious undertaking. Gramsci congratulated the Turin Communists for their prescience and foresight in putting the southern question on a national agenda but admitted he saw no future in manipulating the "magic formula" and waving it like a wand before the peasantry, unless it was made part of a general revolutionary strategy leading to action by the combined class bloc. In addition to prefiguring a new and more mature strategy, it provided an early glimpse of one of his key concepts—hegemony—forged in the crucible of envisaging an alliance between workers and peasants, between capitalism and semifeudalism, with the latter subordinated to the former. Gramsci would work out the detail of this idea later in his formulations concerning passive revolution, where the encounter between the new—capital—and old transferred Marx's conceptualization of formal subsumption from the economic to the political register and beyond.

Gramsci anticipated that resolving the southern question through the formation of a mass class bloc signified an immense project that demanded organization and knowledge. In Italy, he wrote, the peasant question had to be approached through the specific optic of Italian traditions and history, which referred to the typical forms the peasant question has assumed. Specifically, he was pointing to the relationship of the southern question and the Vatican. Winning the peasant masses over to the proletarian camp meant making this relationship a principal consideration in any planning of revolutionary strategy. It required an accurate assessment of class desires, and among the peasantry, finding ways of incorporating them into a larger program. But the issue was already complicated by the regional structural division separating North and South, whereby "parasitic northern banks and industries have enslaved" the peasant masses.[7] Moreover, this enslavement, as we shall see, was bound to the traditional, moral, and affective ties of the church and clergy, which exercised close control over peasant behavior, especially in the South.

The relations between North and South, particularly those provided by the national economy and state, discouraged the formation of a broad middle class and made impossible "any accumulation of capital on the spot," as well as savings. The reason for this deficit was found in the fiscal customs system—notably the reluctance of capitalists to convert their profits into capital.[8] Even more troubling, primitive accumulation in the form of remittances sent by immigrant communities in the United States had failed to fulfill the liberal expectation ("dream") that the inflowing of money would offset the imbalance between North and South by changing the entire economic and social structure of the country. Unfortunately, Gramsci remarked, the state had quickly intervened to "stifle" the anticipated revolution by offering treasury interest-bearing bonds to transform immigrants and their families from passive "agents of silent revolution" into active agents willing to subsidize the state's financial capacity to divert money from more productive distribution in development into "parasitic" northern banks.[9] It was thus the contemporary Italian state, composed of an alliance of northern banking interests and southern semifeudal landowners, that managed to maintain the status quo of an unbalanced, uneven relationship between the two regions.

Hence Gramsci's proposal to bring together worker and peasant under vanguard proletarian leadership employed the form of "passive revolution." By changing the composition of political relationships with different personae—classes—occupying the assigned ranks of authority, it was possible to replace the hegemony monopolized by the bourgeoisie since the nineteenth-century transformation. Two primary hurdles had to be overcome: the ideological disposition of northern workers and the "great social disintegration" of the South. The problem of the entrenched ideological conceits of northern workers has already been mentioned. How to deal with the fixed image of the peasant as lazy and subhuman was a necessary condition of successfully moving to the goal of actually realizing a mass national bloc. Gramsci realized that the South and semifeudalism had been produced by capitalism and that the circumstances of peasant life derived not from na-

ture, as was widely believed, but from history. According to the earlier statement of 1920, the Turin Communists had acknowledged the necessity of
"modifying . . .the general ideology of the proletariat . . . as a national element that lives within the complex of the state and is unconsciously subjected
to the influences of the educational system, of newspapers, of bourgeois tradition." Moreover, complaints of laziness and criminality had become a bourgeois common sense, disseminated in countless ways by the propagandists
among both northern and southern masses.[10] With remarkable ease, such mis-
representations spread throughout the country to become unquestioned, indel-
ible truths. Peasants were, by nature, "biologically inferior," "semibarbarians,"
"barbarous," destined to a natural destiny, "criminal," "incapable"—creatures
of nature. Gramsci accused the Socialist Party of circulating these outsized
characterizations appropriated from the arsenal of bourgeois ideology, which
were ostensibly authorized by the claims of a "scientific" socialism among
northern workers. The proletariat must adopt approved "political effects" if
it is to qualify to govern as a class. This demanded stripping it of every residue of corporatism,[11] erasing every tinge of syndicalist prejudice. As a class,
it was immediately obliged to purge its ranks of all distinctions that called
attention to the specificity of membership in trades if it was to "win the
trust and consensus of peasants," and to rid itself of the habit of exclusively
identifying with crafts, skills, and trades in order to begin thinking of itself
as members of a class of workers. "The metal workers, the carpenters, the
builder, etc. must not only think like proletarians and no longer as metal
workers, carpenters, builders, etc. but they have to think like workers who
are members of a class that aims to lead the peasants and intellectuals."[12]

In the time the southern question surfaced as a major consideration, northern workers had already played their part in factory seizures, and peasants
were actively involved in agricultural workers' strikes whose consequential
splintering into uncoordinated and independent actions had to be overcome.
For Gramsci, the several problems unleashed by southern social disintegration
merely mirrored the absence of "cohesion" among the peasant populace.
Since the peasant masses comprised a potentially great "agricultural bloc,"
the lack of cohesion proved to be the most serious problem facing the
proletarianizing strategy. In dissecting its structure, he saw three layers
within this "great amorphous, disintegrated mass of peasants" that contributed to this traditional incoherence: the peasantry, the intellectuals of the

petite and rural bourgeoisie, and the large landowners and great intellectuals serving their interests. Admitting that the peasants were in continual ferment, he judged them incapable of giving systematic expression to their "aspirations" and "needs." The middle strata of intellectuals was assigned to provide the necessary coherence by serving as the conduit for peasant demands, transmuting vague and diverse impulses into ideological principles honed to animating action from the class base. The large landowners, for their part, were supported by singularly prominent regional "great intellectuals," like Benedetto Croce and Giustino Fortunata. It was this group who presently configured the field of southern ideology, with "efficiency" and "precision" directed to the task of centralizing the rural South into a unity capable of dominating the entire region.[13] With great talent, both Croce and Fortunata represented the capstone of southern reaction.

Gramsci approached the representatives of southern intellectual life with a mixture of sympathetic admiration and critical distance. He viewed its members as symbolizing the most important stratum of national life in Italy. More than three-fifths of the state's bureaucratic personnel were recruited from this stratum, which made it imperative to understand their "psychology." Capitalism, he contended, alters the intellectual stratum everywhere. In the past, the older, traditional intellectual classes mainly acted to organize a society composed of peasants and artisanal workers, whereas the development of capitalism mandated a different kind of organization that encompassed the state, now positioned to attend the complicated demands of commerce. The dominant political class had to form permanent groups of technical specialists skilled in applied sciences. These new technical classes were increasingly empowered to prevail and exercise control over the complex division of labor and articulating the rules of bureaucratic domination of everyday life. Where agriculture still prevailed, the older type of intellectual continued to supply a large body of personnel to the state's bureaucracy. Gramsci added that at the local level, in the villages and small towns, these more traditional intellectuals occupied the rank of intermediaries between peasants and administrations—"democratic in its peasant face, reactionary when facing the big landowners and government."[14]

In this regard, the clergy must also be included as belonging to the traditional group of intellectuals, with a clear-cut differentiation between North and South. The northern priest was usually the son of an artisan or even a peasant who either possessed democratic inclinations or was closely related to the peasantry; his southern counterpart has been frequently less correct in his conduct, often living openly with a woman and exerting his energies in fewer spiritual functions than the northern priest, whose vocation was directed toward guiding family activity. Because of the northern priests' comparatively exemplary behavior, the separation of church and state and program of ecclesiastic expropriations was more extreme in the South, where parishes and convents were able to preserve or dispossess considerable wealth and land. As a result, the southern clergy represented to the peasant the authority and force of a land administrator with whom the peasant must regularly enter into conflict over questions of rent and the payment of interest. In this way, the southern priest often resembled a usurer demanding high interest rates and threatening forms of extortion rather than a spiritual counselor exercising his religious duties. Even in his spiritual role, the southern priest often spent more time manipulating religious sentiment in order to reinforce the exaction of payment. In Gramsci's estimation, he inspired no confidence with his worldly outlook nor exhibited the normally expected impartiality associated with a man of the cloth. "Confession, therefore, exercising a minimal role," the southern priest was filled with pagan superstitions indistinguishable from his supposed Christian beliefs that more often than not subverted his clerical obligations. According to an old saying, "the priest is a priest at the altar; outside he is man like anyone." Gramsci portrayed a society that had remained moored in its archaic countenance that now was designated to become the basis of a new coalition with a capitalist and industrial North, led by the proletariat that represented capitalism, rather than its feudal partner.

Because southern peasants were intimately attached to the large landowners through the mediation provided by the intellectuals, they scarcely were situated to realize the form of an independent, autonomous mass organization, however formal. As a consequence of this historical dependence, peasants always found themselves placed within the ordinary articulation of the state, which meant being subsumed to its apparatus. It was a rare occasion to come across the example of southern organizations steeped in democratic tradition. Only in Sardinia, Gramsci reported, had an exception occurred when returning war veterans had succeeded in creating a more solid, democratic social structure. However, in Sicily large landowners appeared as a more resolute and compact group, whose opposition to democratic impulses was reinforced by industry and commerce. The upshot of this analysis was to illustrate how the upper classes, from Piedmont to Sicily, secured and maintained hegemonic domination in political life by excluding the development of a broader democratizing process that was undoubtedly assisted by limiting economic growth to the North. The foundation supplied by southern intellectuals produced an organization of a "continental South and Sicily" that presented the figure of an immense ("monstrous") agrarian bloc whose purpose was to "oversee" northern capital and bonds and uphold the status quo.

In Gramsci's assessment, the prominent southern intellectuals assumed the task of "prevent[ing]" the cracks and fissures in the putative agrarian bloc from becoming too "dangerous," too explosive, and turning the great disintegration into a "landslide." For this reason he was provoked into concluding that their work amounted to no more than a reaction. The South possessed no tradition or organization anchored in the promotion of "middle culture," even though, he admitted, important publishing houses and academies committed to encouraging erudite scholarship proliferated. What it lacked were institutions for attracting the middle layer of southern intellectuals or vehicles specifically designed to foster the production and dissemination of such a cultural stratum. Such initiatives that have been undertaken to broaden the South's cultural compass in the North invariably have been blemished by a certain "southernism."[15] Gramsci saw in this cultural failure a corresponding closure blocking the path to introducing greater political democratization, which, he confidently believed, would have been nurtured by a widening of cultural possibility. Even so, the "supreme moderators of these initiatives," politically and intellectually, were Croce and Fortunato, who successfully managed to mediate discourse in such a way as to depoliticize the southern question and stunt its revolutionary promise. The effectiveness of such intellectuals attested to not just their "immense" intelligence and acquisition of culture but as much to their capacity to operate within the broader European environment and "world culture," despite their formation in the South. Gramsci argued that they were able to tap into the "restless[ness]" of southern youth and effectively dissuade them from pursuing a revolutionary path by rechanneling their energies to follow a "middle way of classical serenity."[16] "Benedetto Croce," he continued, "has fulfilled an extremely important 'national function' by having detached the radical intellectuals of the South from the peasant masses and having them participate in European culture." In accomplishing this task, he has contributed to the nation's (that is, the state's) mission of subsuming the class of southern intellectuals, and by extension the peasant bloc, to the national bourgeoisie, guaranteeing their continuing fidelity to the agrarian bloc as the principal component cementing the status quo. If the Turin Communists successfully broke with a tradition that had called on the urban proletariat to become the "modern protagonists of Italian history" and appointed them to mediate between certain levels of intellectuals of the Left, positioned to succeed to the status of a ruling class "superior to the bourgeoisie,"[17] Gramsci was also certain that it was essential to the growth and development of a proper class of intellectuals competent to organize for a future takeover of political control. He was obviously referring to the necessary experience in hegemony that would prepare this class for later leadership and, therefore, looked to the eventual "break to occur" in an intellectual class "that is organic in character" and "historically authenticated." It was crucial that "the formation, as a formation of mass" holding left tendencies, was committed to an orientation "toward the revolutionary proletariat." For the "alliance between proletariat and peasant masses requires this formation." But such an independent formation will depend on its ability to destroy the (southern) intellectual bloc that has for so long spoken for the peasantry if a way is to disclose itself for realizing that "proletariat and peasant are the only two national forces and bearers of the future."[18] Gramsci must have detected in the possible coalition vast differences lived and experienced by northern workers and southern peasants. Because it was more broadly an alliance composed of capital and the archaic, bringing with it an unwanted mix of temporal regimes embodied in practices, customs, behavior, and institutions, past(s) in the present or the encounter of the nonsynchronous with the synchronous, the approach offered for overcoming these differences was through slow, organic development of intellectuals within the proletariat, even though he remained strangely silent on the peasants who would be enlisted into the mass national bloc as subordinates to a hegemonic arrangement of political leadership as they were socialized into industrialized agricultural. In this respect, Gramsci's strategy for creating a mass bloc in which peasants would be subsumed to proletarian leadership faintly resembled the operation of formal subsumption in economic matters but in the register of social and political organization.

Yet it is difficult to imagine how the peasantry would be able to shed the entirety of their feudal habits, or how long such a process of casting them off might take. Even harder to conceive is the disappearance of the archaic traces with the final accomplishment of the passive revolution once it had stabilized social and political order and after the traces had already been adjusted to serve a new purpose. The task may have been more daunting than imagined. Any reader of Carlo Levi's account of his year of political exile in Basilicata, just north of Calabria, in *Christ Stopped at Eboli* in the mid-1930s, a little more than a decade after Gramsci had composed *The Southern Question*, will recognize that the South constituted not just backwardness but, more important, an entirely different temporal register. "Christ never came this far [Eboli, where the railway terminated]," Levi's portrait begins, "nor did time, nor the individual soul, nor hope, nor the relation of cause to effect, nor reason nor history."[19] Levi faithfully reported the archaic South Gramsci saw as vital to a unified Italy, its release from the world of temporal standstill only able to be accomplished by unifying with the modern and capitalist North and working together to remove the uneven multiple temporalities represented by and embedded in lived material realities separating regions and its inhabitants from one another. Strongly echoing the kind of combining of the archaic and modern Marx had recommended earlier to the Russian progressives, Levi's text revealed the shadowed landscape of the rural South that Gramsci wished to unite with the industrial North through the practical logic of formal subsumption, now reconfigured to accommodate the specific circumstances of Italy's history and the range of utility broadened beyond merely the economic domain. Too often the appeal, as I have suggested, was valorized by fascists in an ideology that could just as easily transmute a class-based bloc of the masses into an organic ethno-cultural body of the nation purported to have remained intact and unchanged by history since the beginning of the folk. What, in any case, differed was the intervention of time and place. Much of this Gramscian program was explicitly mirrored in the analysis and proposals of José Carlos Mariátegui, whose subalterns became the indigenous native masses, in a Peruvian state clearly divided by manufacturing and agrarian coastal and mountainous regions to form a complex configuration consisting of Inca communalism,

Spanish feudalism, and modern industrial capitalism. Others, elsewhere, would seek to replicate the Gramscian program, not directly of course, but by working through the specific logic of capitalist development in conditions of their time and place to bring together the received with the new, the "then with the now."

Passive Revolutions

Finally, it is necessary now to turn to the broader implications of the Gramscian assessment of modern Italy and the problem raised by the South and the way the stalled transformation and persisting regional division and unevenness provided the occasion for identifying the political form that produced an incomplete revolution he perceived in the "passive revolution." It was, he wrote, "precisely the brilliant solution of . . . [diverse] problems which made the *Risorgimento* possible, in the form in which it was achieved (and with its limitations)—as a 'revolution without a revolution,' or as a 'passive revolution'"[20] or even a "revolution-restoration."[21] In his explanation of Edgar Quinet's use of "revolution-restoration" and Vincenzo Cuoco's earlier idea of passive revolution, what appears to be missing from Italian history is the historical fact of popular initiative. Hence "progress occurs as the reaction of the dominant class to the sporadic incoherent rebelliousness of the popular masses—a reaction consisting of 'restorations' that agree to some part of the popular demands and are therefore 'progressive restorations,' or revolutions-restorations,' or even 'passive revolutions.'"[22]

In his historical scenario, Gramsci bypassed the modularity of the French Revolution, which he saw as a paradigmatic example among bourgeois revolutions, to propose the candidacy of the passive revolution as the general form or "framework" of the kind of transformation Italy experienced, where bourgeois leadership was neither dominant nor the class numerically large. But it needed to be said that when a class presumed leadership and sought to subsume the subaltern remainder, it was acting politically to utilize what was at hand to further its own interests by unifying the national political order according to its own interest. Under these circumstances, the bourgeoisie presumed the status of leadership and sought to subsume the subaltern classes by responding to or giving formal expression to their—subaltern— aspirations. Neil Davidson, in this respect, has recently proposed that

Gramsci saw the French example of revolution as an exception and as an event that functioned to explain why later revolutions assumed the particular form of ambiguity embodied in revolutions-restorations.[23] Davidson is the most recent in a line of interpreters who have not only taken notice of parallel historical trajectories leading to revolutionary transformation in Italy and Japan but also sought to expand the utility of the category of passive revolution to account for a range of revolutionary events that might be included as instances that correspond to its form. His principal argument was that the domination of the bourgeois in many so-called bourgeois revolutions corresponds closely to the political strategy that more often than not depended on recruiting and mobilizing what was near at hand, which would explain the passive form and the ambiguous mix of different classes and political ambitions that constituted the "revolution." Gramsci had already entertained the possibility of extending the category to classify Japan's Meiji Restoration of 1868, which for him resembled both England and Germany.[24] Moreover, he was convinced that the concept of passive revolution would apply to "those countries that modernize the state through a series of national wars without undergoing a political revolution of a radical-Jacobin type,"[25] which meant the further possibility of including other transformations in the world beyond Europe, such as the Kemalist revolution in Turkey, the Iranian Islamic Revolution, and the 1911 and 1927 revolutions in China. I would like to further suggest that if we can accept Marx's definition of formal subsumption as the general form for all capitalist development, with its capacity to generate "hybrid" and other subforms that coexist with capitalist productive practices, then it is not too far afield to propose the category of the passive revolution as an equivalent political form to a production process that privileged suborning what was useful at hand to serve capital's pursuit of surplus value and along the way produce continuing economic unevenness modern nation-states were pledged to eliminate, but perhaps only in the last instance. This would not be a reflection of the economic structure but something closer to an analogue extended to political practices as a parallel political form, since passive revolutions also embodied a mix of political practices and institutions, and their procession of temporal associations belonging to prior social configurations, with newer, contemporary political forms. In fact, Gramsci saw no differentiation between the political program of passive revolution and its economic goals. Since it was an interpretative category, it embraced both. "Passive revolution," he wrote in the *Prison Notebooks*,

> would be brought about through the fact of transforming the economic structure in a "reformist" fashion from an individualistic to a planned economy. . . . The creation of an economy "mid-way" between that of the pure individual type and one that, in the full sense, functions according to a plan would allow the passage to more advanced political and cultural forms without radical and destructive cataclysms of an exterminatory kind. "Corporativism," through its internal development, could either be or become this middle-ground economic reform of a passive character.[26]

Elsewhere, Gramsci explained how the passive revolution worked historically to conserve part of the past.

> What will be conserved of the past in the dialectical process cannot be determined *a priori*, but will be a result of the process itself, and will be characterized by historical necessity, and not by arbitrary choice on the part of so-called scientists and philosophers. And one can meanwhile observe that the innovatory force, in so far as it is not itself an arbitrary fact, cannot but be already immanent in the past, cannot but itself in a certain sense be the past, an element of the past, whatever of the past is alive and developing; the innovatory force is itself conservation-innovation and contains within itself all the past worth developing and perpetuating.[27]

Precisely because formal subsumption was form instead of a thematic and content, it contained the possibility of its future tradition within itself.[28] Because of the form's capacity, indeed its compulsion for replication, its manifestation as passive revolution implied a conception of repetitious historical time in the reappearance of certain political forms necessitated by capitalism that also sanctioned claims to both singularity and comparability. Like the operation of formal subsumption in the realm of economic matters, moreover, there was clearly a hegemonic relationship informing the political configuration of political classes and participants that constituted the "passive revolution" or "revolution/restoration" and the liberal political form of governance that sought to balance the new arrangement of social relations between the "persistence of the old order" and emergent new forces made possible by capitalist development. We know that revolutionary transformations under the domination of a class took onboard both past political practices and personnel from prior regimes now recruited to serve a new kind of political order, environment, and purpose, the coming together of Walter Benjamin's "then and now." Gramsci proposed that fascism constituted the " 'current' or 'actual' form of passive revolution," congealed in a "war of position," freezing the "historical bloc" to imply that this was merely a replication of the phenomenon's content since the form was unchanging.[29] Fascism was the effort to maintain the temporal regime of both capitalism and the original bourgeois leadership ardent to preserve its domination against a new political content threatening to the order of things. Only if the form of passive revolution were directed at reproducing the Jacobin revolutionary model would it be necessary to change its form. While the content of passive revolution will differ according to the circumstances of time and place, the constraining form itself will remain the same. This is especially true of the uneven mix of historical temporalities embodied in its composition—the sense of the pasts' presence and immanence—the form of passive revolution must contain as a condition of its repetition in every present.

In this regard, Japan's Meiji Restoration exceeded Gramsci's own expectation about its suitability as an instance of passive revolution, since its primary purpose from the beginning was to merge past and present, according to the Imperial Charter Oath of 1868, old customs and new knowledge, an archaic presence even more temporally remote and different than Levi's Italian South situated in the capitalist present, under the central authority of a divinely anointed emperor and the state's pursuit of capitalist development at the expense of realizing either social development or widening of the base of political participation. While the preceding Tokugawa regime constituted a form of centralized feudalism, the system began to fall apart in the early nineteenth century with the serious withdrawal of certain regional and religious groups from the central authority in the pattern of centrifugal pulsations, foreigners threatening colonization and peasants accelerating the violence of their protests against market controls of rice. In many ways, the Restoration had to address and find a way to totalize the regional splintering and the diverse temporal orders they were promoting, which meant that the momentum leading to it was constituted of an overdetermination that threatened to undermine both economic development and political order. The first decade or so of the new regime (1870s and early 1880s) was faced with a good deal of popular disorder related to the struggle to dissipate forms of class struggle. Where the Meiji differed from the Italian experience was in its capacity to centralize the fragmented constituencies, even though much of Japan's modern history still echoes with the desire for a more complete revolution. And in the formation of "folklore" there surfaced a long-simmering yearning for regionalism and the revival of nativism in the rescue of custom, crafts production and religious sentiment, the twin axis on which the Restoration forces brought down the Tokugawa order. The great Marxian historiographical debate of the 1930s over whether the Restoration was a bourgeois revolution from the top or an aborted one, resulting in refeudalization and political absolutism, found agreement only in the fact that the Restoration brought with it a "train" of unevenness announced by the persistence of feudal remnants, even as "stunted" and "travestied" forms.[30] Putting the two accounts together would have virtually reproduced Gramsci's notion of passive revolution in form and content, if not necessarily name, and, perhaps, diminish the distinction between social revolution and revolution from the top. It is entirely possible that in the modernizing process the former could take on the form of the latter and "'pre-existing dominant classes' retain their political and social power, so long as their political and social *role* changes."[31] Regardless, the Meiji transformation and transition to a capitalist order was accomplished by a small ruling class, not the peasant masses who were forced to pay for it. It embodied both retrograde elements of the past now serving a different economic system and capitalist modernization with its procession of never-ending new practices to create a society still navigating the temporalities of contemporary noncontemporaneity.

In the end, it seems that one of the real consequences of the form of passive revolution, whether in Italy or Japan or elsewhere, is that it actually defers indefinitely the difficult task of resolving the past and thus necessitates, today more than ever, the demand to find ways to overcome the force of its barrier to the future. Clearly, what emerged especially from Gramsci's formulation of the passive revolution was the untimeliness of the contemporaneous noncontemporary, the forging and fusing of different temporalities of past and present to produce an uneven mix. As I suggested earlier, Gramsci merely transcoded the economic appropriation of capitalism of prior practices into political development, whereby older institutions and procedures were appropriated by a newer bourgeois social order dedicated to liberalism as a way of actually diverting the excesses of more radical working-class transformations. While much of his writings were grounded precisely in history, showing the heterogeneous nature of any present and the synchronicity of nonsynchronous identities,[32] this representation was made explicit in his *Southern Question* and the constant juxtaposition of northern industrial Italy to the semifeudalism of the South.

In many way ways, this problem concerning history and time had already been inadvertently raised by Lenin and Luxemburg, when they contrasted the presence of capitalist production with either a "natural economy" (semi-feudalism) or noncapitalism. In both cases, there was no attention to the empirical fact of temporal unevenness, as such, and its consequences for the accompanying conduct of historical time. By comparison, Gramsci seemed more sensitive to the status of history, and especially the part performed by Italian history in creating the ambiguous arrangement of inaugurating a unified nation-state. Nothing was more important for his present than this particular historical heritage, which became the basis of his conceptualization of the idea of passive revolution. Peter Thomas has proposed that Gramsci's "researches" were driven by the formula "history equals philosophy equals politics" that was "articulated around a redefined notion of praxis."[33] Implementing this formula meant acknowledging that the present could never be identical and transparent to itself. The demands of a philosophically steeped praxis made a necessity of accounting for the historical and political forms of determination. With this approach, the present always appears as the "historical present," as ontology, as Paul Ricoeur and Peter Osborne have defined it. Thomas detects in this formulation the figure of the "noncontemporary present" or nonsynchronous synchronicity, that sense of a present always weighted with the past that Marx earlier envisaged as resulting from a logic that took what it found useful. The point to Gramsci's adaptation was reflected in the broadening of the operation beyond the economic into the political realm and beyond. Whatever the case, elements from the past were subordinated to the pursuit of value. According to Thomas, Gramsci grasped the present as comprising "an ensemble of practices in their different temporalities, struggling to assert their primacy" and making the present "as an *achieved* rather than an *originary* unity."[34] That is to say, the historical present distinguishes the space of struggle between classes and therefore imprints its time as the moment of *zeitwidrig* ("time's turmoil") expressing the tumult involved in the attempt to overcome normal social time and establish a new hegemony. Where this perspective differs from the operation of formal subsumption in the economic sphere is less in the difference of form, which both operations shared, than in the incapacity of capitalism to fully control how the appropriated pasts behave in the present.

Peruvian Historical Palimpsest: Mariátegui's Model for the Transformation of Latin America

If Gramsci pioneered opening the path to the global South and recognized in the Italian local scene the reservoir of forms of vast unevenness between the geographically situated industrialism of the North and semifeudal agrarianism of the South and Sicily, he also marked, as we have seen, the persisting nonsynchronicity of the present and the resulting collision of the tempo and rhythms of everydayness that sharply differentiated the two regions. In making this move to the local, which would inflect the global, it is well worth recalling that his early experience persuaded him that Comintern orthodoxy appeared largely preoccupied with Europe. This emphasis led to recognizing a disjuncture in a program directed toward imposing policies on the world outside Europe or even on its margins at the expense of overlooking and bypassing the specificity of local conditions. This had been a growing problem for a number of thinkers located on the periphery of the industrial West, like Wang Yanan, Mao Zedong, and Uno Kōzō, who increasingly sought to square theory with history, locality, and the circumstances of global capital and the world market. Gramsci, in this respect, observed that in Italy the historical and contemporary conditions actually were too remote from the substance of such policies (as Japanese Marxists learned in the early 1930s) and too abstractly inappropriate for application. For his Peruvian contemporary, José Carlos Mariátegui, the dramatic discovery of the primary importance of local conditions that remained distant from the abstracted imaginaries exported by the Comintern proved to be a revelation in his own short-lived effort to follow the on-site realities of Peru within the larger conjuncture of the interwar years, the emerging struggle with capitalism, and the aspirations for socialist revolution. Mariátegui spent several years in Europe as a political exile banished by the Peruvian government and returned in 1923 to spend his remaining seven years in writing, teaching, and political organizing, until 1930 when he prematurely died. But his productive output and the diversity of themes and interests he raised not only spoke of creative originality but reflected a ceaseless energy that seemed to prefigure a sense of his premature death.

In the time he spent in Italy, Mariátegui witnessed significant events like the strike of the Turin workers in 1920s and attended the Livorno conference where the Italian socialists split and the Communist Party was founded. He could also have observed the temporal immanence shared between the different geographic regions of North and South, which, at the same time, demanded acknowledging the immense difference between northern industrial cities dominated by worker proletarians and an agricultural South inhabited by peasants living under conditions of semifeudal oppression and degradation. Although it is not certain whether Mariátegui actually knew Gramsci, Gramsci's name appears scattered throughout his writings, and Mariátegui's wife, who was Italian, claimed that he had spoken with him. In any event, what would eventually capture his notice in the observation of two different regions sharing a contemporaneity but not identical presents was the recognition that the present lived by southern peasants would not have been any more recognizable to the northern workers than their present would have been to the southerners. For him, this example of contemporary nonsynchronicity would later call attention to its resemblance to the vast separation between Peru's Andean highlands and the coast, with its mines and incipient forms of capitalist development. But even more significant than this geo-economic division was the way he was able to move back and forth in time from a historical present of the republic now committed to capitalist development that still embodied earlier historical temporal forms representing feudal, semicolonial, and semifeudal epochs, and beyond that to reach Inca communal society, thus configuring a composite, vertical structure of layers denoting past historical societies superscripted by later arrivals. This vertically layered structure of historical epochs functioned as a palimpsest, where despite the superseding of layers, traces of earlier forms of social organization, economic modes, and political power were still visible to the present. In short, the palimpsest configuration embodied a panoply of Peru's precapitalist historical presuppositions. Even more important for Mariátegui was Gramsci's grasp of how Italy's southern peasantry were treated as "foreigners" in the modern nation and seen as socially inferior "primitives." Because the peasants of the Italian South were too often perceived in the North as racially inferior or backward, in Mariátegui's reckoning this signaled a kinship they shared with the Peruvian Indians, who suffered from comparable exploitation and oppression. It also meant that the resolution of the agrarian question relied on solving the racial problem.

In both Italy and Peru, history in the form of conditions derived from the remote past coexisted in a dramatic contrapuntal relationship to each other and the specific present housing them, filling it with different historical times "that do not coincide but encounter each other with mutual incomprehension," to create the image of "non-presence of the present,"[35] but actually what had been a sense of an absent presence of past. This mixing or even collision of different times in a present attested to some form of hybrid or formal subsumption defining the social totality in both locations. Moreover, Gramsci's conceptualization of the "passive revolution," as I have already suggested, was simply the political expression of formal subsumption, which pointed toward the possibility of similar mutations in other domains of the social formation (culture, religion, custom, etc.). While Mariátegui saw in Peru's "republic" a legacy of failure in the so-called Independence Revolution, he knew that it fell far short of installing a liberal democratic order since it was characterized by a weak and incompetent bourgeoisie that willingly collaborated with the "landowning nobility" when there should have been conflict between them.[36] In this respect, he observed, the Latin American revolutions failed, owing to this impulse for collaboration among the bourgeoisie, who subordinated liberal principles and interest to the achievement of independence, which, once realized, resulted in aligning their interest with the landed aristocracy. As in Italy, the republican program in Peru, based on a liberal ideology, could not promote principles supporting a resolution of the agrarian problem, which would have required "freeing the land from feudal shackles" and "eliminating the system of large land-owning."[37]

A good deal has been made of Mariátegui's national popular ideology, often as a way of diminishing the place of Marxism in his thinking and even calling attention to a form of Marxism remote from the founding texts. But it was precisely this capacity to seek some sort of accommodation between specific local circumstances and capitalism's global challenge to the promised social revolution that explains Marxism's decision in the interwar period to sink deep roots into the national question everywhere it sought to establish its program. Moreover, this was the occasion that provided the move to deprovincialize Marx: to replace Euro-America as the dominant but provincial provenance with diverse regional contents derived from the "world crisis" that would affect local histories and contemporary situations differently and thus make demands on the scope of Marxian analysis. With activist-thinkers like Gramsci and Mariátegui, especially, we are provided with significant instances of how the spell of the "imperialist" (Western-dominated), analytic holding Marxism in its thrall was broken during the interwar years. Mariátegui, for his part, set his sights on the larger global problem in which Peru would stand in as an instantiation inflecting its movement and resolution. "Capitalism or Socialism," he wrote in his journal *Amauta*, "this is the problem of our epoch." The goal was the future of the "Latin American Revolution," which, he added, "will be nothing more and nothing less than a stage, a phase of world revolution. It will simply and clearly be the socialist revolution."[38] Mariátegui was convinced that even though both capitalism and socialism had originated in Europe, they are not "specifically or particularly European. It is a worldwide movement in which none of the countries that move within the orbit of Western civilization are excluded. This civilization drives toward universality with the force and means that no other civilization possessed."[39] Under the sanction of this future universal civilization, "Indo-America" should not be a mere imitation or copy and "should have individuality and style in this new world order, but not its own culture or fate that is unique."[40] Here, despite employing a strategy that perched its perspective on the national question, he was actually gazing beyond it to the prospect of building a new civilization that would exceed the provincialism of the nation-form and its claims to irreducible uniqueness and special destiny. The stage of imitation has passed with the achievement of independence and the appearance of republican nationhood following the "rhythm of Western history, whose compass has inexorably moved us since colonization." While on the one hand Mariátegui advised moving beyond this episode of imitation that depended on the "European repertoire," on the other hand he wished to acknowledge that socialism was long an American tradition, as evidenced by the fact that the "most advanced primitive communist organization that history records is that of the Incas." With this appeal to an archaic, precapitalist Inca communal organization, he sought to stage a scenario that was capable of linking the most remote experience of communal life to a socialism that was yet to come in his own time. Yet, he warned, it must not be a socialism hobbled by European "parliamentary degeneration and socialist reformation" but one clearly produced by "heroic creation" and enlivened "with our own reality, in our own language."[41] Starting from his Peruvian immediate present, encasing the vertically layered panorama of Peru's historical epochs, Mariátegui believed that he was offered a totalizing perspective of prior historical presuppositions leading back to Inca communism, whose recovery would allow a different return trajectory to the present and make available the outlook for a new beginning to accomplish the great task yet to be achieved.

At the same time, there have been some who have wrongly referred to Mariátegui's rescue of the archaic, Inca communal order as an expression of "Inca utopianism," since it implies some sort of impossible romantic restoration of a prelapsarian "golden age" and thus overlooks the Marxian conceptualization of capital's general law of development and its logic of subsumption, especially the capacity pairing incommensurable practices in the service of producing surplus value and linking the archaic to contemporaneity. In this view, such politicizing of nostalgia also fails to consider the diverse historical moments that constitute an inventory of presuppositions belonging to the remote pasts that play no immediate or direct role in the formation of capitalist society. But when Mariátegui summoned the example of a primitive Inca communism in the American tradition, he had no intention of restoring what had long passed into the archive of historical presuppositions. Its momentary recall in the present was meant to exemplify a way of enlivening socialism that fit into Latin America by giving it its own "style" and "individuality" that would reinforce its capacity to evade the snares produced by imitating the "European repertoire." It had inaugurated Peru's history and made for a history vastly different from the European national narratives colonized people were forced to live instead of their own.[42]

In this regard, Mariátegui related the Peruvian Indians, the Quechuas—the indigenous peoples who identified with traditional communism—to Gramsci's figuration of the subaltern peasantry. These people, he believed, still embodied a spirit of cooperation and a virtually inborn devotion to the land and agricultural cultivation that derived from an archaic historical experience, despite the oppression and exploitation they had been made to suffer. It was also his hope that they would follow Gramsci's agenda and unite with Peru's industrial workers. But this unification, he worried, was an overwhelming task since he realized that the indigenous peoples of Peru and Latin America had experienced a suspension of their "natural evolution" as a result of white and mestizo repression. In spite of the relentless exploitations inflicted on these peoples by foreign colonizers and the retrogressions endured under colonial feudalism (the latafundia system, *gamonalismo*), "the elements of civilization that remain" in these Peruvian communities "are, above all, what survives of the ancient autochthonous organization."[43] "White civilization" has failed to introduce any progress within native culture. His recommendation that indigenous peoples, most of whom were farmworkers and peasants, enter into an alliance with industrial workers represented a fundamental effort to bring the Indian and the surviving traces of their archaic communal order into a capitalist present, to merge past to his present in a social compact, whereby these historical temporal forms would be permitted to retain their own identities in a different present alongside more modern, capitalist expectations.

For Mariátegui, the real importance of Marxism was its openness to accommodating the particularistic aspects of national realities as long as they were cast in terms of the current global situation. Older historical forms would be refigured and assigned a different temporal tense in a present from the past in which they had originated. A Marxism sensitive to the regional specificity of "Our America" was precisely the strategy that would liberate Marx from its dominant, provincial Eurocentrism in such a way as to make available the founder's texts to the world beyond the industrial center of the West. Because Marxism was open to diverse regional historical experiences that historical materialism had to account for, instead of remaining narrowly constrained by a singular and singularizing dogmatic discourse applied to all situations, Mariátegui's attempt to explain problems in a universal idiom was not completely synthesized. Nor could it ever reach this state of completion since each region brings a different set of demands drawn from its own experience and knowledge. Regardless, he strove to forge an understanding of Peru from a perspective of his present that disclosed to him a strategy that, he believed, addressed both Peru and the whole of Latin America that it increasingly stood in for as a metonymical substitute. His strategy consisted of temporal reversal, induced by the current situation of a fledgling capitalist economy undermined by corrosive economic foundations that should have been swept away by an emergent bourgeoisie after the attainment of independence. This situation seemed to be similarly replicated throughout Latin America. But like Gramsci's Italian bourgeoisie, the Peruvian bourgeois class failed to accomplish the necessary removal but for different reasons. The difference he observed was that in Peru there was no genuine bourgeoisie or class independent of the large landowners with which they were aligned against peasant and Indian agrarian interests. In his time, it was already too late for the bourgeoisie to implement adequate reforms designed to break the back of the large landowners—too much time had passed, and he recognized, with others, that the agrarian problem was one that global capital also had to resolve. Under these circumstances, he was prompted to move his attention to the indigenous farmers and the image of Inca rural society, whose traces remained embedded in this class since the Inca were a "rural race" dedicated to the earth. From there he returned to the present but one filled with the resources of the past that might be enlisted in resolving the agricultural problem at the same time that Peru settled the question of race and the status of the indigenous, who were chained to it.

It should be noted that Mariátegui's sensitivity to the importance of the present was inscribed in his book *La escena contemporanea* (1925), which recorded the relationship of the pasts residing in his present and claimed neither "objectivity" nor "an astigmatism." In this book, it is possible to see the sanction for his strategy of temporal reversal. He confessed to the impossibility of envisioning "a panoramic grasp of the totality of the contemporary world."[44] The world, he declared, must be approached episodically by moving from one fact to the next, journalistically and even cinematographically, similar to a photo montage. But "our imagination will always be delayed" by the "entirety of the phenomenon."[45] The theme of a privileged contemporaneity was continued in lectures he gave addressing the "History of World Crises"

(Historia de las crises mundial, 1923-1924) that concentrated on the "crisis of Western Civilization" as it was being lived by the Peruvian proletariat. The problem he foresaw was the presence of a proletarian class that lacked sufficient knowledge and understanding of a world in which it was no longer a spectator but a principal actor committed to changing it. "Now, more than ever," he announced, "the proletariat needs to know what is going on in the world. And it cannot know this through the fragmentary, homeopathic information from the daily news."[46] It is always channeled by the "reactionary press" that works to undermine and deplete the revolutionary energies, organizations and men to disorient the world proletariat.[47] As a result, "the fate of all the workers of the world is in play," he added, "in the European crisis." This world crisis was as much in the interest of the Peruvian workers as it was of the workers of the Far East. It had been choreographed on the European stage, but its consequences reached all Western civilization, and ultimately to the marginal and colonial societies like Peru. In this way the countries in the colonial periphery are linked to the "orbit of this civilization" because of the connections that launched economic colonization imposed by British, North American, and French capital. Moreover, he looked to what was described as the "internationalization of the life of humanity" and the "historical reality" of material connections that have connected all people into a solidarity."[48] It is this crisis the proletariat must apprehend, "that part of the proletariat whose historic role it is to represent the Peruvian proletariat in the present instance."[49]

Mariátegui perceived the crisis not simply as a product of capitalism but rather as the result of capitalism's response to the post–World War I era and its effort to recover the wealth dissipated and lost in the conflict. The attempt to rebuild Europe's states was calculated to require a disciplined "regime of rigorous fiscal economy, of increasing work hours and salary reductions."[50] Resolution of the crisis demanded a "rollback" of proletarian gains won earlier, to which, he insisted, they simply cannot acquiesce. This solution accentuates the implementation of another round of austerity and sacrifice from those least able to sustain such a harsh economic regime. Moreover, the great tragedy of European countries has been the determined cancellation of concessions made to socialism. Both the economic gains won by the proletariat and their hard-earned political victories have been targeted for elimination by the forces of reaction. With this new assault, Mariátegui recorded, came the arrival of fascist dictatorships in Italy as a prefiguration of even worse things to come. If the crisis was thus a combination of economics and politics, it was, above all else, ideological, inasmuch as the "affirmative, positivist philosophers of bourgeois society" have fallen into rapid decline, along with nationalism and historicism confronting the challenge of a destructive relativism and skepticism. In his thinking, this new intellectual descent proved to be the "most profound," most severe symptom of the "crisis" since it exceeded economics to threaten the totality of bourgeois civilization itself—that is the whole of Western civilization.[51] But Mariátegui's sure dialectical impulse also identified in this epochal decline "the rise of the proletariat," which could only emerge "by virtue of the decadence" visited on Western civilization. The clearing away of the rubble of bourgeois civilization required by the resolution of the crisis would expose the way to fasten on to the "reality" of contemporary noncontemporaneity that lay before the present.

In Mariátegui's stratigraphic history, with its vertical embodiment of coexisting layers of different historical societies from Peru's past inscribed in the present, the most important historical residues were those representing the original Andean indigenous communities. These he viewed as a carryover of an archaic communal order founded on agricultural cultivation. Here was an inflection of Marx's consideration of the precapitalist or archaic formations based on common ownership of the land. The subsequent layers consisted of colonial feudalism, brought by the Spanish who drove the Indians into the sierra, varying forms of semifeudalism, and a republican present committed to capitalism. Since this scheme was neither temporally linear nor premised on a causal relationship between a before and an after, the vertical layering implied no other relationship between the strata than the time when they appeared. But all were copresent in and with the now, so to speak, contemporary with it but not synchronized and identical with it. What attracted Mariátegui to this most remote historical configuration was that its communal structure in which peasants were both proprietors and cultivators of the land pointed to a historical trajectory that was set off course by the trauma of foreign colonization and the genocide that reduced the Indian population to a fraction of what it had previously been. Yet, he was convinced, this historical presupposition had not disappeared in the wake of destruction and degeneration inflicted by foreigners. Its indistinct outline could still be discerned in the successive historical forms resulting from the conquest and colonization. The archaic form was replaced by the legacy of European feudalism introduced through the agency of colonial oppression and coercion brought by the Spanish, with its still powerfully present and active latafundia system in the Andean highlands (where it remained virtually unchanged down to Mariátegui's present) and in the hacienda of the coastal region. This system mutated in hybrid forms like semifeudalism and semicolonialism, which often depended on coercively impressing Indians into work service and importing blacks from Africa into slavery for the same purpose. The last but still incomplete historical form was the implantation of the modern capitalist economy, with concomitant linkages to certain coastal areas that remained relatively free from the specter of feudal dominance exercised by the *gamonal* system of "large landowners" or "local bosses." It is important to notice that some of the elements of modern capitalism derived from mercantilist or merchant capital of an earlier era preoccupied with mining and the extraction of precious metals and gems.

For Mariátegui, the fundamental problem of Peruvian social reality was the land, which he directly linked to both the agrarian question and the Indian problem, specifically, the racial divide—thus identifying economic deprivation with racism.[52] In his seminal essay of 1925, "The Land Problem," included in his principal collection of essays *Seven Interpretative Essays on Peruvian Reality (7 ensayos de interpretación de la realidad peruana)*, he dismissed an older humanitarianism toward the indigenous peoples promoted by the sixteenth-century Dominican missionary priest Bartolomé de Las Casas (1474–1566) as "outdated" because it ignored the "economic problem."[53] Condemning the argument simply as "abstract humanitarianism," he recognized that if this defense of the indigenous was permitted to continue in the present, nothing would happen to change their contemporary circumstances, demonstrating, along the way, a clear rejection of linear historical causation. Apart from the romantic associations attached to this legacy, Mariátegui was persuaded that the perspective provided by the present required abandoning the approach recommended by Las Casas centuries ago as a necessary condition for implementing a program based on the primacy of the socioeconomic problem that confronted the landless peasantry. "Nothing," he asserted, "is more evident than the inability to understand, with the help of economics, phenomena that dominate the process of formation of the Peruvian nation . . . it does explain its roots. This is clear in our epoch and if for

some the epoch seems rigid, that . . . would be because of the logic of economics."[54] Elsewhere, he insisted, "we are not content with demanding the
Indians' right to education, culture, progress, love and heaven. We start
by categorically demanding their right to the land."[55] On this theme, he
reminded his readers that this "thoroughly" materialistic demand did not
prevent Peruvians from admiring the "great Spanish friar."

Bringing the problem of the land immediately to the surface simultaneously entailed coupling it with the agrarian question. The right outcome to
the problem of land and agriculture could be realized only through the "liquidation" of the still surviving remnants of feudalism in Peru. In this connection, Mariátegui's critique and analysis of the current situation echoed
Gramsci's reflections in *The Southern Question*. The Peruvian highlands, like
the Italian South, remained captive to the oppressive regime of large-scale
landowners and bosses. The process of liquidation should have been completed earlier, and while a few palliative laws came with the inauguration of
the republican state, there was no follow-up. The reason for the failure to
promote effective land reform lay in the persistence of a weak bourgeois class
throughout the duration of a century's republican history, which, like their
southern Italian counterpart, managed to produce no genuine bourgeois
class—"a true capitalist class."[56] Mariátegui reasoned that the older feudal
class simply disguised itself as a republican bourgeoisie in order to retain its
privilege after independence. During the republican period the large land-
owning class has, in fact, enlarged the extent of its holdings, despite constitutional constraints and the development of the "practical necessities" of a
capitalist economy. With the continued survival of feudalism in the heart of
the republic, there is the inseparability of the "large estates" and "servitude."[57]
The question troubling Mariátegui's analysis was knowing that there was
nothing radical in the process of breaking up large estates into smaller
units, since it was a program that originated in liberal ideals. Contemporary
history already showed this process of breaking up estates in Eastern and
Central Europe, which Mariátegui described as the "ramparts of feudalism," through acts aimed, in principle, at restricting landownership and the
size of plots. In view of the failure to enact adequate land reforms in Peru—a
problem Gramsci recognized in southern Italy—the issue had now become
linked to the "survival of the community [in Peru] and the demands of practical socialism in Indigenous agriculture and life."[58] The time had passed to

sweep away the feudal hangovers that continued to undermine the agricultural livelihood of the peasantry and with it the nostalgic reenactments of the colonial past and the romantic aura that had settled on the feudal legacy to shield it from being seen for what it actually was.

What Mariátegui's analysis sought to demonstrate was how "economic foundations" from prior pasts persisted in Peru long after the elimination of the Spanish "medieval" legacy. Survival of these debilitating vestiges, he observed, was rooted in the retention of class interests, which had not been eradicated with independence. As long as the agrarian question remained unresolved, the structure of a democratic and liberal constitutional order would continue to be destabilized by the semifeudal economy undermining its new foundations. Unlike other regions confronting a similar agrarian problem, the Peruvian circumstances Mariátegui described appeared more complicated because of the presence of the indigenous, yoking the problem of the land economy to race. In Peru, he claimed, the indigenous population constituted "a race of farmers," identifying contemporary agricultural workers with their Inca forebears.[59] Through these contemporary indigenous, he moved back, beyond the historical environment shaped by colonial feudalism to an archaic order that preceded its time, developed and sustained by the Inca, who were "rural people" devoted to agricultural cultivation and animal husbandry. In the remote shadow of the Inca, he saw the contemporary indigenous, just as he saw the present in the past. Rootedness in agrarian life, the common idiom shared by the Indians of the past and the present, originated from the deeply held conviction that "life comes from the earth" and produced the specific culture of the region. Mariátegui pointed to the vast public works projects undertaken by the Inca (*Tawantinsuyu*) for agricultural purposes—notably irrigation channels and agrarian terracing of the Andes, monumental works on a pharonic scale that necessitated a centralized political authority, as in China, capable of organizing and mobilizing immense armies of labor. The magnitude of such achievement, he asserted, mirrored the high degree of economic organization and technological innovation reached by archaic society.[60] But it was the land and its cultivation that commanded principal attention, then and now, in a society founded on communal ownership and a religion of sun worship.

The significance of Mariátegui's recovery of this foundational historical stratum was driven less by a romantic or quixotic impulse to recover some distant golden age than it was to awaken and enliven the present. For the present, where its ancient silhouette was still visible in the life of the indigenous, it closely resembled Walter Benjamin's designation of a "primal history," figured in the form of a communal order which, admittedly, had been forged by a political autocracy and symbolized by this precapitalist "agrarian communism."[61] Collective ownership of cultivable land by sets of related families was divided into individual and nontransferable plots; common ownership of grazing land, water, and forests was controlled by tribes (*marka*) or marks, as Luxemburg put it, that were usually associated with a village and employed cooperative labor and permitted individual appropriation of harvests and produce. With the destruction of this economy and its culture, what had been the premises of a historical trajectory, of what Marx called *becoming*, leading to the formation of a commune-based civilization became the ghostly inventory of historical presuppositions of what might have been but no longer are related to what follows. Yet they do not altogether disappear, even though they are "gone and past" (*Grundrisse*). Although this "autochthonous" form of agrarian communism disappeared under the impact of the foreign assault, nothing adequate replaced it. The thriving population of ten million or more and its "efficient organic state" were wiped out through the instrument of systematic genocide and thrown into servitude and dependence.[62] The colonizers erected a partially artificial and foreign economic basis, invariably reproducing their own interests. What the episode illustrated was Spain's inability to appreciate the economic value of people, the "human capital" inherent in the indigenous and its investment in agricultural production.[63] Spanish colonial policy aimed at exterminating the population and enslaving the remainders. Driven by an economy of extraction and theft, the Spaniards were first interested in the acquisition of precious metal and stones and installed an incipient mining industry by converting agricultural cultivators into miners. "Within a naturally feudal system," Mariátegui wrote, "agricultural labor would have converted the Indians into serfs linked to the land. Labor in the mines and cities would make them into slaves."[64] This is what he meant when he accused the Spanish colonizer of devaluing human capital. In addition to making Indians into slaves, the Spaniards imported Africans and later Chinese to supply the need for labor and servants to the viceroyalty court and its Spanish population located on the coast. But the significant contribution of Spanish colonialism was its implantation of feudalism in Peru, even though it was defective because of its heavy reliance on slavery and extraction rather than production and the creation of wealth. In Mariátegui's critical account, the abject servitude of the Indians under both Spanish feudalism and an apparently worse "creole feudalism" was not improved with the establishment of the republic. The republic has simply sanctioned the "ascent of a new ruling class that has systematically taken their [Indian] land."[65]

Both feudalism and its mutation, semifeudalism, have survived well into the republican era, principally within the precincts of the agrarian economy. The institutional retention of the large estates not only testified to this inheritance; the legacy was manifest in primary forms of capitalism such as wage labor in exchange for services. The Andean region, Mariátegui remarked, exemplified the discipline of typical servitude. He was persuaded that in the "transition to capitalism," wages are exchanged for labor, and where there is no proper form of salary regime, there is no capitalism. But the capitalist concentration also creates latifundism with the absorption of smaller properties by the larger enterprises. As a result of this process of incorporation, the capitalist latifundia, employing exploited labor for production, involve salaried work and stood in sharp contrast to the operation of the feudal estate, where even though the day laborers receive a scratch of land, they are nonetheless obliged to work the lord's lands without compensation. Under these circumstances, the cultivator remains a serf since the republic has been reluctant or unable to break this entrenched *gamonal* system. By contrast, the coastal estates and their labor systems have in fact become capitalist enterprises, but the landowners continue to preserve absolute authority, despite the fact that workers are nominally paid wages. Mariátegui was describing the beginning of "formal capitalism" in an environment in which feudalism continued to endure in one form or another and in a relationship based on a regime of absolute surplus value or labor. In this arrangement, workers who "received" land as a form of payment still "served" the lord's lands as serfs. If the workers received wages, the lord of the hacienda still exercised absolute control over their lives. The point Mariátegui seemingly failed to directly see was how these practices signified the operation of formal subsumption in the creation of surplus value.[66] Even though the nature of hacienda labor was salaried, the latifundia sought to "conserve the spirit of the *encomendero*" charged with the function of incorporating land into royal domains (during the colonial period) by making them productive and proselytizing the indigenous population, which was put to work. Trying to instill a spirit of managerial control, however, was not the same thing as the use of coercion that actually accompanied the position as it was executed by the conquistador who occupied it. Rather, it was closer to a new relationship wherein the older practices were materially suborned to capitalist development and the further attempt to preserve the "spirit" of the older system merely indicated the nature of the changed circumstances. Because the state in the republican era had failed to reach these levels of social organization and production, especially in the more remote regions of the country, feudalistic practices were allowed to continue intact; but in other areas, such as the coast, capitalism was aligned with feudal political control that insulated worker's lives from the feared possible contagion of proletarian doctrine. Mariátegui was describing a scene dominated by immense unevenness and untimely temporalities that determined the rhythms of life and labor, a scene entrenched in the logic of capitalist development.[67] Moreover, bourgeois indolence and the absence of a "capitalist spirit" ultimately bankrupted a large number of coastal haciendas that fell into the hands of creditors and forced them to revert to colonial/feudal practices that "regulated production to the European and North American markets."[68] Other failed enterprises were simply taken over by foreign companies. "Our latifundia, our landowners, whatever their illusions of independence, are, in reality, intermediary agents of foreign capitalism."[69]

Recalling Gramsci's analysis, Mariátegui claimed that liberal policy in Peru had fallen far short of formalizing the relations between capital and labor and the authority of the state in a context suffused with feudal remainders.[70] The difference between Italy and Peru was that if the latter resembled the Italian South, the former's North was more advanced and regionally embedded. As late as 1929, Mariátegui observed that "industry is still very small in Peru. Its possibilities for development are limited by the condition, structure, and character of the national economy, but it is even more limited by the dependence of economic life on the interests of foreign capitalism."[71] Convinced that the formation of a proletariat must come with the development of capitalism, he was equally certain that "the industrial proletariat . . . has to realize its obligations of solidarity with the peasantry of the hacienda.".[72] Failure to establish unity between worker and peasantry came from the weakness of the state to eliminate the vestiges of "indenture" and "share-cropping" still practiced by the large landowners, which vigilantly resisted the establishment of a free wage system. These regimes of work represented forms of bondage and servitude, originating from the semislave traffic in coolies. It was through these forms of semislave labor that the figure of feudalism was able to cast its shadow to partially eclipse the development of capitalism.[73] In some regions along the coast, wage labor merely replaced sharecropping, tenancy, but had no effect on the status of workers, who remained in a state of bondage. Here, Mariátegui compared the Peruvian system of "indentured" labor (yanaconazgo), differing from one region to the next but essentially identifiable with "precapitalist methods of working the land as observed in other countries[,] with semi-feudal agriculture. For, example Tsarist Russia."[74] Evidently he saw in the formation of the semifeudal the form and sign of capitalism's developmental logic that disclosed further a glimpse of the process of how appropriating received practices from prior pasts was put into the practice of serving capitalism. Thus the Russian system of "paying for rent by work, money, or crops as [it] exists in Peru."[75] This system (otrabotki) intervened between older practices of bonded labor that relied on violence and "free labor" distinguished only by economic obligations and therefore functioned as a transition precisely because it combined features of the old and the new wage form. The persisting "nature of agricultural property," with its continuity of forms of tenancy coupled with servitude, resulted in constituting "one of the greatest obstacles to the development of national capitalism" in Peru. It led to absentee landlordism, living off the rents from their properties, "without providing any work or *intelligence* to the country's economic activity." Moreover, these landowners correspond to aristocrats or rentiers, and their hereditary proper rights resemble "feudal privileges." The tenants have no inducement to improve the value of the land, and while they aspire to someday to become owners, whatever they may add to increase the value of agricultural land benefits only the landowner[76] While agricultural production on the coast made accommodations with capitalism, it had not been sufficient to make up for the "ineptitude" of extant feudal practices in the highlands, showing no progress toward the creation of wealth. Once again, the contrast returned to making distinctions between feudal and semifeudal, whereby the latter had already encountered capitalism that resulted in its mutation, while the former remained frozen in the lockstep of a "patriarchal," primitive type of feudal "landowner."[77]

A further roadblock to development in Peru and Latin America in general has been the alignment of feudal and bourgeois over their shared "contempt for the Indians, as well as Blacks and Mulattos."[78] Mariátegui did not overstate the importance of the relationship between race and feudalism's persisting fortitude in certain regions, a staying power that exclusively depended on exploiting Indians, where wage labor was "nascent"[79] and usually "deformed," cultivation anchored in a primitive manner on poor soil (since the best land was reserved for the large estates and forced to provide free service to the owners).[80] In the end, his intense support of the indigenous and their identification with the surviving traces of a former Inca communism and tradition of "cooperation" they still embodied mediated his observations on the economic structure of colonial feudalism and its subsequent refashioning into a semifeudalism. This economic structure proclaimed the eventful encounter of capitalism and precapitalist formations and modes of production to project the complex figure of "synchronous nonsynchronicity." It presented an image of society constructed on the shifting ground of coexisting different contemporaneities that that would define the content of Marx's conception of the social and the nature of capitalist society. In a very real sense, Mariátegui demonstrated how the semifeudal mutation represented both the sign of formal subsumption and the society it wrought into a permanent transition caught in the constant collision of pasts in presents that are never completed but always left open; not a society distinguished by a polarization of opposites and the successful overcoming of one by the other, nor the grand transition from a noncommodity community—feudalism—or any comparable tributary system to market society or one faithful to exchange. If Mariátegui sought to show how his palimpsest, extracted from the humus of Peru's history, could represent the historical circumstances of Latin America, he was also aware that its rich texture of layers would yield a mode of analysis capable of laying the foundation for a socialist transformation in the conception of mixed temporalities that would define the future. But in the end this future still remained within history, as he explained: "We confess, without scruple, that we are in the domain of the temporal, the historic, and that we have no intention of abandoning them. We leave the spirits incapable of accepting and understanding their epoch to their sterile afflictions and tearful metaphysics."[81]

4

THEORIZING LATE DEVELOPMENT AND THE "PERSISTENCE OF FEUDAL REMNANTS"

wang yanan, yamada moritarō, and uno kōzō

Although Rosa Luxemburg foresaw the eroding effects of the penetration of capitalism in noncapitalist zones, both the political-economic and cultural consequences of colonial dispossession, the on-site experience was recorded and addressed by others who lived it. The rapid pace of seizure of colonial possessions crested by the time of World War I, and expropriating and extractive powers of imperializing colonial nations settled down in the interwar decades to analyze and assess the baneful effects on subjected societies. Specifically, attention turned to determining the deficits that resulted from forcible dispossession and late entry into the world market. On the part of imperializing powers, there appeared a chorus of regret that began to complain that the colonial project was too expensive, while in the colonies there surfaced incipient nationalist movements demanding independence. In Asia, only Japan managed to successfully to escape the direct consequences of imperial colonization by becoming an aggressive colonizer itself in the late nineteenth and early twentieth centuries. Despite evading the direct ill effects of colonial expropriation, Japanese opinion saw the nation precariously balanced on the periphery of industrializing capitalism and embarked on a developmental trajectory since the 1870s that had introduced the coexistence of surviving practices and institutions from a prior feudal order that now were seen as "remnants and vestiges" and that, for many, constituted an immense block to the full realization of a completed capitalist order. For those who perceived in these unwelcome survivals the specter of an unresolved past in their new present as the force that would lead Japan to a retrograde refeudalization and a politically destructive absolutism, the achievement of a mature capitalism was envisioned as a necessity for the transition yet to come from capitalism to socialism. War and destruction in the 1940s and a subsequent military occupation afforded those who believed that the spectral remnants of the past overcame the prewar imaginary the opportunity for a second start. What they achieved was simply the reproduction of the prewar past in a more perfected form in a different temporal register

In China, the rampant colonizing process of diverse European powers prevailed in the coastal areas and selected regions in the interior to produce a political patchwork that was named semifeudalism and semicolonialism. And in India, already colonized for some time, England remained the hegemonic power despite the growing murmur of an anticolonial nationalist sentiment on the horizon that was already pointing to how colonial dispossession had undermined indigenous industries. In all this, it was recognized that these ancient societies had come to capitalism late, and their entry into it was frequently involuntary and often carried out under force or its threat. Such "lateness" inevitably led to classifying these societies as backward and inferior, despite being immanent with a "modern" present, and existing in another temporal register that signified an unbridgeable time gap between advanced modern nations of Euro-America and the rest of the world languishing in the backwaters of modern civilization. "Lateness" did not necessarily imply irretrievable backwardness, but it introduced the imperative to "catch up" in order to enter the time of the modern present and thus close the temporal cleft. In societies like China and India, the colonial factor was often deemed to be the cause for retarding growth, whereas in Japan, lateness brought advantages inasmuch as imitating the model of a mature English capitalism in the late nineteenth century enabled avoiding early stages and experiences of capitalist development that now belonged to its remote past. It also pointed to the fact even though Japan, for example, experienced a long feudal duration, it had failed to produce capitalism. What lateness involved was attentiveness toward the special circumstances of the particular encounter with capitalism, as both Antonio Gramsci and, especially, José Carlos Mariátegui had already demonstrated, not some mechanically repetitive compulsion forcing a society to adopt a standard template replicating the same processes everywhere. In other words, the historicity of experiencing meant adjusting a model at a particular moment of maturation of capitalist development that would mark its contemporaneity and shared copresence. To be sure, the constraints inflicted by colonialism would seek to displace this possibility through forms of violence that emphasized "backwardness," driving the colonized back to the temporality of an everyday not yet contaminated by the historical intrusion of capitalism, as both Rabindranath Tagore in India and Yi Tae-jun in Korea demonstrated. In some instances, as in the case of Japan, the old formation in Okinawa was purposely restored in the nineteenth century in order to retain received land and labor relationships in the production of sugar. And the regular appeal to archaism in a number of societies became an index indicating the degree to which the reinventing of the past to support capitalism constituted a creative adaptation of formal subsumption. Among analysts like Wang Yanan, Yamada Moritarō, and Uno Kōzō, there appeared to be a shared critical stance toward the utility of the "Asiatic mode of production" (AMP) and its capacity to explain the historical present China and Japan confronted in the interwar period, even as they differed somewhat in their respective assessments of the role played by surviving "feudal remnants" in their own societies.

If it is reasonable to suppose that Marx and Engels conceived the figure of the Asiatic mode of production to explain the difference between the development of capitalism in Western Europe and its absence in the world beyond (that is, Asia),[1] it is plausible to suggest that its utility and applicability eventually fastened onto the colonized portion of the world in the nineteenth century that was being involuntarily drawn into the world market. On numerous occasions, Marx and Engels changed their minds about what made up this difference that delayed a comparable development. The leading explanatory candidate was ultimately the absence of private property in these societies represented in more contemporary examples of "Oriental despotisms" Marx identified with Turkey, Persia, India, and China.[2] In the vast literature on the AMP, few accounts have entertained the possibility that Marx envisioned the figure as a methodological model. In many ways, the concept of the AMP resembled and even behaved like Marx's totalization of capitalism in *Capital*, in the presumed form of real subsumption. It should be recalled that when Marx posited the totality of capitalism as consisting of only capital and labor in his attempt to clarify the process of expanded reproduction, he was putting forth a model, a proto-ideal type. In both instances, a model was being configured (or constructed) that would allow him to account not simply for the difference between Western Europe and its outside but for an act of totalizing that would enable grasping the figure in such a way as to see it and its constituent structure in its totality. What I am suggesting is that the Asiatic mode of production was more form than empirical historical content, more a methodological device than a completed historical and empirical reality. The confusion between an existent historical reality and a projected model was undoubtedly the source of the misrecognition that identified all societies classified under the category of the AMP as appearing homogenous and looking like one another, as would all examples of an achieved capitalism. In fact, the constant changes in thinking about the figure repeated attempts at adjusting and refining the model more precisely. As for its utility, it was only with colonial acquisition in the late nineteenth century and after that it eventually became the means to clasp an evolving empirical reality. The effect of this growing identification of Asiatic mode of production and colonies of former imperial civilizations like India and China, especially, (and later the Islamic world and Africa) was to commit these societies to the permanent register of temporal "standstill," "vegetate . . . to the teeth of time"[3] and endless repetition, lacking accumulative development over the course of time that, as in Western Europe, led to the emergence of capitalism. A harsh judgment, to be sure, and one that pointed more to the conceit of capitalism rather than Marx that found its way into bourgeois social science dedicated to development and modernization (purposely misrecognized as economic growth) and the demand for "catching up" in order for such societies to join the modern present. "That such an empire [China] should at last be overtaken by the fate on occasion of a deadly duel in which the representative of the antiquated world appears prompted by ethical motives, while the representative of overwhelming modern society fights for the privilege of buying in the cheapest and selling in the dearest markets—this, indeed is a sort of tragical couplet, stranger than any poet would have dared to fancy."[4] But in fact, the AMP became the basis of what might be called a colonial mode of production. A view that condemned noncapitalist societies to an earlier time, as if they still belonged to the childhood of history, languishing in a shadowed, static past to the modern present, presumed that only development leading to the installation of a capitalist order could overcome the vast and uneven temporal disparity. The obvious conclusion was that no substantial internal development had taken place in these regions over the blank seriality of a long duration since the time of archaic origins, excepting only changes introduced from the outside. What the history of these Asian societies consists of is a "history of successive intruders who founded empires on the passive basis of [those] unresisting and unchanging societ[ies]."[5] Hence the paradoxical result of temporal stagnation of Oriental despotisms and the myriad small, self-reproducing village communities under Oriental despotisms' authority, despite the level of civilization they were able to realize as late as the eighteenth century. Whatever else recent, broader application of the concept beyond Asia or worldwide archaic communities in Peru, Mexico, and even Polynesia signifies, it still testifies to the modular function of the Asiatic mode of production and the promise of typifying a certain modality of society for subsequent historical and empirical research. What, of course, was lost in the subsequent recognition of different forms of civilizations and societies was the development of different cultures with their own conceptualization of history and time. The importance of reconfiguring the AMP as the "passive basis" of a colonial mode was the figuration of categories like semifeudal and semicolonialism that sought to describe the circumstances of the particular penetration of capitalism in the colony.

Japan's development as an independent nation-state rather than a colony put it outside the framework of the AMP. Even so, Marxists retained a certain fidelity to the usefulness of the concept, despite its unsuitability to Japan's recent history. Although Japanese showed some interest in the AMP, it came to an end after 1931 with the Comintern's decision reached at the Leningrad "Discussion on the Asiatic Mode of Production" to discount its veracity and discourage its further application.[6] Its explanatory force was exceeded by Yamada Moritarō's powerful account of the frozen transition from Tokugawa feudalism to a combined economic refeudalization and political absolutism under the Meiji oligarchical regime, which, for the "Lectures Faction" (*kōzaha*), produced a veritable counterrevolution. I will consider Yamada's powerful interpretative template below, which closely followed Marx's sketch of capitalism in *Capital* and showed how it was derailed from the classic course represented by England. Its appeal to this model, which more or less situated Japan within European historical development, shut down any serious consideration of the Asiatic mode of production as the key to Japan's subsequent evolution of a capitalist society, despite Yamada's scorching critique of the inhuman effects it inflicted on the Japanese worker. The historian Hani Gorō, whose own work on the Meiji Restoration was aligned with the partisan *kōzaha* position associated with Yamada's template, wrote an important article in 1932, just before interest in the AMP in Japan closed down because of a combination of factors composed of shifts in Comintern policy and the domestic oppression of the Japan Communist Party. Hani's article "The Form of Capitalism in Asia" (1932) focused on an analysis of the particularities of Asian society—its difference from the West—and its claims to universality. He was especially concerned with the effects of Western/Japanese imperialism in Asian countries, which reduced their claim to universality to degraded forms of Asian particularity that became another name for backwardness, a view shared by the Chinese thinker Wang Yanan, as we shall see. After 1933, Japanese interest in the AMP dwindled and vanished, except for stray, short articles like the one Hani wrote in 1940 for a historical dictionary that sought to extol its contemporary utility for understanding world history. In many ways, Hani was still concerned with the question of Asian universalism, but by this time he was forced to remain silent on the consequences of imperialism imposed on Asian society. He was particularly concerned with emphasizing the importance of fundamental laws that would lead to the progress of the scientific study of history. Specifically, he was referring to the methodological role played by "productive forms in the modern study of history."[7] These productive forms or forces of production moved history and society and accounted for changing development. In a general sense, he was recapitulating Marx's definition of historical materialism and the vocation attributed to the modes of production articulated in *A Contribution to the Critique of Political Economy* (1859). This preoccupation with productive forms (or forces) resulted in progressive developments from archaic communalism to contemporary capitalism within a general world history.[8] As for the Asiatic mode of production, he acknowledged it had become a problem. Its special character appeared in the possible plural forms identified with it that defied the unwavering linearity noted in world historical development, such as the ownership of slavery or community-owned land or state centralization demanding various forms of income extraction like a tributary system that had not yet differentiated land rent from taxes, and so on. What seems significant here is how Hani hinted at seeing the AMP as simply another tributary version of extraction and exploitation, like feudalism, which, again, was close to the formulation that Wang envisioned seven years later. Hani was troubled by the stagnation of forms between an undifferentiated, primitive system of slavery and agricultural slavery and how it continued thereafter to haunt a later present. He concluded that in the present the idea of the Asiatic mode of production had broadened as a research method in the scholarly world, but it was still necessary to wait for the "great quantity of concrete understanding of reality" related to the history of India, China, and Japan to appear and illuminate its role in their current circumstances, which was to suggest that it still possessed methodological value in the understanding of these contemporary societies. Yet it is important that Hani did not differentiate the colonial status of China and India from Japan's independence but instead saw Asia, the "Orient," as he called it, as a unity. In the early postwar, the historian Ishimoda Shō proposed that while the Asiatic mode of production probably brought China into the wider compass of world history, Japanese proponents of the AMP before the war had effectively discounted Asians and seriously disregarded their circumstances. In a moving response to the Chinese Marxist and participant in discussions in the earlier Chinese social history controversy, Guo Moruo, titled "The Theme of Historical Studies in Crisis—Response to the Appeal of Guo Moruo," Ishimoda denounced the theory of the AMP on the ground that after nearly two thousand years of historical progress in Asian societies, they were still being condemned to lasting "stagnation," and he wondered what logic authorized this evaluation.[9]

In China, the Marxian social history controversy, by contrast, resorted to employing the model of the AMP in the effort to periodize China's long history and explain the transition to capitalism.[10] The debate surfaced in the tumultuous years between 1927 and 1937, when revolutionary pitch in China reached a new register that ultimately ignited a civil war between Communists and nationalists during the decade. According to Arif Dirlik, the majority of participants in the social history controversy were not professional historians, as such, but young intellectuals who had already been active in

political life since the May Fourth years (1919). In their hands, political action merged with the emerging social revolutionary agenda of the Chinese
Revolution to provide historical practice with a practical vocation. Exposure
to the intellectual and political tradition of May Fourth during the formative
years of their lives constituted the necessary experience that molded both the
nature of their political commitment and the choice of historical practice as
the means to expressing it. In assessing the failure of revolution in 1927, dissi-
dent social historians explained that the cause derived from their defective
view of conditions in the present. Still, "the question of contemporary society
provided the link which connected revolution to history,"[11] anticipating a later
Gramscian plaint that declared "all history is contemporary, that is, political."

Soviet Comintern strategy was intimately implicated in directing the revolutionary impulse in China in the late 1920s, and with the failure of the
revolutionary movement in 1927 its China experts adduced that its collapse
stemmed from a fatal incapacity to recognize that the country exemplified
an instance of an "Asiatic society." What this meant is that the formulation of
a revolutionary agenda could no longer derive its strategy from the experience
of a vastly different Western Europe but now demanded the consideration of
an alternative set of possibilities as the basis of a new revolutionary strategy
that conformed more closely to China's historical circumstances, which lay at
the heart of contemporary society. While Soviet political leadership balked
at this suggestion because by 1928 it denied the necessity of an antifeudal
agrarian revolution, the problem, nevertheless, stoked historical controversy
and sparked greater interest in the figure of the Asiatic mode of production.
Although the interest lasted until 1931 or thereabouts because of the Comintern's decision to shelve its claim to the status of a social formation attributed by its proponents, in "the course of the discussions, the Marxist
periodization of history was subjected to an unprecedentedly thorough
re-examination."[12] And issues of China's historical particularity continued
to persist in Chinese historical writing throughout the 1930s but were usually superseded by efforts to conform to Soviet interpretations of Marxist
periodization to demonstrate that Chinese society had successfully followed the universal "laws" of development that Marx had discerned in
Europe. As a result of the preoccupation with periodization, historical practice lost its initial revolutionary ardor, as well as its commanding interest in
the relationship between contemporaneity and the historical present. What

disappeared after the early 1930s was not an interest in historical materialism, as such, but the conviction that the vocation of historical analysis had an immediate and compelling relationship to revolutionary strategy and action.[13]

The Chinese fixation on periodization and the certainty it offered with its temporal march of definite stages associated with modes of production brought China into a wider world of historical development. There was no agreement over whether the AMP constituted a social formation in its own right, with its own dynamic driving the pulsation of development or a transitional bridge linking the stage of primitive society and slavery. Many, including Guo Moruo and Wang Yanan, favored this latter view. With Wang it was often difficult to distinguish the AMP from feudalism. Even though he was critical of the former figure, elements associated with it managed to leak into his analysis of early Chinese feudalism: "China's socio-economic development never escaped from the common categories of human world history; rather it belongs, along with other non-Chinese Asian societies, to these categories. In this sense, the 'Asiatic Mode of Production,' which has been seen as exceptional, simply does not exist [as such]."[14] But what appeared evident is how China's long history of feudalism disclosed signs of the presence of private property, even surplus capital and labor in later periods, a development that later was retarded and distorted by a combination of the residues of earlier modes and Western imperialism and finance capital. This perspective of the frozen combinatory of the premise of formal subsumption and capitalist practices was named semifeudalism. Finally, the AMP opened the door to nationalism, or reinforced its prominence and especially the claims of uniqueness and exceptionalism that could have a duplicitous relationship with imperialism. Owing to its static spatial countenance and the apparent absence of the movement of historical time, the AMP prefigured, if actually not inspired, all those later, postwar claims to an alternative modernity. In this respect, it is correct to look on the AMP as the path through which Chinese could enter the broader arena of world history by participating in a putatively universalistic scheme of development; at the same time, the privileging of the country's singularity revealed the strong pull of particularism, resulting in a combining of world revolution and national revolution, what later proponents of the revived Asiatic mode of production in the 1980s would call "Marxist historiography with Chinese characteristics," echoing Deng Xiaoping's prescient plaint, "socialism with

Chinese characteristics."[15] Perhaps the Chinese experience represents the final culmination of what was called national Marxism in the interwar period, ironically enabled by the AMP, which elsewhere had died a natural death but was rejuvenated to assume a new role: instead of throwing up remnants as roadblocks undermining China's economic growth, its purpose was switched to providing cultural stimulus that enhanced China's sense of national *amour propre* and reinforced both its claim to singular exceptionality and a strong central state. The real problem was that while Marx and Engels referred to precapitalist "Oriental society" and an Asiatic mode of production, along with others throughout scattered passages, its later proponents failed to remember their cautious warning that what can be known of pre-bourgeois forms is invariably mediated through the prism of later political economy. This observation prompted Marx to suggest that the "pre-bourgeois forms of social organization of production are treated by political economy in much the same way as the Fathers of the Church treated pre-Christian religions."[16] This meant that institutions, like religions, that came before were seen as "artificial," and those of the bourgeois were considered as natural.

In the end, the debate over the status of the Asiatic mode of production in China's history produced neither a consensus on whether it was a social formation or a mode of production or a stage of primitive history, and even less agreement over how it affected China's "transition" to capitalist modernity. For most participants in the discussions, the Asiatic mode resembled either some form of primitive communalism or an all-encompassing power or central state that presided over semiautonomous communities. In this regard, the Chinese economist Wang Yanan (1901–1969) departed from this preoccupation and returned to the continuing force of the discussions inaugurated by the social history controversy in his writings on China's economic history, especially its commitment to the scheme of periodizing that situated an uncommonly long feudal transition originating well before the common era. In his contribution, feudal remnants were joined to the formation of semicolonialism, dominated by what he called the "comprador-bureaucratic class" that served as runners for imperial and colonial agents who colluded to stunt China's economic growth. It is instructive to note that Wang's recuperation of the problem of periodization meant returning to the question of feudalism and how it had ultimately constituted a barrier to China's capitalist modernization. In the context of his text (late 1940s), this issue of a persisting feudalism, which had been vigorously debated earlier, troubled Chinese interpreters principally because it was linked to the conviction that "external and political forces" inhibited the economy's capacity "to destabilize" the peasantry by revolutionizing the forces of production expected of feudalism. Specifically, this expectation referred to feudalism's aptitude to nourish the "sprouts of capitalism" and generate its subsequent growth.[17] In the later revival of the discourse on the AMP (1980s), this argument no longer possessed historical relevance, and the appeal to it shifted responsibility from feudalism to the peasantry itself. According to Timothy Brook, "the critique of China's past (and present) the AMP allows is thus far more sweeping, and its rhetorical force more potent, than the feudal persistence view."[18] Given the intimate association of a powerful, oppressive central state attributed to the renewed figuration of the AMP, it is plausible to suggest that a state once identified with mobilizing mass armies of workers for public works projects could now turn to dedicating itself to constructing a world-class economy as simply another comparable state promoted public works program. Within the discursive framework of the AMP, the sponsorship of large-scale public works projects in the past and the building of a contemporary global economy would satisfy the same economic and political goals of the state and political class.

Periodizing Semicolonialism

But in the time of Wang Yanan, an interpretation founded on the long duration of Chinese feudalism enabled him to categorize China's encounter with capitalism as a form of semifeudalism that would explain the damaged growth and development because of the presence of external factors. Contemporaries in Japan like Yamada Moritarō and Uno Kōzō also remained silent on the AMP and returned to assessing the role played by feudalism: Yamada envisaged the presence of feudal remnants as the principal singular contradiction distorting capitalist development in Japan and causing a refeudalization leading to political absolutism; Uno, on the other hand, discerned in its survival clear-cut benefits for the development Japan's capitalism. By contrast, Wang proposed that the local manifestation of semifeudalism in China inflected a global process of continuous unevenness, driven by this form of primitive accumulation. In this respect, the construal of primitive accumulation was not constrained by a fixed temporality or period in which it occurred, succeeded by capitalist accumulation. But like the operation of formal subsumption, from which it was often indistinguishable, primitive accumulation would necessarily have to rely on practices belonging to early or prior modes of production to generate a configuration constituted of a mixture. Owing to its formal nature, primitive accumulation was capable of renewing itself under different and altered historical conditions to coexist with capitalist accumulation. Where this theorization departed from Uno's valorization of the tenacious survival of the "medieval village" and *shōnō* (petty agrarian) management in the epoch of modern capitalism in Japan was that semifeudalism, in the political form of "semicolonialism," would continue to delay the development of capitalism at China's expense and continue to accrue benefits to those classes like the comprador-bureaucrat and foreign capitalist. In this sense, it is possible to imagine Wang's move to categories like semifeudalism and semicolonialism as an investment in forms capable of embodying the Luxemburgian perception of how capitalist accumulation will invariably require noncapitalism. An even greater contrast between Wang and Uno shows up in Uno's ambivalence over the status of primitive accumulation, on which I will say more below.

Wang Yanan, like many of his contemporaries involved in discussions on the state of the contemporary Chinese economy, was forced to reach back to a remote historical past to identify a putative feudal formation to chart the "necessary" transit to capitalism. He settled on a feudalism whose duration extended interminably from dynasties that possessed all the substantiality of historical imaginaries, existing well before the common era and reaching down to the nineteenth century and even beyond. Unable to locate the empirical origins of feudalism, Wang put forth the following hypothesis: "the system in the Western Zhou of using multiple lords to prop up the ruler was the origins of the Chinese feudal system." Furthermore, since this early feudal system originated from an underdeveloped slave system, the social structure contained a "surplus of free workers from the village commune, family slaves, and clan slaves," who subsequently "blocked the development of European style serfdom," resulting in the creation of a system of tenancy.[19] In this passage, there is the shadow of the Asiatic mode of production lurking in an immediately prior slave system and in the existence of village communes. By contrast, Uno's identification of the "medieval village" derived from the Tokugawa period (seventeenth century), and its centralized arrangement of feudal power immediately prior to Japan's modern transformation in the 1860s represented the tail end of a long tradition Marx had already compared with Western Europe as an even more pure form of feudalism found nowhere else. Regardless of the way different lived historical circumstances mediated the encounter of capitalism and noncapitalism, the logic of development was basically similar and resulted in bringing together in a coextensive configuration different practices and relations from early modes and experiences with new necessities promoted by capitalism that replicated the process by which capitalist production continually subordinated (if not always assimilated and metabolized) the old to augment the new. In this way, the logic of the developmental process producing significant moments of temporal and material unevenness in both China and Japan mirrored a pervasive global unevenness but with different local effects. Both thinkers, like their predecessors, were concerned with the nation-form and the national question and the necessity of confronting the current situation. Each sought to offer an explanation of its contemporary status in the global configuration and assess the nature and shape of the present conjuncture that had gathered disparate forces in the 1930s and early 1940s to create a momentary unity leading to economic crisis, fascism, and war. More often than not, such an analysis of the current situation inevitably involved resolving the national question, which in societies like China meant addressing the problem of national liberation and unification and in Japan, as Uno discovered, disclosing its kinship with the "global agrarian question."

Wang Yanan lived through the tumultuous and turbulent interwar conjuncture, during which he translated Adam Smith and Marx and wrote Marxian-oriented works on historical materialism and commodity capitalism. The decade of the 1930s, it should be recalled, had already produced the famous debate on social history in China, which had sought to appraise the status and utility of the Asiatic mode of production, China's remote feudal experience, and determine the country's location in the currently obsessive preoccupation with a linear trajectory that required identifying and fulfilling the stage-driven transition from feudalism to capitalism. There were also resonances in China of the Japanese historiographical debate on the development of capitalism in Japan and the effort to determine whether the Meiji Restoration of 1868 was genuinely a bourgeois revolution or merely a reactionary counterrevolution producing refeudalization and political absolutism. In China, it seems evident that Wang had assimilated the principal issues raised by the social history debate and even the arguments promoted by Karl Wittfogel's early writings on China's economic history and his Chinese followers like Ji Jiaoting and others that envisaged China as a "hydraulic society," committed to the apparent necessity of constructing large-scale public works projects demanding the recruitment and organization of surplus labor for the building of canal networks and other programs related to irrigation and the control of water. Wang's close reading and grasp of Marx's principal texts and understanding of the general currents of world history permitted him to avoid the excesses of these contemporary interpretative strategies that bordered on stretching the AMP into a global phenomenon, whereby "Oriental despotism" was reincarnated into Stalinist bureaucratic despotism. Instead, Wang turned to his contemporary present as the necessary condition for explaining its sociohistorical foundation, which he designated as semicolonialism and semifeudalism. Writing in the late 1940s, Wang saw in China the outline of a larger conjunctural configuration that corresponded to what Lenin had first enunciated in 1916 in his powerful pamphlet *Imperialism, the Highest Stage of Capitalism.* While the conceptual force of this pamphlet, proposing the development of a relationship between finance capital and imperial expansion, was used in earlier debates in the China of the 1930s, and most notably by Mao Zedong, who saw in it the occasion for forging new revolutionary tactics in the Communist struggle against the contemporary Chinese state, Wang visualized the coupling of imperialism and finance capital as a global structural index inflected in China's dialectical confrontation with global capital.[20] In Lenin's original conceptualization of the category of semicolonialism, there were a number of central considerations that subsequently informed Wang's later efforts to expand on its analytic utility in his quite different present. Lenin perceived several elements in capitalism:

1. "The uneven and spasmodic character of the development of individual enterprises, of individual branches of industry and . . . countries," which he cited as "the fundamental and inevitable conditions and premises of this mode of production."[21]

2. Recognizing the need to export superfluous capital to "backward countries" as an outlet for investment, he saw in the acquisition and possession of colonies what seemed to the imperial powers a natural conduit for the export of capital.

3. The present constituted "a peculiar period of world colonial policy," related to the latest development of finance capital. What distinguishes it from capital's past is the "intensification of the struggle for colonies" and a "division of the world" according to a transition of capital to finance capitalism.[22]

4. The "boom" in annexation by 1914 resulted in a global division among colonial, semicolonial—Persia, China, and Turkey—and noncolonial countries. Lenin was convinced that Persia would soon become fully colonized, while China and Turkey were also well on their way.[23]

As for Russia, it belonged with those countries classified as lagging because of economic backwardness "in which modern capitalist enterprise is enmeshed . . . in a thick web of pre-capitalist relations."[24] This was a reverberation from *The Development of Capitalism in Russia*, where he had already arrived at this conclusion and supplied ample empirical proof of its veracity. Even among imperializing countries, Lenin perceived the existence of uneven or asymmetrical practices and the formation of incommensurate social relations that clearly pointed to the way the logic of capital developed as manifest materializations of coexisting mixed practices in the production process. If countries like Russia and Japan were marked by lingering pre-capitalist relations and labor practices, harnessed to capitalist accumulation, these circumstances defined the nature of semicolonialism even more, which he considered as exemplifying the "transitional forms which are to be found in all spheres of nature."[25] While Lenin was right to see in the colonial situation—and its semicolonial hybrid—the occurrence of the mix between pre-capitalist and capitalist practices, he was, I believe, wrong to imagine this process as merely "transitional" since the logic was embodied in a form, not a time-bound content, whose effects could be found everywhere capitalism appeared. It would lead only to itself in another register.

For Wang, "backward countries invaded by imperial powers" are destined to become semicolonies, what Lenin described as the "middle stage" of development toward full colonization. If they do not become full-fledged colonies, they can only follow this path: "the original feudal structure experiences the gradual penetration of commercial capital from imperial powers."[26] This was no simple separation of two different economies and political practices. Wang discovered that these uneven economic relationships were embodied in the continuing interaction between the development of capitalist accumulation and what was passed off as primitive accumulation. Politically, the relationship was inscribed in the formation of what he and others at the time named as the "modern comprador-bureaucrat," who presided over a hybrid economic order that combined "the thick web of precapitalist social relations" and newer capitalist relations and practices to become a "semicolonial" and "semifeudal" society. The importance of this hybridized class, combining Chinese bureaucratic experience with their new function of serving as agents for imperial powers, lay in their capacity to facilitate the process of capitalist expansion in China, persuading Wang to easily identify, has had Lenin, the extension of foreign capitalism with imperialist seizure. By the same measure, the mediation supplied by this class meant that national capital was inhibited from growing and accumulating, which resulted in stalling or freezing the Chinese political economy into a permanent standstill. "We have," Wang, charged, "good reason to view China's semifeudal, semicolonial-bureaucratic economy as a typical model of these types of [backward] societies. That is, we can proceed from the premise that China reflects the future of other semifeudal, semicolonial societies which are stuck in a half-dead, half-living state," a gloss echoing Marx's own grim prognosis in *Capital* that called attention to the "suffering" caused by both the living and the dead.[27]

There appear a number of interesting implications in Wang's theorization of China's slippage into what seemed to promise permanent semicolonial, semifeudal status. Even though comprador-bureaucrats failed to be constituted as a bourgeoisie, they often functioned analogously to them. The structural arrangement over which they presided resembled a version of political hegemony similar to the form that Gramsci recognized in northern Italian domination over southern semifeudalism and semicolonialism. The comprador-bureaucrat differed primarily in the fact that as a class they were intimately linked to foreign capital and were positioned to line their own pockets at the expense of undermining national capital accumulation. Given

China's contemporary historical circumstances, foreign wars, imperial seizure and a climactic civil war in the mid-nineteenth century, the progressive division of the country into colonial spheres of influence, and the reliance of the "imperialist . . . upon comprador-bureaucrats and the large landlord class to extend their rule to every corner . . . of Chinese society," he was sure that the imperialists and their Chinese class allies shared an identity of interest targeting the exploitation of profits. "So much so," he added, "that they collide and overlap, to ultimately form a single battle-line."[28] The resulting division of labor disclosed that the control of the comprador-bureaucrat class was entrenched in a regime committed to "primitive accumulation," while the imperial powers were based on the expansion of capitalist accumulation. The other interesting implication of Wang's analysis is reflected in how he chose to privilege China's contemporary condition as semifeudal and semicolonial as a model for all "backward" countries—a negative judgment reversing Marx's appraisal of how England's development "only shows to the less developed the image of its own future."[29] In Wang's evaluation, the economic structure of semifeudal, semicolonial societies was a unique manifestation, which led to either full colonial status or the path of realizing commercial capital gradually as it penetrated and took command of the interstices of the feudal structure. Seemingly attached to the status of irretrievable backwardness for societies like China, he reasoned that the invasion of capital through the introduction of commodities invariably inhibited and blocked the expected transition to a capitalist system. Foreigners dominated the production of commodities, in spite of being made in China, undermining the capacity of nascent native manufacturers to compete. What instead happened was a permanent stalling of capitalist development by congealing a hybrid arrangement that discouraged discarding feudal elements that were no longer beneficial rather than "preserv[ing]" those that proved their utility. Reversing the order to suppress those capitalist elements that were seen to interfere with the comprador-bureaucratic agenda resulted in favoring only those practices dependent on comprador capital. However, Wang probably could not have been able to make this determination and was, I believe, merely describing the logic of formal subsumption, which he recognized was anchored in primitive accumulation.

The problem that Wang was required to face was the extended existence and duration of historical feudalism in China. In engaging it, he inadvertently raised some serious questions concerning the claims made by Marxian historical analysis, as it was understood at that time, and its reliance on temporally linear narrative explanations. He wanted to show the relationship of the stubborn legacy of political and economic characteristics of China's long-lasting feudal structure to the subsequent formation of comprador-bureaucratic capitalism. The ostensibly long occupancy of feudalism in China had been a principal preoccupation of earlier interpreters in the social history debate, and scholarly opinion agreed that the purported transition from "slave production" to "feudalism" occurred around the time the common era began. Stretching the epoch of feudalism in China into a *longue durée* was a way to satisfy the desire to synchronize the Chinese experience with the "path of world historical development."[30] But this effort to situate China in a temporal frame derived from stagist Marxism, shaped by the figure of Western feudalism with which it was supposed to achieve equivalence, constituted a narrative form that already sought to eliminate temporal unevenness. Moreover, it sacrificed the possibility of entertaining vastly different and viable historical trajectories capable of explaining China's present more precisely. Wang, in employing a measure of time derived from another's experience, had already risked misrepresenting China's history. We should recall that for Marx, the history of capitalism was preceded by suspended historical presuppositions, "gone and past," and "belong[ing] to the history of its [capital's] formation" but "in no way to its contemporary history." Capital's antecedent history is effaced (but not eliminated) once it creates its own presuppositions. Hence, the stagist form of emplotment Wang adapted to China's precapitalist history managed to replace the vacated space of that forgotten historicity of precapitalist formations that capitalism and its conceptualization of calculating time removed. In fact, the concept of time employed to chart the linear passage of feudalism to capitalism was itself mediated by capital's time accountancy as it increasingly became involved in measuring the magnitude of labor time in the new factory environment, with its assembly lines, greater regimented work discipline, and so forth. In this temporal leveling, making the remote past identical to a capitalist present, what Marxists like Wang overlooked was the role that Marx accorded to the form of historical presuppositions. Luxemburg had glimpsed their role in her grasp of a historical figure consisting of layered pasts, and Mariátegui, as we have seen, envisioned the historical presuppositions as embodied in political-economic formations lying on top of each other to form a palimpsest—all preludes lying beneath capitalism. Had Wang Yanan moved in this direction rather than binding China's long history to a feudalism originating in the Western Zhou (1029–771 B.C.E.) and continuing on a "one-way street" in one form or another down to the present, but actually elongating the figure of Western feudalism, he might have been better situated to explain the specific Chinese instantiation of past in present, exemplified by the comprador-bureaucrat alignment with foreign imperialism, as merely a particular accenting of the generalized form of semicolonialism China expressed because of historical presuppositions derived from its own remote precapitalist past.

Be that as it may, Wang proposed there was no reason to presume the simultaneous emergence of capitalism in all parts of the world. Nor was it possible to "assume, by extension, that . . . the social systems of the ancient and medieval worlds were the same around the world." His major complaint focused on the attempt to tie slave production to feudalism, without considering the possibility of other forms of primary producers as specific to certain times, places, and circumstances under which the surplus was expropriated through exploitation. His own hypothesis hazarded recuperating what he objected to in accounts he criticized as "undialectical." As suggested, he located the origins of China's feudalism in an archaic time of the Western Zhou dynasty practice of using multiple lords to bolster a hegemon. Emerging out of an undeveloped slave system, irregularly distributed, the social system, he suggested, contained a surplus of "free workers" associated with village communes, family slaves/servants, and slaves attached to specific clans. The presence of the preponderant pool of "free workers" inhibited the development of a class of serfs resembling those found in Western Europe that caused the creation of widespread tenancy during the succeeding Spring and Autumn period of Warring States. In this way, feudalism in China was transmuted into an arrangement of power dominated by tenant farming and rent collection rather than a structure based on land allocation and the granting of salaries. In time, this mode of feudal exploitation was replaced by centralized bureaucratic control, which, accordingly, produced the following characteristics:

1. Because it was a feudality founded on a "natural economy," engaged in agriculture and household handicraft manufacturing, peasants were not

simply subsistence cultivators but also producers of their own goods and cash crops and turned over the surplus product to the "landlord-aristocrat-bureaucratic" class under the guise of "rent" and "taxes," which the state distributed to its officials as "salary" or "pay." Wang believed that this process led to the "commodification" of surplus product, if not forms of labor itself. The scale and scope of this commodity economy expanded, due to accelerating demand that encouraged the organization of the received feudal system around a centralized structure of power directing a circulation economy vastly different from the classic forms of feudalism.

2. Land still constituted the basis of social power and wealth, and where China's feudal experience departed from Europe's example was in augmenting a procedure of relatively free sale of land and unrestricted use of tenant labor. Direct producers could acquire only small parcels of land, while the majority of landholding was monopolized by the exploitative classes, even though they managed to extract small harvests. A major portion of the harvest was still skimmed off as "tribute" by the ruling political classes.

3. Since landownership conferred status, it became a coveted object of acquisition among different groups, intensifying the process of peasant exploitation.

4. In this arrangement, the emperor stood as the largest landowner and with his retinue of officials and aristocrats they all competed to extract as much as possible from commercial activity, which often led to profitable organization of monopolies.[31]

This system was maintained intact as the Chinese political economy up to the time it encountered capitalism in the nineteenth century. Wang was certain that its longevity produced promising results he identified as the "sprouts of capitalism" already manifest in the eighteenth century. But he also understood that the vitality of this protocapitalism was always in peril of being undermined by the unrestrained extravagance among the ruling classes, intensification of exploitation, and high interest rates on lending that opened the way to rebellion. The penetration of capital hastened the collapse of the Manchu-Qing state, he proposed, and the consequent combination of a feudal structure and imperialism collaborated to permanently "stall" development and channel its remains into the form of "semifeudalism" and "semicapitalism." What seems interesting about this new alignment of imperial capital and a received "feudal structure" is that, on the one hand, it spurred capitalist development controlled by foreign powers that accelerated the logic of formal subsumption, and, on the other hand, it simultaneously fostered the function of retaining what may be called feudal remnants or left-over residues that could be utilized in the service of capitalist production. Wang captured its logic in the following observation: "Evidently, the residual elements of the traditional economy are being restructured by the capitalist commodity economy, and at the same time, they constantly act as a series of constraints upon the elements of the capitalist economy, either by contesting or adapting to them."[32] Here was the capitalist logic taking over what it found useful but with a difference: the appropriations acted to curb the new political economy and limit growth through the hybrid structure of semifeu-dalism, semicolonialism. A better description of the dialectical logic of formal subsumption could not be made, especially in view of the fact that this imbrication of capitalism and Chinese feudalism ultimately implied the parallel but continuous interaction of the global and local, drawing together both the unevenness of the historical present and geographical diversity. The profit accrued from capitalist enterprises went to the imperial powers, while the exploitation directed by the comprador-bureaucrat benefited both foreigners and their Chinese "partners"—which, in Wang's thinking, seriously affected the accumulation of national capital. Under this double exploitation reflecting the collusion of capitalist production process and "feudal" forms raking off surplus product, it is difficult to imagine how deeply inscribed this coexistence of different temporalities has been in modern China's political, economic, and cultural unconscious. It is even harder to calculate the extent of discordance this form of unevenness inflicted on social life and subsequently was capable of producing throughout the twentieth century. In Wang's reckoning, the penetration of imperial forces could not have transformed China into a capitalist country.[33] It is, instead, transforming it into a semicolony and then full colony and converting the country into a supplier of raw materials and labor power and a place to "peddle" and dump manufactured goods. The depths of this comprador depravity was reached in the regime of the "ruthless" Jiang Jieshi (Chiang K'ai-shek), which probably reinforced Wang's conviction that China was destined to exist in a permanent state of unrelieved or patriarchal exploitation, especially constituted of small producers of simple commodities bound to the pursuit of capitalist expropriation. What concerned him most was the paradox of a society that has followed "the same path of experience taken by all capitalist countries"[34]—that is, the general form of all capitalist development—but that regretfully has been at the same time "stalled along the path too long now." Clearly, the problem dogging China had been the "compradorization of merchant capital" and its "reliance upon extra-economic forces," notably on "unequal exchanges, its close ties to the bureaucracy," and the arbitrary way merchants act in setting prices to exploit the peasantry. The deeper they penetrate the rural interior and remote areas of the country, the greater the opportunity for exploitation, and it becomes evident that this form of accumulation relies on coercive methods and is not random at all.[35] What worried him about this alignment of expropriation and exploitation was that it signified permanent bonding of "so-called primitive accumulation" and capitalist accumulation, processes that were immanent to each other even as they embodied and reflected different and often conflicting temporal rhythms between then and now in a same present they cohabited. In the end, the freezing of an uneven history captive to the prospect of unscheduled untimeliness, the simultaneous interactivity of primitive and capitalist accumulations, typified a permanent global process found everywhere capitalism had managed to establish its production system. The direction of China's experience had been contaminated by yoking it to a political overdetermination of negative forces in which the interest of foreign imperialism willingly cooperated to bolster the retention of a moribund and somnolent "feudal" order well beyond its time. In an interesting reversal of Uno Kōzō's recommendation that the present must call on the past to resolve its problems, Wang recorded how the past and its history continued to contaminate the present and prevented it from moving on.

Theorizing Temporal Difference

As the central residues of a long-standing feudal structure in China were kept on an artificial life support that contributed to "stalling" the development of capitalism and forfeiting the prospect of national accumulation, in Japan the relationship between feudal residues and capitalism proved to be a compatible combination competent to produce a more successful outcome. At least this is what economist and theorist Uno Kōzō believed. To be sure, the historical circumstances each society faced were considerably different: China burdened by imperialist dispossession, leading to territorial fragmentation and a declining, corrupt dynasty in the nineteenth century that would explode in an incomplete revolution, warlordism, and civil war in the next, whereas Japan at the same time already successfully transforming itself into a modern capitalist nation-state to become a major imperial power in the twentieth. Japan avoided the imperial colonialism that divided China through the fortunate coincidence of geographical distance and historical necessity expressed in the preoccupations of colonizing nations: Great Britain, France, and Russia's involvement in the Crimean War and the embroilment of the United States in its own Civil War. The difference also dramatized the notation of late development and the need for an adequate explanation of the temporal distance between Marx's *Capital*, preoccupied with the earlier experience of capitalism's appearance in England, and Japan's later transformation in the nineteenth and twentieth centuries. In Uno's thinking, the lateness of the event of development allowed Japan to assimilate a model of a much more realized capitalist political economy represented by the England it encountered after 1868. Yet the initial impulse compelling Uno in the late 1930s and early 1940s to supply an account of the nature of Japan's capitalist formation was the challenge ignited by the intellectual debate over the character of the development of capitalism in Japan. Sparked by the promise Marxism offered for social theory in the late 1920s and early 1930s, this debate attested to its prominence in Japan as a social theory capable of explaining the total process of social change and providing an accompanying political critique of the current Japanese situation. It is no exaggeration to say that Marxism dominated the intellectual scene during these years, before the state shut down the Japan Communist Party (JCP) and subjected all progressives of varying stripes to a process aimed at eliciting renunciations of their affiliation.

The fundamental problem set by the debate on Japanese capitalism was both how to determine the effectiveness of Marx's analysis in a different time and place and the need to explain the intricate interweave between history and theory. In pursuit of these twin but related purposes, the debate proceeded to produce a veritable historiographical archive of empirically informed work on the social and economic history of late Tokugawa and early Meiji Japan that tried to show the circumstances under which capitalism appeared and developed and whether it signified the realization of revolution. The difference between the two positions lay in an interpretative strategy based on the premise that capitalism developed from a dynamic propelled by internal or domestic forces and contradictions advocated by the *kōzaha*, or Lectures Faction, associated with the JCP and a counterclaim that presumed that despite the agency of domestic forces, the development of capitalism was also enhanced by importing its mature operations from abroad, promoted by the *rōnōha*, or Labor-Agrarian Faction of independent Marxists. Even so, the principal impulse behind the debate appeared to be more concerned with seeing through a program committed to constructing a social theory that would bridge the gap between theory and practice. At stake was the question of whether Japan was sufficiently prepared for socialist revolution or merely fated to remain locked in a form of semifeudalism. Discussion fell into opposing camps that proposed that Japan's transformation in the nineteenth century laid the groundwork for revolutionary readiness as against a more negative view that advised that the country was still hostage to feudal remnants deflecting the development of a completed capitalism. It was also reflected in the contemporary production of these vestigial forms as a response to the accelerating pace of competition posed by world capitalism.[36] The Lectures Faction clearly favored the latter interpretation, while the former was articulated by Labor-Agrarian partisans. But the basic difference between the two main perspectives was said to be a conflict between economics and politics. Uno Kōzō, who sympathized with the *rōnōha*, perceived that the Labor-Agrarian Faction was more engaged in considerations relating to the economic question of Japan's capitalism, while the Lectures Faction was preoccupied with the political effects of the still-born revolution that distorted later development. For the proponents of the *rōnoha*, the Meiji Restoration qualified as a bourgeois revolution or soon after acquired its trappings, whereas the *kōzaha*, closely associated with the Japan Communist Party and thus subject to changes of directives from the Comintern, represented the transforming event as a counterrevolution, refeudalization under forms of "political absolutism" embodied in the establishment of an imperial bureaucracy. Yet this division failed to conceal a more complex and knotted array of disagreements.

The Specter of Refeudalization

The theoretical critique of the Lectures Faction was formulated by the economist Yamada Moritarō (1897–1980)[37] of Tokyo Imperial University in *Nihon shihonshugi bunseki* (Analysis of Japanese capitalism, 1934), which supplied the principal template for the development of what he called "Japanese-style capitalism." In promoting a Japanese-style capitalism, the state relied on utilizing a "Japanese-style rationality" instead of adopting an established method of operations based on applying a technology requiring the implementation of direct mechanization or capable of strengthening and supplementing manual labor; the procedure resorted to creating an organizational structure composed of a "strict reshuffling of . . . foremen" positioned to combine the general framework of work with "semifeudal-like work forms."[38] This particular rationality underlined a predilection for emphasizing the bringing together of workers according to their regions, targeting industrial specializations and manufacturing processes. Where one lived is where one worked: "This was the objective necessity imparted to the proletariat."[39] What this immediately revealed was the intermingling and combining of older labor practices with newer requirements demanded by industrial capitalism, purposely using what was at hand to serve the pursuit of surplus value. The most obvious result of this organizational rearrangement of "semifeudal" labor practices was to increase surplus labor. "Japanese capitalism," Yamada wrote, "regulated the necessity to openly construct a broad system concentrating on the military—key industries—on top of the broad foundation of agricultural slave-like petty cultivators; it was established to automatically reproduce and routinize the path leading to the process of reindustrialization."[40] In this way, the "military-like semislave system model" shaped the particular type of Japanese capitalism and, according to Marx, realized a form that accelerated the "utmost severity 'of civilizing overwork' " superimposed "on top of the barbaric cruelty of serfs and slaves."[41] With this observation, Yamada was not only referring to the operation of formal subsumption, even though the process is not named, as such, but also suggesting that its implementation resulted in a system of layering the new on top of the old, pasts in the present, to initially overdetermine the quickening growth of surplus labor and exploitation and to ultimately fuel the development of temporal unevenness. But he apparently overlooked the temporal consequences of this new system of layering and the aggressive utilization of the past in a new present. In fact, he was convinced that the pure Japanese type drove out other developmental models like those represented by English capitalism, which appeared as the "fatherland" (*sokoku*) of free competition and departed from the German example, which represented the home base of "concentrated monopolization." In his narrative account, the Japanese example resembled the Russian variant, a classically negative route dedicated to "a militarized agricultural slave—semi-agricultural slave system which, in any case, divided world historical meaning."[42] Yamada failed to acknowledge that none of these forms of capitalism avoided a developmental process founded on the appropriation of received practices that were subordinated to the organization of the capitalist pursuit of surplus value. There was no genuinely pure example of capitalism, even though Uno sought to conceive of a theoretical model, perhaps as a response to Yamada's condemnation of the Japanese experience as uniquely "distorted" and incomplete. But Yamada's appeal to the category of semifeudalism signified a state of incompletion that would remain permanently as it was, frozen in the tracks of its initial trajectory.

Since the category of semifeudal Japan's capitalist development set it apart from representatives like England and Germany, the process of reproduction would work differently. In Yamada's reckoning, semifeudalism generated not expanded accumulation, as Marx had thought, but a simple form of repetition based on semislave labor. Here, he detected a connection between "production rotation" (*seisan senkai*) or "organizational exchange" (*henseikae*) and "permanent reproduction" (*kidō saiseisan*).[43] Production rotation referred to using received organizational, institutional, and labor practices from the Tokugawa period by converting them to now serve the expansion of a capitalist economy dominated by key military industries. Because workers usually worked where they lived, the rotation system might have also involved using agricultural workers to produce resources for the new military industries, as well as for their own subsistence and reproduction, which would have lessened production costs. What I am suggesting is the possibility of implanting a reproduction cycle whereby workers would also rotate places of employment between manufacturing and agriculture on the basis of a seasonal schedule. Yamada remained silent on the question, even though he provides both empirical evidence and a framework for its plausibility. The interesting problem is that Japan did not have to pass through a long and horrific period of primitive accumulation, as Uno later recognized, even though Yamada was convinced that the condensed transformation of the older Tokugawa production system into Meiji capitalism constituted Japan's modern economic rite of passage through primitive accumulation that brought irreparable hardships and inflicted unprecedented harsh sacrifices on the population. But the unfolding of the process was not nearly as long England's duration of primitive accumulation, which threw untold numbers into destitution and permanent unemployment and, along the way, criminalized whole sectors of the population. In this regard, Uno Kōzō was probably right to suggest that because of the nature of Japan's developmental experience and its timing, it was possible to retain the "medieval villages" longer, thus keeping people still employed in either full-time or partial farmwork, thereby providing for their own subsistence and reproduction until industrialization was ready to recruit its labor force at the beginning of the twentieth century. In England, Marx observed the long wait, virtually three hundred years, until manufacturing and heavy industrialization were in a position to begin hiring workers in large numbers. By that time, he added, the long, painful experience of primitive accumulation had been virtually forgotten. For Japan, the shortness was a constant reminder of its permanent cruelty.

Although Yamada's thesis proved to have a powerful effect on the production of historiography, the work privileged the peculiarities or special characteristics of Japan's capitalist development according to its own rationality, which, since the 1880s, consisted of a basis or foundation dominated by the state's efforts to channel Japan's initial industrializing impulse into military hardware and equipment. Because of this initial industrial direction, he was persuaded that the Meiji Restoration was directly provoked by the pressure (*gaiatsu*) exerted by advanced capitalist nations bent on colonial expropriation that forcibly consigned Japanese capitalism to occupy a "worldly low status" based on procedures that followed a path that "structurally condensed the capitalist process," squeezing it into its special semifeudal character composed of wage labor and land rent.[44] In Yamada's accounting, this emphasis on military industries constituted the principal purpose, the "key," as he put it, to driving Japan's industrialization after the Meiji Restoration and became the form of a "fixed determination" that would not change.

Part of this decision was shaped by an experience that, since the late Tokugawa period, was fueled by news of England's imperial intervention in China during the Opium War in the 1840s and a growing fear of the imminent danger of foreign colonization eventually spreading to Japan.

At the heart of Yamada's analysis was the status of form (*kata*), which, he believed, was fixed in the late Tokugawa transition to a semifeudal order centered on manufacturing committed to "militarist organization" as the "key industry." This fixed form continued into the Meiji period, permanently cementing the late Tokugawa anxiety over the threat of foreign colonization that had compelled the necessity to erect a coastal defense network that became a permanent fixture of national security policy. Put another way, the heritage of fear articulated in the prior feudal epoch became the organizing principle of Meiji modernization. It was also accompanied by the fixed forms of labor that Yamada characterized as "semiserf" and "semislave." Thus the new capitalist system transformed former guild workers into "semiserf slave-like wage workers and semifeudal contract workers." Independent Tokugawa handicraftsmen were transposed into manufacturing workers, and the form of the older "artisan" (*shokuin*) was transmuted into contract workers resembling wage earners.[45] This changeover was accompanied by the conversion of "petty cultivating agricultural slaves into semiserf-like farmers."[46] The new forms were really revisions of an old content now joined to the wage form—more or less old wine in new bottles. But Yamada, it seems, misunderstood how Marx had used the concept of form. As suggested earlier, Marx envisioned form as open and flexible and not bound to or by any fixed determination. With Yamada, the operation appeared to close the distance separating form and content by making the latter indistinguishable from the former. The form of manufacturing and labor regimes that evolved in the late Tokugawa period thus hardened into a fixed content that remained unchanged down to his present in the 1930s. Accordingly, Yamada's vision was constrained to the extent that he could not see beyond the relationship between the establishment of a "tenacious unified embodiment of key industries" and the subsuming of the Tokugawa system of wholesale dealers (*tonya*) of domestic/household (simple commodity) industries. This referred to the existence of petty manufacturing, combined with traditionally small and large workshops involved in cloth and garment production; it also included various attending forms of labor such as the "semislave-like petty cultivating peasants," constituting the main body of cultivators within the peasantry, together with the "use of the feeble labor power of the old, children and women," who were merely "supports [*hashira*] that rescued the middle peasants and upper strata from ruin."[47] Portrayed here was the world of the "wretched thatched cottages" of production (what Marx in *Capital* called *Jammerhöhlen*, loosely "misery or miserable hollows") now recruited to distinguish the pure Japanese form. Moreover, these workshops of silk production reorganized the majority of poor peasants within the class of "semislave-like petty cultivators" under a system of commercial capital that also resembled the older practice of wholesale dealers who relied on handicraft manufacturing in these "wretched thatched cottages." The same could be said of the thread manufacturers. "Together, these semislave peasants dominated and controlled the characteristic labor system of the pure Japanese form."[48] The changeover to rotation conformed to procedures belonging to industrial capitalism that was completed with the reorganization inserting the wretched cottage system into the production process. The older Tokugawa organization of thatched cottages, along with its workers, became the basic components structuring the new military industrial complex of Meiji Japan. It must be considered, Yamada explained, that while this system became the fundamental premise accounting for the "prosperity of Japanese capitalism"—"the establishment of industrial capital"—it also disclosed the basic circumstances of its "catastrophic [*hakyoku*] character."[49]

While Yamada was describing the general law of capitalist development by detailing how the initial thrust of Japan's capitalism relied on subsuming the commodities of small producers who became wage earners and utilizing protomanufacturing practices and institutions from the past, he was unbending in insisting that this developmental system stopped because it was fixed at its point of determination. It stopped developing where it began, at the point when the flexible form coagulated into a concrete content. It was the converted system's stalled character that guaranteed automatic realization of the stationary process of reproduction. In this way, what originally were practices enlisted by capitalist development acquired the status of "feudal remnants" from a prior mode of production, undermining and postponing further progress leading to the realization of a mature and completed capitalism. Yamada was convinced that these defects would finally inhibit the anticipated transition to socialism. In his understanding, the modern framework of Japan's industrial endowment in place constituted an enduring reproduction of the "semifeudal property ownership and a semiserf system consisting of subsistence cultivation" of the late Tokugawa period. This fixed form was "personified" in the "key industries of the military structure," disposing institutions toward "production rotation" (*senkae*) where "semislave petty peasant cultivators and semislave wage workers were made the soul of the labor [force]."[50] The whole structure of Japanese capitalism was permeated by this fixed form of labor.

Yamada's contention was that the changeability of a form into a congealed remnant derived from the Tokugawa response to the double threat posed by the appearance of foreigners in Japanese waters and the continuation of domestic peasant upheavals (*naiyū gaikan*). What this double-edged political trauma induced was the form of a "Great Fear" that shaped the Meiji decision to transform the old order by directly addressing both the challenge of colonization and the necessity to reorganize the political economy and stabilize social order. As a result, Yamada easily overlooked how these earlier forms, already symbolizing feudal fetters, testified to the growth of capitalism. This initial misunderstanding led to his inability to acknowledge that after rapid political reorganization erected a centralized nation-state, these inherited "semifeudal forms" would in time be mediated by the capitalist production process just as they would, in turn, mediate capitalism. This missed step explains why he concluded that the Meiji state merely continued and enlarged on the prior Tokugawa policy of building a coastal defense system by embracing a broadened program aimed at the manufacturing of military hardware for national self-defense. On the one hand, the new state privileged the goal of "military preparedness" in order to "prevent the resistance" expected from the laboring stratum, which had been transmuted into "semislave peasant cultivators" and "semislave wage earners," and, on the other, it pledged to defend the nation against the imminent threat of foreign invasion from advanced capitalist countries. A strong military presence would also enable Japan to forge market acquisitions and secure steel in China and Korea. The "rigid" unity informing the military structure was expressed in implanting steel production for munitions and weaponry, naval arsenals (already begun in the Tokugawa period), railways, and the formation of a financial oligarchy assigned to manage the new machine industries (*zaibatsu*) and to initiate new enterprises devoted to shipbuilding, mining, and so on.

In this scheme, more or less completed by the turn of the century, semi-feudalism became the sign of backwardness that proclaimed the absence of a developmental logic driving capitalist production to new dialectical mutations. It is important to infer from this state of declared backwardness that the symptom of temporal disparity between capitalist Japan and other capitalist nations, which had secured development by presumably shaking off the past, meant that Japan was consigned to live an eternal past in the present because of the "turn toward an abridged form of structure . . . reflecting the nature of a militarized semiagrarian slave system." This destiny implied the occupation of a permanent time-gap, existing in a different present from those with which Japan was immanent.[51] Underlying this sense of a state stalled by the past was the political conviction that the Meiji Restoration was never a genuine bourgeois revolution. Neither was the Japanese state that it subsequently established built on the formation of this class of "semiserfs" and "slaves" or even on the social basis of "free workers," which presumably would have been made available had the experience of enclosure taken place. There was not even a landlord class that was ever capable of realizing some measure of embourgeoisement. In fact, it was a counterrevolution, an aborted transition that relapsed into refeudalization to make the past into a permanent present. But this was a political conclusion that overlooked an economic analysis to the extent that it inverted Marx's own characterization of the general rule of capitalist development and diverted the transition to capitalism into the deep groove of a semifeudal order, neither fully feudal nor capitalistic. In fact, Yamada, following Engels, proposed that the construction of a strong state, personified in a "pure military, police mechanism," originated in modern, large-scale industry based on "political necessity."[52] Regardless of the effort to separate politics and economics in Yamada's analysis, it should be said that there was a deeper connection between how he interpreted the economic development of capitalism and the political conclusion he drew from it that Japan had been transformed into an absolutist state. Where he was correct was to see in absolutism the political analogue to his economic analysis that consigned Japan to permanent semifeudalism. Just as it was possible to convert older economic institutions and practices to serve a capitalist order devoted to military industrialization, so too was it plausible to imagine the implementation of a political form founded on the appropriation of received political practices, institutions, and conceptions of authority that would serve the establishment and development of a capitalist system of production. When Yamada described the Japanese economic process as a "structural condensation" within capitalism, he could have also been describing the political form of absolutism. In his reasoning, political absolutism derived from refeudalization of Meiji, to provide the framework for the later formation of fascism his contemporary the philosopher Tosaka Jun named as "Japanese-type fascism." In this regard, the Meiji slogan of "Wealth and Power," working and dying for the nation, actually pointed to a capitalist nation-state committed to national defense and imperial expansion constituted of revived political remnants from the country's long past employed to reinforce the achievement of these national goals, dramatically personified in the refigured divine emperor and imperial institution (which Yamada never mentions) and the implementation of a network of national religious shrines valorizing self-sacrifice in the defense of the fatherland.

"The Agrarian Problem" and Late-Developing Capitalism

I have noted that Yamada Moritarō's contemporary and colleague the economist Uno Kōzō (1897–1977) was also preoccupied with the particular character of Japan's capitalist development. However, his interest was motivated neither by a conviction in the possibility of a "pure form of Japanese capitalism" nor by a belief in the unyielding fixity of forms in the face of capitalism's development and dialectic of history. If Yamada appeared as the proponent of Japanese exceptionalism—which is, I believe, at the heart of Lectures Faction historiography and has haunted its universalist aspirations—Uno sought to portray the development of capitalism in Japan as a local inflection of a global process similar to the experience of other late-developing societies since it followed the same economic laws despite the mediating contaminations exercised by specific historical circumstances. While he agreed with Yamada that Japan's capitalism differed from the experiences of other countries like England, France, and the United States, though not necessarily Germany, the difference resulted from the moment of encounter rather than fulfilling self-referring directives seeking to satisfy a revolutionary stage theory constantly being revised by the Comintern. Despite the separation of the Labor-Agrarian Faction from the JCP and Comintern, Uno, especially, took the Soviet emphasis on feudal remnants seriously. However, he never went so far as Yamada to see in their retention in the present a barrier to further development. Similarly, it can be said that Yamada undoubtedly overstated the emphasis on the feudal remnants and attributed to them a force that ended in the detour of a classically "pure Japanese form." With Uno, the important event was Japan's late embrace of capitalism that qualified the country for the status of a "late-developing nation" (*goshinkoku*).[53] Capitalism everywhere, he proposed, developed from its own interior movement according to economic laws. But this movement would always be mediated by the temporality accompanying the "importation of machinery as the characteristic method of capitalist industry."[54] This observation raised the prospect of accounting for the time differential between Japan's adoption of capitalism in the late nineteenth century and its appearance in sixteenth-century England, and what it meant. Uno explained that the capitalism Japan imported from England had matured and was vastly different from what Marx identified with the advent of "primitive accumulation" in the fifteenth and sixteenth centuries. As a result, there was no reason for Japan to pass through the "process of so-called primitive accumulation" since it had assimilated a model of English capitalism that had already completed the earlier phase that broke up the agrarian village and set loose an army of unemployed "free workers." By contrast, as noted, Yamada had tried to make the case for "direct primitive accumulation" in the early Meiji period, conforming to an orthodox Marxian periodizing scheme that classified it as a one-time event, which had precipitated disturbances among miners and outbreaks over the construction of telegraph lines that resulted in appropriating farmlands.[55] (Many of the disturbances over the construction of telegraph lines necessitating the expropriation of farmlands were initiated not merely by peasants but by *shizoku*—former samurai—who may have been protesting their recent declassing but were also opposed to the pace of modernization.) But Yamada felt compelled to find an equivalent correspondence between the stages that Marx attributed to England's passage to capitalism and Japan's later arrival. Moreover, the state was involved not only in direct seizures of land but also in employing differing forms of slave labor. This was particularly true of the appropriation of "convict labor," which, Yamada asserted, constituted "a concentrated representation of utilizing the slave labor system that laid the foundation for the period of the primitive accumulation model" that the state "carried out widely from the beginning of Japanese capitalism."[56] The contrast between Yamada and Uno was sharpest at this point since the former was certain that Japanese capitalism fixed its necessary characteristic when it constructed a "system of key industries" focused broadly on producing military hardware based on erecting a "semi-agricultural-slave system of petty cultivators." The original model of Japan's capitalism was thus rooted in military industries and "slave" labor that accelerated the severity of both, expressed by the "so-called civilizing of 'excess labor'" and the barbarizing of the agrarian slave system. In this sense, Japan's pure form of capitalism constituted a vast departure from the English model based on "free competition," the monopoly concentrations of the American and German models and every other older style of capitalism because it "fetterized" the development of labor power.[57] With Uno, every experience of capitalism was modularly different because of the response to the agrarian question that revealed something about each nation's development at a certain moment but nevertheless still constituted a problem for both national and global capital to resolve.[58] Each nation sought to solve the agrarian question as a problem of national development, even though it was a difficulty that required the intervention of global capitalism to resolve.

What caught Uno's interest was the discovery that capitalism, at least in the "classic" English example, was based on the separation of agriculture from industry.[59] Yet this pattern of development, dating from the starting point in the sixteenth and seventeenth centuries, was no longer applicable for "late developing nations," which adopted a more mature or advanced form in the nineteenth or twentieth centuries. The real consequences of bypassing the grosser effects of primitive accumulation permitted maintaining the prior medieval village intact in a society like Japan and intentionally delaying the alienation of large numbers of peasants from their means of subsistence. With this observation, Uno proceeded to elucidate a process of developmental difference that came into view from observing the actual temporal lateness of Japan's reception of capitalism. Lateness by no means ever implied a qualitative judgment announcing inferiority or backwardness but merely a different time and trajectory in the historical process. The measure of difference was only quantitative, chronological. In the Japanese experience, the difference was inscribed in the decision to sustain the medieval village and the subsumption of small commodity producers to the pursuit of value. Although the agrarian village forfeited handicraft production, which once formed a subsistence fit with agriculture, it is natural that peasants would be induced to commodify some portion of their products: "while such an invasion (*shinnyū*) would increase agricultural production, it would also result in the loss of tranquility and independence by depending on the market."[60] But, he warned, its retention never meant that the village would automatically become "commodity-economy-fied"[61] with the appearance of capitalism. Only capital's production process could realize that accomplishment. However, the "medieval feudal relationships" lost their basis. The process of capitalizing the countryside occurred gradually, to be sure, but inexorably. For capitalism to manage the foundational production sector of the country's economy, it was vital for it to inhibit the behavior of older feudal relations that could hinder its operations. The problem was less in the implementation of "new capitalist production relations" directly involved in managing other sectors of the country than in "acknowledging" that these forces now formally corresponded to this new arrangement.[62] "Substantively," Uno reasoned, "even though production forms of the past survive transitionally or midway [in the capitalist present], we cannot say that they are formally [*keishikiteki*] the same relics [as they were in the past]." Nothing was permitted to interfere with the process of new production relations, which simply meant that older practices in the new present won a new lease on life by being subordinated to capitalism. Here, he had no trouble acknowledging the persistence of "remnants" (*zanzombutsu*) and their capacity to "influence" the development of capitalism. But this was merely following through the logic of formal subsumption as the rule of capitalist development, without naming it as such, and verifying that older relations of production were no longer directly involved, even though the "influences" of the remnant still constituted a primary factor in the development of productive power. By the same measure, the management of *shōnō* (petty farming) slowly encumbered the commodity economy, first losing its basis to capitalist industry and then experiencing the inevitable transformation of labor power into a form capable of being utilized by capitalism.[63] This important transformation did not immediately result in the achievement of the wage labor form. The outcome of Uno's effort to account for the initial contact between capital and the countryside and the corresponding role played by the feudal remnant was to show that no contradictory collision occurred between productivity and relations of production. Standing in the way of actuating this process was the absence of an adequate theoretical understanding of how history behaved, a grasp that avoided being reduced to positing fixed polarities separating feudal from capitalist societies. In fact, Uno, as I suggested earlier, seemed to sense precisely the blindness of much social theory after Marx that sought to displace his analysis of the complexities that constituted the social by appealing to models based on unbridgeable oppositions between premodern and modern. The anticipated inevitable progression from the former to the latter in these theories presumed a view that disregarded the possibility that the process actually drew in the active involvement of the past in the present as a necessary condition of the modern. Uno was objecting to the "fictitious" dissolution between a feudal past and capitalist present into two separate societies in which their interconnectedness has been broken and the uneven mix is absent.[64] By the same measure, he added, it is not possible to decisively assess them as if they occupied the same level of basic social relations. The so-called theory of forms (*kata*), in an obvious swipe at Yamada, disregards the conditions within this change from one social order to another. Here, Uno was pointing to how an analysis of the changes in the economy of petty cultivators that ignores how basic social relationships affect those surviving social relations from the past end up disregarding objective laws that function behind fundamental social relations. His colleague Sakisaka Itsurō, an economist and a translator of Marx, who wrote a savage critique of Yamada's principal work, pointed to the obvious dialectical relationship set up by the introduction of capitalism in a feudal environment and the formation of a different form of the social composed by an uneven mixture of incommensurables, coexisting different practices and even relationships, some new, others "feudal," yet each constantly interacting with the other, changing and being changed. These coexisting incommensurables, moreover, signified different temporal historical associations that resonated with their own rhythms, ways of doing things and thinking, even though subordinated, producing constant asymmetries of unevenness. Owing to the character of late development, Uno proposed that in its starting point with primitive accumulation and its subsequent developmental process, "the process of individual revolution" differs considerably to visibly mark both the "remarkable development of capitalism" and the "necessity to realize the dissolution of older social forms in a comparatively slow manner."[65] If his adversaries in the Lectures Faction looked to the necessity of charting a route to revolution, Uno's preference came closer to Gramsci's recommendation of a nonrevolutionary strategy to move slowly.

Uno's concerns concentrated on the process that led to the dissolution of the agrarian village in England and the position it occupied in triggering primitive accumulation by forcibly separating large numbers of people from their means of subsistence and throwing them into the labor market. He was convinced that this experience was no longer applicable to latecomers like Japan, which have taken divergent paths in the dissolution of the agrarian village. Lateness in Japan failed to dissolve the agrarian village and set loose large numbers of people as "free workers" searching for a new means of subsistence and employment in new nascent industries that would not be ready to absorb them until the period of World War I. Because he was committed to examining the consequences of late development in countries like Japan and Germany, he believed that the impulse to capitalize could be comprehended only by concentrating on the relationship of the modern state and capitalism and their mutual interdependence if both were to survive. Once capitalist production was inaugurated, it demanded a mode of operation according to its own laws of development.[66] In late-developing countries, there was an inevitable temporal hiatus between capitalist demands and political requirements representing disparate interests. If this gap was allowed to interrupt or hamper the reproduction of capitalism and deny its significance, which Uno recognized constituted the "foundation of the modern nation-state," it would have thus threatened the viability of its very existence. Not only did late developers like Japan see the stakes of national survival bound to this relationship, the apparent pressure exerted by advanced capitalist countries necessitated a further inducement to implement effective policies designed to protect embryonic large-scale industries for rapid capitalization. Here, Uno perceived the immense distance between England's protectionist policies in the seventeenth and eighteenth centuries and those undertaken by Germany and Japan in the nineteenth. Accordingly, late developers like Japan employed the joint-stock system, created in the "background" of protectionist policies and veiled by them, to realize a greater concentration of capital. In this scenario, finance capital became predominant and ultimately changed the form of capitalism itself to necessitate a new kind of political response from the state directed at accommodating this new content. The representation of industry as developed by the modern state in late-developing countries like Japan and Germany "concealed the necessity of developing capitalistically," even though this had been the case.[67] In this connection, Uno, who had earlier counseled caution against any explanation seeking to exceptionalize Japan's capitalist experience, admitted that even if local circumstances eventually function to instantiate and inflect the global problem, the adulterations of history would work to mediate specific national developments of capitalism everywhere despite following the same economic laws. Moreover, he added, no capitalist development anywhere was possible unless it was accompanied by some ready-at-hand preparatory ground of accumulation.

Agriculture, which was in process of dissolving, had to be recalibrated to account for its renewed political significance and its breaking-up process terminated. But in Japan this process had already slowed, and cultivators remained on the land and thus linked to their means of subsistence. "Agriculture," he advised, "that remained within the sphere of production of direct consumer items such as grains lingered as its prior form and was only gradually invaded by capital as it assisted the process of reproduction of capitalism."[68] Even with the slow dissolution of the agrarian village and the gradual integration of agricultural production into the national economy, the village in Japan was unhurried to undertake responsibility for large-scale capitalist management. Uno was only interested in showing how the process of dissolution occurred in a late-developing country that avoided the trauma of primitive accumulation England had experienced three centuries earlier. Japan's importation of capitalism required neither the capitalization of agriculture after the historic separation of the direct producers nor the preparation of a relative surplus population to satisfy the requirements of large-scale industrialization. The problem Japan confronted has been rapid development—catching up, as Uno put it—that has not always fulfilled the proper prerequisites for capitalism's development, which it displaced onto the agrarian village. Hence the village remained committed to "small-scale agricultural production" in contrast to the appearance of large-scale industrial enterprises in the cities and provided the recruiting ground for male and child labor when urban industrialization required it.[69] However, capitalism prevented the continuation of unalienated land feudalism. Communal lands attached to the feudal economy were either nationalized or sold freely, and in this way the villages underwent the gradual commodification of the countryside and lost control over household industries traditionally connected to agriculture, which increasingly were "dispossessed by the large businesses of the cities." The outcome was that the village, in time, witnessed the decline of one sector of the feudal economic base in the *shōnō* management and experienced the dilemma of living through retention at the same moment that its economic foundation was being undermined. Given the circumstances of the late arrival of capitalism and the adoption of a more mature form of industrialism, the logic of its development gradually resulted in the erosion of the medieval agrarian village order at the expense of being forced to assume the burden of resolving problems created by capitalism. Uno portrayed an arrangement in which peasant households were now simultaneously obliged to manage small-scale farming and compelled to enter a commodity economy and turn over a portion of what they produced. While villages continued household manufacturing, they became more dependent on buying raw materials for agriculture as commodities. Even land now had to be bought.[70] Despite the material changes, Uno recognized in the subsuming process how the peasant's life remained intact. At this juncture, his observations paradoxically converged with Yamada's: "Whether the small-scale farm management under feudal relations, where the peasant himself is . . . possessed by land or a farmer is self-managing [*jiei nōmin*] who possesses land, it is, in any case, premised on a direction of union of land and producer. . . . In our country, agrarian villages must assume the burden of several troubling problems [in the countryside] together with the development of capitalism in the cities. . . . Without understanding the problem, capitalism itself has imposed misses the extent to which such development has inflicted sacrifices on the countryside,"[71] since the countryside must see the erosion of traditional practices while being forced to resolve problems capitalism has unleashed. One of the problems on which Uno remained silent was reproduction and the degree to which peasants were obliged to assume responsibility for providing for their own partial subsistence when engaged in capitalist manufacturing enterprises. It is conceivable that they rotated between fields and manufacturing, which may well have forced them to take on the additional burden of providing for partial subsistence when they were working in manufacturing, which would have resulted in a lowering of wages. It is possible, in any event, to conclude from this perception a description of the effects of subsumption in the countryside and its disruptive impact on traditional practices, which the native ethnologist Yanagita Kunio had already detailed in *Tōshi no nōson* (City and village, 1929). Yanagita's work likened the countryside to the emptying out of a colony compelled to continually supply resources to the metropole. Although Uno seemed reluctant to name this process and its new arrangement "semifeudalism," which he considered merely as a slogan, he was willing to concede that "routinization of the so-called feudal system was maintained on the basis of [retaining] feudal relationships that cannot be said to be immediately feudal."[72] If the feudal economy continued to demand higher rents, the persistence of tenancy, with taxes still being paid in kind, and feudal ground rent (retained elsewhere as well, such as England), none of this was any longer rooted in feudal social relations as such.[73] Yet such practices acted as reminders of feudalism and reinforced something akin to what might be called a "feudal unconscious" that manifestly surfaced in Japan's capitalist modernity in "thought," "sentiment," and "customs" that resisted erasure.

With this observation, Uno not only identified the core of the logic of subsumption—the preservation and continuation of the form of older precapitalist practices and ways of thinking alongside newer ones that had taken command over time—but imaginatively extended the limits of the "general rule of capitalism" beyond the economic sphere to other areas of social and cultural life dominated by the involuntary interaction of conscious life and the force of other, unconscious habits and modes of behavior. Just as Yamada shows that his political analysis is founded on an economic accounting aimed at demonstrating refeudalization, so Uno's appeal to the primacy of economics illustrates related political consequences that cannot be separated from it. His identification of a surviving feudal consciousness without a feudality to support it signals the kinship and calls attention to the political conclusions derived from his particular economic narrative of the late development of capitalism. Acknowledging the presence of the "substance" of a feudalism no longer based on the imperatives of feudal social relations, Uno attributed this mutation to "economic competition."[74] But he also followed the opinion of his contemporary, the journalist and "public intellectual" Hasegawa Nyozekan, who had proposed that while the feudal system's "lingering life is preserved even in modernity," this avatar must still be distinguished from "feudality" (*hōkensei*).[75] Writing in the immediate postwar years, Uno claimed that feudal custom, thinking, and sentiments continued to remain observable among the general population, not only in agrarian villages. The reason for this sturdy survival cannot be explained solely by ascribing it to a "despotic police state derived from the Meiji epoch," as supposed by the Lectures Faction, the military, or imperial bureaucrats, even though each, in his own way, embodied the authorizing principles of political hierarchy that empowered him, an admission Uno seemed not want to make. What struck him most was the presence of feudalism as a form of absence in a different present once the system had been materially eliminated and the knowledge that this tendency had not been avoided in the most advanced capitalist nations. "But in our country this disposition has been remarkable."[76] If capitalist countries have not yet liquidated older feudal habits and thinking that apparently lie below but close to the surface of conscious life, Japan has gone further because the basic problem, from the beginning, has been that there has been a concerted effort to preserve them.

Unlike other societies where interpreters had to conjure up an imaginary feudalism and its transition to capitalism to satisfy a rigid orthodoxy, Uno and Yamada were on good ground since their referent was the Tokugawa order that had existed immediately prior to Japan's capitalist transformation in the 1860s and 1870s. Marx had earlier ratified Japan's "purely feudal organization of landed property . . . and small-scale agriculture, [which] gives a much truer picture of the European middle ages than all the history books."[77] But that feudalism did not necessarily lead to the establishment of capitalism or yield vital components for its formation. The survival of residues and vestiges is not necessarily bonded to the experience of a prior feudal system, as if they were natural remainders and excesses that will soon become a ruin and pass into the landscape. In this regard, any patriarchal system will do. The perpetuation of the old and habitual in the new present signifies the general condition of subsumption found everywhere capitalism has established its program of production, and, as I earlier suggested, this bringing together and combining of incommensurables not only makes the present into a fractured heterogeneity but also differentiates the modern social from all those theorizations that still seek to distance the capitalist now from its other to literally homogenize it as genuinely modern. Uno's own accounting of Japan shows only a partial commodification of the countryside,

with the preservation of the agrarian village in one form or another as a sign
of the incapacity to bring about the complete dissolution of feudalism and
the imposition of capitalism's complete control. Moreover, the installation
of commodity production within the *shōnō* household industries clears the
path to greater commodification and the inauguration of the wage form. But
the production of commodities failed to yield an entirely new social system.
"Even though employed labor was carried out," Uno observed, "it meant nothing more than an assistance to family labor. If one speaks of capitalism's
influence that extended to the villages, it was something that stopped at its
external character. It was not something that accompanied a transformation
from within its [village life] interior."[78] With the compartmentalizing of the
space of two different temporalities lived externally and internally (and inadvertently recuperating the philosopher Watsuji Tetsurō's conception of the
"double life" [*nijū seikatsu*]), Uno did not directly visualize the temporal consequences of this observation and the possibilities it offered for inducing conflict, nor, in fact, did he express any sensitivity to the rhythms regulating
them on an everyday basis that required an awareness of the constant navi-
gation involved. Even more important was his inability to envision what other
contemporaries had already grasped, which was the relationship between an
adopted external culture and a still persevering interior life shaped by the
world of feudal thought, sentiment, and habit.

But what Uno did point to was how the coexistence of partial capitalist
practices alongside traditional ones in the countryside—a half self-sufficient
and half commodity-centered economy—supplied the guarantee for sustain-
ing older forms of thinking, feeling, and habitual ways of conduct. This
would be the case whether inheritance was specifically feudal or any tributary political and social form. The only difference was one of degree: in
Japan, this legacy was apparently preserved with a vengeance. In a discern-
able dialectical reversal, the force of older practices, despite their subordination
to capitalism, acted on the new—in all domains of activity, economy, politics, and society. In other words, "the feudality of our country's agrarian villages," Uno proposed, "is not a feudality as a system; even though it is one
that appears in thought, sentiment, and customary habit in peasant households; it is the reason why it can't be settled."[79] Through the agency of capitalism, these residues are only partially metabolized and modernized in the
legal system that accompanies them. But the tenancy of this feudal uncon-

scious works to undermine precisely those relationships that capitalism has endeavored to establish as the political promise of a democratic society. Uno agreed that the "feudal character" imprinted on the relationship between small producer and landlord, the feudality of the agrarian village and the past it embodied, continued according to "despotic political control."[80] While this could be easily torn down for a more democratic order, it was far more difficult to uproot feudal control maintained by the "feudal thinking of small producers," by *shōnō* management, and shake the country loose from its iron grip. If he seemed to be offering a pessimistic forecast for postwar Japan's "democratizing" moment, he was correct to exemplify the dialectical nature of the structure of capitalism and the co-evality of pasts that became parts of its present that demonstrated the process everywhere capitalism encountered a society's past it sought to surpass. Uno here, I believe, inadvertently caught sight of the complex question of subjectivation, which would occupy a principal position in the democratizing agenda of postwar Japan, as well as prefigure later postcolonial preoccupations. Like Yamada, he was indifferent to problems of consciousness and even ideology. He shared with Yamada a conviction that Japan's historical experience produced remnants, surviving residues resituated to function in a new and different present. The difference was that Yamada's remnants were material manifestations, external, while Uno's leaned toward the internal and psychological makeup of the Japanese. However, both forms exerted coercive pressures. It is interesting to note, in this connection, that Uno's conception of the persistence of feudal thought, sentiment, and custom resembles Tōsaka Jun's conceptualization of the ideological basis of a Japanese variant of fascism, which emphasized archaism, the retrieval of past social relationships and morality to guide the present. What was overlooked in Uno's discourse was the temporal discordance the new configuration necessarily demands and the possible collisions it would incur when the past was required to resolve the problems created by the present. In the Japanese case, Uno was able to portray the operation of subsumption resulting from the special circumstances of the late adoption of capitalism and the effects it produced as instantiations of a global process that will happen everywhere but always with a difference founded on specific local conditions. It was for that reason that he saw in capitalism's history everywhere the obligation put onto the past to solve problems created by the present.

5

COLONIAL/POSTCOLONIAL

The years after World War II witnessed a marked shift in Marxian and non-Marxian discussions concerning the order of capitalist modernization away from explicit considerations of the effects of capitalism in the noncapitalist colonial periphery to an assessment of the afterlives of colonies in the wake of decolonization and the achievement of new nationhood. With the passage of colonialism to the new nation also came the enforced status of the postcolony, as if it were a necessary stage that automatically accompanied the accomplishment of nationhood as a permanent reminder of an unwanted past in the new present and an unyielding stigma destined to fetter the future. The new register of the postcolony referred first to the chronological moment that ambiguously signaled both an end of colonization, as Aijaz Ahmad recalled for us years ago, and a beginning on a new and uncharted course toward attaining the nation-form. As a chronological moment, the postcolonial thus involved the confrontation with a host of political, economic, and social problems that demanded immediate attention, if not resolution, as a premise for continued national existence. These problems came from the immediately prior colonial past of the new nation and constituted a vast, heterogeneous material "heritage," a living and ongoing historical archive of remnants, that bonded the new nation to its past and former colonizing power, especially to antecedent forms and combinations that were already working to prefigure the shape of the new society. Given the purpose and duration of colonization, this entailed recognizing that the colonized were already forced to endure and navigate their way through multiple lives, differing spaces, and temporalities. By the time of decolonization, the metropolitan centers and administrative sites of most colonies were already mixed social formations, microcosms of cosmopolitanisms and capital accumulation that had become familiar fixtures of everyday life. The contrast between those who approached decolonized regions and new nations as still weighted with the colonial legacy and postcolonial theorists who sought to displace the colonial heritage is found in the way the former recognized the persistence of mixed social formations and the formative role played by capitalist accumulation while the latter, who, in some extreme instances, were bent on discounting the presence of capitalism as simply another Western-imposed metanarrative that had smothered sensibilities and imaginations, set about putting into question its universalistic claims.

Some of these theorists have argued that the prefix "post" modifying the colony and the emergence of the "new nation" in the space vacated by the banished colony authorized a break from the immediate past to inaugurate the condition of what Leela Gandhi has called "postcolonial amnesia." This transfer became eventually evident in shifts in the meaning of the term "postcolonial." What originally had described and marked the temporal moment of decolonization and its aftermath was replaced by the process of uncovering a new sense of subjecthood and what constituted it. Induced by a growing disappointment with the new nation, this turn to probing the effects on the colonial experience of subjectivity set off a preoccupation with the psychological consequences of foreign domination and oppression aimed at releasing an essential difference colonization had largely ignored, resulting in the repressing of the precolonial past and motivating the conditions of collective amnesia. But such a maneuver of recovery was realizable only as a discursive aspiration that could never overcome the massive material reminders of the past—remnants from colonialism and a country's precolonial history—situated in the new national present. The discursive figuration of postcoloniality appeared in the 1970s and 1980s as one of the manifestations of the "cultural turn," assisted by the adoption of poststructural interpretative strategies that constituted an effort to "dematerialize" Edward

good

Said's colonial discourse in the name of "radicalizing" it.[1] The new discourse on postcoloniality thus turned to restoring the forgotten past of the postcolony, in order to resolve the question of its relationship to the present as a means of moving beyond it. An interesting prefiguration of this postcolonial move was the Japanese effort in the pre–World War II decades to find a way to use the national past to mediate the excesses of Westernization. Implied by this "return" was the perception of a stalled present that could only be unmoored through a recovery of the difference that had been repressed or forgotten as a basis for reconciliation with the present and the start of a real new beginning. In the postcolonial discourse, this interpretative tactic was psychoanalytic rather than historical (which so much poststructural philosophy eschewed) and aimed at configuring the identity of the former colonial subject in its difference and parity as a form of self-reconciliation and empowerment rather than in oppressed inferiority. But it remained a desire in the discursive register that was ultimately undermined by the very burden of disappointment with the failures of the postcolonial nation once they became a reality. Such a discourse seemed more of a response to the residual reminders of massive economic, political, and social materiality from the colonial past, now residing in the center of the new postcolony, which the new nation would be expected to overcome, in spite of its deeply embedded impossibility. In this sense, there was a wide split between what Leela Gandhi has identified as the discourse's offer of a therapeutic and a new sensorium and the kind of society that the postcolonial new nation had already become.[2] Postcolonial discourse wanted to return to the inaugural moment of the nation to recover the lost or forgotten past as a condition for a proper beginning, even though it had already left the starting post. It was a therapeutic for an imagined or possible alternative society because the colonial past had never really been forgotten or lost.

After World War II, attention turned to former colonies like those in South Asia, Africa, and to some extent Latin America, the latter long decolonized, even though it was not treated as such by the capitalist West. The Cold War contest between differing forms of development promised modernization makeovers of Third World countries, notably those that had recently been decolonized—between capitalist and Marxian (Stalinist version) claims that often appeared as reverse mirror images of each other. In this chapter, I will consider how the colonial past and the problem of capitalist production was figured as a vital historical problem of the new nation and then will turn to a few writers of the postcolonial persuasion and their effort to imagine a post-colonial mode of production that would embody difference.

Production/Reproduction

According to the French anthropologist and specialist on West Africa Claude Meillassoux (1925–2005), colonial history portrays the vivid spectacle whereby labor has been forcibly driven from the countryside to the cities rather than the incidence of "expropriation."[3] Under these circumstances, it would be difficult to distinguish between the economic and the political to determine which of the two is the least violent technique with which to increase labor power. Meillassoux's observation reverts discussion back to the colonial historical "heritage" and the initial encounter between the domestic economy and capitalism. In his reckoning, the domestic economy, despite being "crushed, oppressed, divided," was still able to provide the basis of succeeding economies since the "domestic relations of production have not completely disappeared. They still support millions of productive units integrated" to some extent into capitalism. Meillassoux's particular target was the economist Samir Amin, whose conception of uneven development, drawn from dependency theory, appeared to be authorized by the presumption of a global division between center and periphery and who, as a result, employed an explanatory strategy that sought to show how exchange and circulation, rather than production and the exploitation of labor, accounted for the expanding wealth of the developed world (center) at the expense of the underdeveloped Third World (periphery). Amin has simply furthered this strategy by continuing to bypass Marx's emphasis that posited the "wealth of imperialist countries deriv[ing] from the exploitation of workers in these satellite countries and not from international trade"[4] by advocating the role played by unequal exchange as creator of value. This remark registers a significant critique of circulation as a producer of wealth and economic unevenness attributable to the neglect of a production process pursuing value based on the exploitation of labor power. While sensitive to the presence of lower wages among workers in the "periphery," it allowed Amin only the latitude to propose that the intensification of labor power producing the disparity evolved from the exercise of political means or noneconomic coercive factors in former colonial locations. It could also have been the attempt to reimplant regimes of absolute surplus value, alongside work based on relative surplus value, which then might have depended on the reliance on the application of noneconomic modes of coercion. But he remained silent on this. If Amin understated the significance of the mixture and combining of precapitalist and capitalist practices, emphasizing the abstracted and homogenizing binary of world systems capitalism (center) and localized periphery that overrode local identities and the specific problems they faced, Meillassoux sought to restore the presence of prior production practices in the present and the specificity of the local at the level of empirical concreteness. He was persuaded that the analysis of one "superceded but tenacious form of production is not irrelevant for the understanding of the present."[5] It is precisely this attentiveness to the tattered remainders from prior forms of production, what Meillassoux named as the "domestic mode of production," that provided the pathway for him to return to the primacy of the production process in former colonial regions of West Africa but also explain the logic of formal subsumption and especially how earlier forms emphasizing the reproduction of the "domestic community" were coupled with capitalism.

Meillassoux returns analysis back to the general rule of all capitalist production to grasp the circumstances of the formerly colonized world, where postcolonial is still simply a chronological continuation of the colonial and the dominant mode of production, conforming to embryonic economic enterprises that remain only formally capitalistic. Even though these embryonic capitalist enterprises are distant and remote from the larger world economy, it is their formal nature that still permits participation in the broader capitalist sphere. In some instances, enterprises were implicated in the general development of capitalism without their prior mode of production necessarily being in full sync with the capitalist system. This would include plantations throughout the former colonial world, from the Caribbean to Asia, where in many cases free labor, as such, did not yet exist. Under these circumstances, it is thus conceivable that instead of the existence of separate dual economies or sectors, there was constant necessary contact and communication between the old and new, which, in Meillassoux's excursus into the encounter of the "domestic community" with colonial capital, demonstrates the continuity of interaction once colonialism officially left the scene.

For Meillassoux, the domestic community constituted the "basic cell," recalling Marx's description of the commodity, in a "mode of production" composed of similar communities devoted to "economic and social production" and the reproduction of specific relations of production.[6] While undoubtedly not actually timeless, time seemed to be displaced in the process of reproducing what we might call archaic exemplars that function to hold off the intrusion of timeliness and the figure of change. Despite Meillassoux's concentration on anthropological fieldwork in Africa, his decision to bind production closely to reproduction could have referred to any society that had reached a similar point of encounter with capitalism. Such communities, especially agricultural communities, which looked upon land as an "instrument of labor," were ultimately directed toward producing sufficient goods for both subsistence and self-perpetuation.[7] In this environment, he found the necessary correspondence between "relations of reproduction" and relations of production, a relatively seamless totalization of a world of practice: "the necessity to reproduce . . . relations of production, which are linked through the production of the producer, squeezes them up into ties within an institutional framework."[8] When this arrangement is contrasted to capitalism, it is evident that its guiding mode of production relies on controlling the "means of reproduction . . . and not over the means of material production."[9] The importance of Meillassoux's account of the inseparability of production and reproduction forming the infrastructure of the domestic community, rather than kinship, is that the cost of reproducing labor remains undifferentiated from the institutionalized constraints that have equated production—substance—with reproduction—perpetuation. The coming of colonialism forced the separation, which led to the recruitment of forced labor that would determine the level of wages by now calculating the cost of reproducing labor power.[10] Paradoxically, this change had the effect of replicating the "separation" Marx described in the archaic scene in *Grundrisse*. In this transaction, Meillassoux discounted the role played by supply and demand in the calculation of wages.

The decisive alteration came with the end of colonialism. Where colonial entrepreneurs once freely employed force to recruit workers and could expect the colonial administration to assume the cost of labor, new "national" structures were erected to determine the level of wages offered in order to induce recruitment. But labor's cost and the augmentation of higher wages now had to be undertaken by private companies. It was still necessary to underwrite the cost of policing, which in most cases was covered by the capitalist state. Meillassoux is surely correct to see such political practices as merely noneconomic, when they were directed to reinforcing the established structure devoted to exploiting labor and realizing profit. The problem he perceived in the early years of decolonization was the relationship between wages and the available labor pool. Workers from predominantly rural areas would invariably return home once they earned enough. Forms of rotational labor, marking the early stages of capitalist development in numerous regions, meant that workers frequently had access to agricultural land that would supplement their subsistence wages. This was particularly the case of enterprises that paid low wages and did not necessarily involve the industrial sector. The differentiation of workplaces accounted not only for wage differentials but also for the necessity of workers to navigate different temporally based demands. It was one thing to work on the land, where the constraints of time were determined by climate and seasons, and another to work under the discipline of clock time in a factory. Since the agricultural workday was not regulated by averaging the magnitude of time necessary for producing a commodity, it required an entirely different temporal regime. Rotational workers moving from one temporal regime to another were required to negotiate different forms of existence and work disciplines between the everyday and workday, invariably risking the incurring of an entanglement of times and an enlargement of possible collisions, as brilliantly recorded by Chinua Achebe (in *Arrow of God*), who describes how colonial (and bureaucratic) time, mediated by clock, collided with the lunar time of the village communities. Agricultural and factory work demanded observing different calculations regulating work time. Such multiple temporal regimes also raised the more complex problem of measuring their effect on the lives of the workers. In a sense, this materialization of temporal unevenness recalls Marx's reflections concerning the initial development of capitalism. The continuation of older practices serving the pursuit of value would change nothing in the external lives of the worker. If the production of uneven times represented by involvement in coextensive different labor practices led to the gradual differentiation of sectors, it is still possible to presume that the constant overlapping contributed to the ongoing process of reconstituting the received social order into a heterogeneous and fractured complex composed of capitalist and noncapitalist elements. This is exactly the world Meillassoux illustrates in postcolonial West Africa.

For Meillassoux, the fracturing and heterogeneity of time marks the relationship between low wages and reproduction. His own perspective targeted explanations offered by writers like Samir Amin, who, as we have seen, concentrated only on the industrial sector, already projecting an image that concealed more than it revealed by neglecting to consider the diversity that would have had to be included in any effort to calculate average wages. In Meillassoux's view, the agrarian question, whose resolution Uno believed was central to global capitalism and which was displaced or simply overlooked by writers like Amin, is brought back for consideration. Persisting underdevelopment, Meillassoux argued, came from continuing forms of exploitation of labor, which, given the new political states in Africa and Asia, required taking into account workers in the agrarian sector. Amin, on the other hand, emphasized the primacy of classes and production by states and circulation in the arena of international exchange. Such a strategic shift invariably endangered comprehending how "underdevelopment" is produced "from a transfer between economic sectors operating on the basis of different relations of production."[11] If the transfer of value "explains" the realization of profit, it falls short of elucidating the means involved in enabling its creation. Here, Meillassoux additionally pointed to how such theorization is unable to explain the crucial "paradox of agricultural economy in countries exploited by colonialism." Moreover, the paradox cannot be resolved by appealing either to explanations founded on the premise of supply and demand or to capital's diverse organic compositions: since these new nations are primarily characterized by subsistence agriculture, they only partially belong to the capitalist realm insofar as the subsistence economy supplies labor power and commodities to capital's sphere of circulation. But it also remains outside of the sphere of production at the same time, and capital has thus overlooked the prospect of investing in this economic sector when the law of development would have obliged it to do so because labor power, made accessible by family exploitation, was cheap and productivity low, so that returns would have been relatively high.[12] In fact, one of the anomalies of development in postcolonial nation-states has been this departure from the historical path Uno Kōzō had identified in Japan's nineteenth-century adoption of capitalism, whereby the agricultural sector and "medieval village" were allowed to remain intact but not necessarily separate from the sphere of capitalism as its productive activity was gradually integrated into the capitalist economy and its population held in reserve until industry was able to begin expanding its workforce and determine its needs. The divergence was undoubtedly stimulated by both conjunctural differences and what capitalism found useful for subsumption. Meillassoux's response to these circumstances was to rethink the status of wages within the framework of primitive accumulation. Here, he detected a division between subsistence agriculture and capitalism, which meant that the former remained external to the latter's sphere of production. Even when capitalism showed some inclination in investing in agriculture, the relations of production still stayed tied to the domestic sector, not the capitalist. While he imagined a division between the two economies, since the relations could not constitute two branches of capitalism, the relationship was secured through a referral to primitive accumulation and capitalism's propensity to appropriate what it was able to find from earlier practices. At the outset, it need not have been one or another since the various forms of subsumption would tolerate differing combinations where labor practices may combine or coexist alongside or behind newer capitalist production procedures. Building on Rosa Luxemburg's insight concerning the mutations proliferated by capitalism and the resources supplied by noncapitalism, imperialism fixed relations between domestic and capitalist economic modes. In this way, Meillassoux was steered toward focusing on the utilization of received traditions governing reproduction that promised the offer of cheap labor power as a form of subsidizing the cost of capitalist production; that is to say, he saw in customary forms of African reproduction customs and procedures that were capable of being harnessed to the capitalist production process. In this equation of the old and new, imperialism probably commanded the process of production while reproduction continued to be bound to the present now dominated by the domestic mode. Even though the consequences of this appropriation reflected the "cause of underdevelopment," by transferring responsibility for reproduction from subsistence to subsidizing the production process (lowering wages) when workers rotated from the agricultural site to the scene of manufacturing and back, the practice must have been similar to any historical conjuncture that brought together primitive accumulation and the inauguration of capitalism's general rule of development. Moreover, Meillassoux proposed that this system would have replicated comparable effects on the exploited and benefits on the exploiters. By the same measure, the rotational cycle must have regularly appeared time and again whenever and wherever capitalism established its command of production, continuing down to the present at even faster and expanding rates that it must be considered, like other mechanisms of capitalist reproduction, to be "inherent in capitalism itself."[13]

For Meillassoux, what remained uppermost was the logical sequence of modes of production marching to a progressive destination rather than the actual encounter of contemporary modes of production "as they meet." Behind this observation clearly lay the imperative of formal subsumption, and especially the production of possible hybrid combinations the operation was capable of generating. Yet he was cognizant, like Marx before him, of capital's necessity to project a system of exchange that, despite its isolated appearance on the surface, "rests on capital as its foundation," in fact is dependent on it and performs as a "necessary illusion."[14] Meillassoux's revised formulation proposed that "if labour-power is reproduced, even in the capitalist system, within the framework of domestic social relations, this means the heterogeneity is organically involved in the capitalist mode of production (while the domestic mode operates on the homogeneous relationships)." Under this combinatory, "insofar as some modes, organically and not residually, contain elements of others within their structures, they cannot be considered homogenous and could not fall within the same category as the domestic economy. . . . Neither capitalism nor feudalism is exclusive of the domestic economy, for they rely on domestic relations to reproduce themselves."[15] With this understanding, he has raised the crucial question of what remains of a form configured by an original mode of production once it has absorbed elements from another. This is especially the case when there appears a heterogeneous mix rather than the destruction of one mode by another, a problem that had been avoided or overlooked by Marxian interpreters content with the positing of stages or modes of production and their progressive replacement by the new of a preceding and now completed phase. This interpretative strategy was invested in the valorization of linear historical time, recalling for us nothing more than the tired image of a moving train heading toward the realization of a scheduled destination and point of arrival, at which it stops, unloads and picks up passengers, and continues anew the journey to the next station. Meillassoux's research confirmed not the imagined clean break between one stage or another, or of differing modes of production and successive replacements, but instead the messier mix of differing modes morphing into hybrid combinations forming the heterogeneous and fractured social order of capitalist modernity. Meillassoux has forcefully argued for a view that locates the "immediate" interests in a certain historical moment, to avoid "discouraging" the forcible separation of different modes of production as they meet and interact with one another. Luxemburg, it might be recalled, already foresaw the advantage of preserving local forms of practice and frames of knowledge, which referred to the "domestic sector producing subsistence goods" and the necessity of continuing and extending primitive accumulation beyond the initial moment of contact (between the received and new). "Modes of production," according to Meillassoux, "are not only 'articulated' at the level of class alliances between capitalist and corrupt lineage leaders, but also organically within the economic sphere itself."[16] When in the encounter between different modes of production, one may seize domination over the other and, as Marx accepted, especially in preserving received domestic relations of production and reproduction and in their persisting overlapping, they will remain intact and "qualitatively different from the capitalist mode of production."[17] In this process, the "domestic mode" is at the same time retained as a means of social organization pressed into serving value for imperialism, which contains a reproductive system not simply limited to economic practices but implicating religion, culture, and custom. It is gradually undermined because its means of reproduction is depleted to satisfy the capitalist exploitative imperative. Accordingly, these constraints, in time, change the nature of the older mode of production and the world it embodied, which attests to the heterogeneity of a social filled with coextensive and co-eval times. The introduction of labor time denoted the adoption of a conception of quantitative time calculation measured by the clock and meant it was situated alongside its absence in subsistence agriculture. The result forced a bifurcation of lives that Meillassoux passed over in silence, but thinkers elsewhere have described as "double living" or living comparatively.

Meillassoux rejected the dualism that has empowered the discourse on development and its claims associated with the production of underdevelopment that has reduced the image of the colony to an impoverished expression of capitalism.[18] Because he was persuaded that the proper context for viewing the conditions of colonial and postcolonial exploitation was projected by the force of primitive accumulation, he was able to dramatize and expand on the encounter of capitalism and noncapitalism and the ways the former was able to draw on and utilize the resources of the latter in its pursuit of value. The principal factor in capitalism's desire to outdo prior experiences of exploitation, feudal and patriarchal tributary, and extract labor-rent and surplus value was the role played by reproduction. In his research in West Africa, Meillassoux uncovered capitalism's reluctance to undermine the domestic economy, especially subsistence agriculture, which was immediately aligned with the process of reproduction. Capitalism confronted a practice that would literally subsidize its productive process, save its investment expenditures, and realize labor rent and surplus in ways that would effectively exceed traditional forms of exploitation. But realization of this advantage went against the premise that capitalism reproduces its own labor power from a population "freed" to be recruited for this purpose, what Marx early described as creating its own presuppositions and thus configuring the environment for the production process. As such, the wages it paid for work could not fall below the cost of the social reproduction of labor power. If they fell below this level, it would undermine the capacity of workers to reproduce.[19] Contrary to this cherished principle from capitalism's folklore, Meillassoux was able to confirm that in areas like West Africa this rule was consistently ignored, and the "historical development of capitalism" up to the present "has contravened this law by a continuous and sustained absorption of population deriving from the domestic sector of production."[20] In fact, his reference to the context supplied by primitive accumulation allowed him to put it on a footing with the historical experience of capitalism, wherever it has sunk its roots. To be sure, the argument Meillassoux put forth would seem to compose a picture of historical development that contradicted the model found in *Capital*. In actuality, however, it affirmed the general rule of all capitalist development, its unconstrained penchant for appropriating what it found useful in the old mode of production. Paradoxically, this was how Meillassoux concluded his reflections on imperialism as continually feeding off the reservoir of precapitalist formations that constituted a permanent, rather than transitional, reflex of its production process. Although the argument inflected the centrality of singular local circumstances in West Africa, it still represented the general and ongoing presence of primitive accumulation expropriating land and expanding capitalism's sphere of activity to "produce and renew parts of labour power" by enlisting a vast army of workers, who were not necessarily dispossessed of land and their means of subsistence.[21] Capitalist entrepreneurs knew that the size of the labor force could be enlarged by inducing migrants who were nearby to work in new enterprises part of the time and return to their fields for the rest. The growth of the labor population inevitably sharpened awareness as to the long-term problem of maintaining the reproduction of labor power, and this opened the way to devising mechanisms designed to integrate workers into capitalist relations. In certain regions of West Africa and Asia, before fully industrialized urban zones, workers maintained physical, social, and psychological ties to the land, especially with families, clans, and villages in the countryside. While the domestic mode of production was undermined in the initial stages of establishing colonial enterprises and farms, the land was eventually exempted from uniform appropriation and large numbers of people remained in situ, as Uno described peasant households in the Japanese countryside, and continued to carry out "self-sustaining modes of production."[22] Ultimately, Europeans fell on the "mode of exploitation" that utilized the production experience of the domestic economy. In Africa, where the domestic mode differed from others, especially those based on class, collective labor was employed as "organized cells of production," both more exploitable and more efficient, insofar as preserving the land made available surplus labor.[23] At this point, it is important to pay close attention to the collective nature of labor in this context, which represented work that actually belonged to the community. This refiguration of communal work reflected the intimate identification of production and reproduction, the joining together of working in the present to ensure the future of the community. It also disclosed the capability of the community to expand reproduction beyond the mere economic guarantees it offered, to include other aspects of social life, custom, ritual, religion, and culture. In the world described by Meillassoux, these spheres of activity have not yet been differentiated into semiautonomous domains of the social order, and this meant they were conceivably still vital to work. Meillassoux's perspective allowed the closing of the relationship between different kinds of work and other activities when he suggested that the labor power of the producer applied to "immediate sustenance," use-value, making it unassimilable to abstract labor. Just as the measure of time is irrelevant in those interludes, when the subsistence farmer enters the capitalist sphere, it is difficult to imagine that the abstraction of time and labor are not mediated by the conditions of the domestic mode in countless ways that require genuinely specific empirical research. We can only guess at the nature of life under these conditions, which, if made accessible, might permit making comparable identifications in the more distant past experience of capitalism's history. The complexity of these negotiations between past and present is so great that it seems obvious that the easier approach is merely to employ determinate stages wherein the old is replaced by the new in an endless narrative of progress.

Subsumption

While the anthropologist Claude Meillassoux examined the consequences of willful exploitation of labor under colonial and postcolonial circumstances, focusing on how the noncapitalist sphere was utilized in the form of supplying resources for the reproduction of African labor engaged in capitalist production, this crucial observation could be made of other instances where capitalism first established its production process. It was manifest in the early phases of capitalism in Japan, as Yamada Moritarō inadvertently revealed, and probably in all those regions where agriculture dominated the shape of social relationships and was preserved, as both Antonio Gramsci and Uno Kōzō noted, until that time when industry had sufficiently developed and was positioned to assimilate segments of the agrarian population into the industrial labor force. In the case of South Asia, this observation pointing to the realization of formal subsumption in a new register appeared only after decolonization, with the writings Kalyan Sanyal. Before Sanyal's intervention, historians of South Asia explored the terrain of nineteenth-century India searching for signs of the initial encounter of capital with domestic agricultural production (under colonial rule) and manifestations of capitalist practice. But most historians were willing to disavow and even understate what lay before them as nothing more than signs of semifeudalism, not necessarily evidence of an evolving capitalism. If the proponents of semifeudalism believed that dual or separate economies coexisted, they were also bound to be disappointed. With Jairus Banaji, a historian of comparative agriculture, we have one of the first attempts to construct an interpretative strategy directly capable of confronting the prospect of identifying formal subsumption and tracking its itinerary as it appeared in the nineteenth-century agricultural scene of the Indian Deccan region under the jurisdiction of British colonial administration. Banaji's intention targets the views of historians of a certain "tendency," who, he believes, misread the signs of capitalist development as reminders of precapitalist formations and proof of the continuation of semifeudalism. The very practices historians had denoted as intrinsic to feudalism or some variant of it, according to Banaji, disclosed what Marx had claimed as the way labor was formally subsumed by capital within a context of continuing "primitive accumulation." It is interesting to note that this study was carried out and published in the 1970s. Even though contemporary to Meillassoux's research, there is no indication that either knew of the other's work. It seems equally significant that these two accounts on India and Africa, produced virtually at the same time and concentrating on a colonial heritage after decolonization (even though Banaji's essays addressed the colonial nineteenth century) in the chronological postcolonial moment, came into view on the cusp of the discursive explosions of postcolonial strategies that moved away from political economic analysis toward preoccupations with irreducible cultural identities, stabilities, and the dismissal of history. The most extreme limit of the postcolonial critique was reached in the dismissal of history as simply another historicism that eliminated possibilities for entertaining "difference." Postcoloniality pursued a vocation that sought to replace the historicity of the colonial moment and its afterlife with a compensatory theory that shifted attention to memory, subjectivity, and singularized experience in the present as the basis for expectations of the future. It is unclear whether Banaji was responding to this shift or ignoring it in his magisterial essay "Capitalist Domination and the Small Peasantry: The Deccan Districts of the Nineteenth Century" (1977). What appears evident is the embedded nature of capitalist social relations in India as early as the nineteenth century, if not before, that were more deeply rooted in material life and practice than any discursive metanarrative of capitalism.

Banaji has concentrated on a critique of three more or less separate interpretative strategies, which had dominated Indian historiography on economic and agrarian history. At the time he wrote, these strategies on the Indian colonial endowment were destined to soon be overshadowed by postcolonial theory and its critical thrust against all complicities with Western metanarratives. Banaji apparently was uninterested in a perspective that authorized the importance of the "cultural dominant" and more attentive to how the received historiographical strategies had mishandled historical specificity by overlooking Marx's powerful formulations on the "logic" of all capitalist development. His principal critical objective was directed at Indian Marxists who clung to more doctrinaire positions that privileged a view of development as a form of "semifeudalism." Plainly lacking in these formulations of Indian Marxists was the suggestion of a developing capitalism in India and its intentions leading to the realization of the stage of a "bourgeois revolution."[24] Despite this historical impasse, Banaji pointed to political activists who had engaged in struggle against the bourgeois state and responded to forms of capitalist exploitation in the countryside. One immediately thinks of early Gramscians like Partha Chatterjee and Kalyan Sanyal's later *Rethinking Capitalist Development*, a work that cites discussions of the "neo-Gramscian" desire in India to implant the figure of a "passive revolution" rather than reproduce the singularity of the classic Jacobin model.[25] Although Sanyal does not go so far as to propose a "passive revolution" as the political analog of formal subsumption, he still favored the nonrevolutionary route. This preference suggests a configuration of an analytic prism through which to grasp the "maneuvers of capital vis a vis pre-capitalist forces" and the means by which they might be "captured."[26] With the neo-Gramscians, Sanyal was drawn to this nonrevolutionary route rather than to the more orthodox Marxian views of historical change recommending the modularity of England and France. While his critique of doctrinaire Marxism, disavowing the development of capitalist social relations, opened the path for a more productive discussion, it failed principally because of his refusal to consider Marx's own explanation of capitalism's developmental laws. Sanyal's commitment to "postcolonial" capitalism was too rooted in the irreducible promises of cultural exceptionalism, leavened by postcoloniality's misplacing of Marxism as another Western metanarrative coercively imposed on South Asia from the outside and reflecting the force of the colonial past.

Banaji identified a second "current" that had been more sensitive to the occurrence of capitalist relations in India, but this current also proved deficient because of its neglect of Marx. Finally, he considered the utility of "dependency theory" that was beginning to envision India as already incorporated into a capitalist world system characterized by bourgeois social relations. This he dismissed because of its "historical impressionism" and dearth of specificity.[27] Instead, Banaji turned to pursuing a course that successfully circumvented a more traditional Marxian reflex based on denying the emergence of capitalist development and forms of social relationships by summoning Marx's formulations on "formal subsumption" and the diverse ways capitalism was able to incorporate older practices and put them into the service of producing value. In spite of his willingness to concede that the practice of capitalist social relations remained recessive throughout nineteenth-century India, they could be nevertheless sighted, he maintained, in regions like the Deccan.

It is both a tribute to Banaji that he early sought to rescue Marx's important formulations concerning the logic of the production process and yet a mystery why so much of Marxism has continued to overlook their capacious utility in historical practice for identifying how the activity of subsumption fosters the production of unevenness. The principal objective of Banaji's critical intervention was to dispute a vulgate version of Marxian historiography in India until decolonization, which had classified the country as developing a variation of "semifeudalism." Historians had usually defined semifeudalism according to an inventory that consisted of "unlegal sharecropping system," operated by small tenant farmers sunk in permanent indebtedness, exploitation expressed by a combination of total landowners and money lenders who act as lenders to these small tenants and provide partial tenant access to the market.[28] Against this "standard" view, Banaji proposed that it was incorrect to have classified such features as signifying semifeudalism because they were considered as "incompatible" with what ordinarily has announced the entry of capitalist relations of production.[29] The decisive factor in reaching this conclusion was the presence of "sharecropping," which resembled a "feudal-type of exploitation" and the role it occupied in the institutional forms of production relations associated with the definition of semifeudal. But, as seen in our consideration of Wang Yanan and Yamada Moritarō, the classification of semifeudal encompassed a broad range of probabilities that already includes transmuted forms of capitalist and precapitalist practices. To suggest the prevalence of semifeudal circumstances of production already strongly implied the accompanying coextension of other forms of production practices, from which Banaji has drawn, pointing to the specific formative moment of commercial or merchant capitalism in India and its capture by traders and moneylenders who "played a decisive role in town and countryside."[30] There is another compelling reason that Banaji does not directly address that pertains to the historical status of feudalism in India. The utilization of categories like semifeudal involves the existence of some form of feudalism in India, even if truncated or immature, and therefore the accompanying progression of stages in the unfolding of modes of production. Moreover, it is difficult to imagine any kind of feudal form without bearing in mind the privileged place accorded to the category of transition, which promised to transport a society to capitalism. Indian Marxists who identified with the semifeudal perspective were conceivably drawn to a historiographical narrative dominated by the centrality of transition because it offered an exit from the feudal and entry into capitalism, eventually leading to the realization of socialism. In this regard, semifeudalism represented only a partial transitory state that still necessitated the enumeration of features they considered as integral to the definition. But if India had reached the halfway point of semifeudalism, what would the other half consist of—what mode of production(s) would join the semifeudal to make it whole and unified? What made it "semi"? By contrast, Japan possessed a recognizable feudal institutional experience, despite its failure to evolve into capitalism, whereas Chinese interpreters struggled to find a feudal parenthesis in China's long imperial history that originated in the pre–common era (the Western Zhou!) and whose elongated duration stretched out to the nineteenth century. If the concept of feudal itself were subsumed under the classification of tributary systems, the problem would have disappeared, only if the commitment to the defining "transition itself," the motor of modernity, was surrendered for other forms of passage capable of explaining the transformation from prior, precapitalist forms of production to capitalism. As for the Indian case, Marx was already on record for having discounted India's claim to a feudal stage when he rejected M. M. Kovalesky's promotion of this thesis. Despite Marx's reliance on Kovalesky's *Communal Landownership* (1879), the occurrence of feudal forms presumably introduced by the Muslim conquest, he rejected the proposition because Kovalesky had forgotten serfdom, evidence for which was absent in India.[31]

For Banaji, the problem posed by Indian historiography required clearing up the "erroneous conception of 'intervention in the process of production'"—that is, the necessity to investigate Marx's "views of the relationships in question." Banaji's complaints against Indian advocates of the semifeudalism argument recall for us the Japanese historiographical debate between the *kōzaha* and *rōnōha*, as the former, articulated by Yamada Moritarō, upheld "tenant farm rent" as incompatible with capitalism that reflected a residue of feudalism, in ways closely resembling the Indian Marxist rejection of "sharecropping," "bondage," or "moneylending" as manifestations of the irreconcilability of feudal relations with capitalism. This differed from the *rōnōha* presupposition that refused to count such residues as simply expressions of belated petrified forms. Rather they were able to situate them within what Uno described as "commodity-economic determinations."[32] In other words, they already belonged to the sphere of capitalism. Similarly, Banaji was bent on showing that these putative feudal emanations were folded into the "capitalist process" with India's gradual involvement in the emergent world market, the construction of a transport system, and the evolution of capitalists from the ranks of moneylenders and usurers. It is this acknowledgment that coaxed him to explore a system of production that existed in certain regions in nineteenth-century India that clearly qualified as capitalistic.[33] The relationships in place in the Deccan should not be viewed as instants of the "disintegration" of its small production economy before and after the 1860s "cotton boom," the evidence usually mobilized to explain "semifeudalism"; instead, such developments should be apprehended through the lens of Marx's formulations on formal subsumption and its diverse subforms. While this perspectival shift enabled Banaji to return to a Marx that seemingly was overlooked or ignored, it also significantly brought into focus Marx's forgotten "general rule" for all capitalist development.

Banaji's analysis was distinguished by "two stages in the historical process," whereby capital seizes prior labor practices and subordinates them to the creation of surplus value. The first is the formation of formal subsumption of labor to capital, and the second is the realization of "real subsumption," which refers to the completion of the commodity relation and capital's capacity to produce its own presuppositions, marking its installation as a mode of production. Formal subsumption occurs with the initial encounter of capital and the "small producer" and Marx's identification of the historical process of "so-called primitive accumulation," the moment when the received process of production is invaded and taken over without subjecting it to technical transformation.[34] It is also initially associated with the demand to extort "absolute surplus value," which necessitated lengthening the workday as much as possible. Even though real subsumption introduced the regime of "relative surplus value," depending more on the application of technological means, there is no reason to assume either that labor was less extorted or that exploitation lessened. Moreover, there is no additional grounds to suppose that forms of "absolute surplus" cannot coexist alongside the most technologically advanced production practices. This is not an argument Banaji would want to accept since he seems committed to actually separating capitalism itself into discrete stages in the forms of extortion and exploitation of small producers whose growing indebtedness to moneylenders for advanced loans made their agricultural output hostage to repaying interest. Marx, it should be recalled, renamed the payment of interest as surplus value. Although the appropriation enacted by formal subsumption, Banaji writes, may "develop outside the framework of a specific capitalist mode of production," Marx recognized on several occasions that even if or when labor has been suborned to the pursuit of value, it may just as likely remain intact as it was before. The distinguishing feature of formal subsumption lay in an unrestrained ability to appropriate prior labor practices at the same time as it took onboard the various forms of exploitation previously used to squeeze small producers. This capacity to take over older forms for the creation of value calls attention to how the bourgeois system sought to realize totalization by commanding elements it still lacked, presupposing the development of a totality that "consists precisely in subordinating all elements of society to itself, *or creating out of it organs which it still lacks. This is historically how it becomes a totality*."[35] In other words, the act of appropriating the near-at-hand for a new purpose required disguising it in such a manner as to make it appear it had sprung from capitalism instead of a prior history. But at the same time, capital was obliged to make it appear that nothing really had changed, except the "soul" of the worker, which remained out of sight. The conditions of labor were already available in this initial phase of capitalist development, and the historic process leading to the moment of transfer was not produced by capital, as such, but the antecedent historical presuppositions for it. Marx, here, is referring to availability of labor at "a certain level of skill, instrument as means of labour etc." in the first period of capital. What appears important is that this "historic process is not a product of capital but a presupposition for it."[36] Hence "production based on exchange value and the community based on exchanging value . . . all presuppose and produce the separation of labour from its objective conditions."[37] In this process, Marx pointed out that exchange of equivalents between buyer and seller "proceeds," but now this relationship constitutes only a "surface layer of a production which rests on the appropriation of alien labor without exchange but with the semblance of exchange." While this is founded on capital, "when it is regarded in isolation from capital, then it is a mere *illusion*, but a *necessary illusion*."[38] Behind it is the real relationship required by capitalism, which involved the appropriation of "alien labour" without exchange, whereby labor was severed from property and made to appear as if nothing really had changed. It was, I suspect, this domination of formal subsumption, its production of mystification, that induced the misrecognition of forms of exploitation as belonging to feudalism instead of capitalism, even though they had already found a place in the evolving capitalist mode of production. In this regard, Lenin had already revealed a glimpse of this process when he reminded populists that certain forms of handicraft industry did not represent a precapitalist mode of production but were, in fact, beginning to reflect capitalist principles. Neither Banaji nor the proponents against whom he directed his criticism had recognized this "model" of the logic of formal subsumption in *Grundrisse*, even though his analysis of the Deccan small producers clearly shows he understood how it operated.

Under the regime of real subsumption, all older forms are suspended. Banaji, here, has merely followed a stagist scenario (more on this later), where formal subsumption is replaced by a more advanced form. But we know that Marx was convinced that its logic possessed the capacity to express forms of production alongside capitalism or without it. When formal subsumption becomes identical to the capitalist production process and even supports the development of more advanced forms (real subsumption) and the "pure motion of capital itself," it can only be concluded that the real has dissolved the formal. However, it is difficult to imagine how appropriated elements that have become integral to capitalism are necessarily reproduced in succeeding registers to become "alien" to what they once had been part of. Banaji's response to this "paradox" is to argue that despite Marx's commitment to the logic of formal subsumption, he first observed that "real subsumption" replaces "formal subsumption."[39] Later he changed his mind. Marx never wrote that a replacement takes place but rather that a "transformation" of the labor process and its actual conditions occurs.[40] Yet a "transformation" does not automatically imply a successive move to a next stage or even the replacement and elimination of what had been subjected to a process of transformation. This explanatory attraction inspired by the logic of formal subsumption is both the great strength and the weakness of Banaji's analysis of the Deccan. Its power resides in its capacity to conserve and consider the importance of older, precapitalist practices used by capitalists; its weakness is mirrored in his decision to emplot this development as linear and stagist. Although Marx readily acknowledged how "real subsumption" chronologically followed "formal subsumption," this was not construed as the progressive march of stages but functioned only as an explanation of how the former "arose" in the context created by the latter. Banaji based his argument on the proposition that the general form—formal subsumption—is not adequately developed "because the labour process remains external to capital . . . and therefore the individual capitals are not bound together by any objective fragmented social interconnection. The labour process remains technically fragmented, or decentralised, whereas the pure movement of capital posits a centralisation of the social means of production and labour power."[41] Capitalism thus becomes capitalism only when it invades and occupies every pore of the social system and establishes a determinate mode of production proclaiming the installation of the industrial factory organization. Banaji joins all those Marxists who have eagerly and prematurely announced the realization of capitalism in order to get on to the next stage and, most important, the transition to socialism. Risking a certain circularity, this argument consigned the faint murmurings of capitalism's appearance to the regime of formal subsumption, fragmented, incomplete, unrealized, captive to small-scale production. This was the world of absolute surplus value, retaining its "small-scale individual character, or it is embodied by 'small capitalists who differ only slightly from the workers in their education and their activities.'"[42] To escape this apparent tautology, and the relentlessly progressive linearity characterizing this narrative, Banaji would have had only to accept the possibility that the two systems coexist, are co-eval, as Marx advised, and that even in Banaji's present and now we can easily point to the maintenance of regimes committed to absolute surplus value alongside those devoted to relative surplus value in countries like India and Britain, to name only two among many, where the last instance has not yet been reached. After all, why else was Marx prompted to declare that formal subsumption can coexist with or alongside the most developed forms of capitalist production?

Banaji's accounting of how "monied capitalists" in the Deccan were able to dominate and extort small cultivators in the effort to skim off surplus manifests one of the earlier examples of how the general rule's processes operated. In this scenario, merchants and usurers who became moneylenders still represented merchant or commercial forms of capitalism, who were able to exercise limited control over small cultivators' means of subsistence and what they produced, without dominating the immediate "process of production."[43] This was accomplished through their willingness to advance raw materials or instruments of production in return for repayment of high interest. In time, these budding capitalists acquired ownership of the cultivators' means of subsistence and output of seasonal production. Even before this recounting, Banaji brings to our attention a prevailing contextual configuration of unevenness composed of local, regional, and global markets. The Deccan had been hit by depression and sectional poor harvests. Accordingly, the crisis began to abate in the 1850s, and the expansion of the commodity economy had already started. Commodity production was initially concentrated on food grains for large local markets like Bombay and Poona. Later, the expansion was overtaken by a "boom" in cotton production, which moved all prices upward on the global market. At the same, this development began to reflect changes in the division of labor in the Deccan and the increase of arable of land to create a veritable "commercial revolution" by the end of the century.[44] "Thus," Banaji writes, "the commodity economy was the basic premise of the revenue-system, just as the expansion of the market formed . . . the nucleus of its programme of 'civilising' the country, that is, introducing the bourgeois mode of production."[45] In addition, commodity expansion meant the transmutation of labor power into a commodity and, along with it, the transformation of small cultivators into wage earners now serving capital, in short, "proletarianized." For small cultivators, the crush of paying assessments plunged large numbers into the immiseration of deeper "indebtedness," an exploitation accelerated by the state-exacerbated famine in the late 1870s, ruining large numbers of subsistence producers.

Banaji's susceptibility to the lure of stagism, signaled by his emphasis on the moment of formal subsumption, reflects a willingness to overlook in the category its status as a form rather than a limited historical stage or even a duration situated in a larger trajectory. While inclined toward noticing instances of unevenness reflected in the formation of multiple markets and in the process of making small producers into wage laborers, his larger narrative faithfully follows a linear and progressive temporality. Frequently in Banaji's plot there appears a reference to a larger narrative of capitalist development, acclaiming the emergence of the world market and economy, which allowed distancing the concrete *particularity* of capitalist development in the Deccan from the "deeper context of an expanding capitalist world economy," existing "alongside" it.[46] He is right to emphasize particularity, its instantiation of the specific forms of capitalist development wherever it established its production process. However, its juxtaposition with a wider referent raises the problem of a relationship between the two contextual orders of local and global and the resulting uneven relationship they produce. In his critique of the Andre Gunder Frank–Immanuel Wallerstein conception of world-system theory, Banaji suggested that world capital is a general determination that managed to dissolve the "concrete processes by which capitalists relations evolved . . . in the abstract identity of world-capitalism."[47] Yet, this "world economy" constituted both a general referent or wider context and one that represented the end point—possibly conforming to the category authorizing the world of "late capitalism"—and a corresponding stagism, an all-encompassing abstraction that will assimilate all claims to particularity and temporal location. It is best embodied today in the advanced forms of finance capital, which, as I have suggested earlier, seem more tolerant of older practices and have no need to eliminate them. It is this broader conception of a stagism that Banaji's narrative has inflected in the developmental phases observed in parts of the Deccan.

As a form, formal subsumption continued as the general rule of the capitalist process, exercising a capacity to exceed historical closure demanded by stagism (and, as we shall see, Dipesh Chakrabarty's dreaded "historicism"). Similarly, Banaji, I believe, disregarded the difference in times between a capitalism that had to wait for the elimination of feudal fetters in England's fifteenth and sixteenth centuries and one that, through the agency of a later colonialism in the nineteenth century, was a more advanced or mature form. Moreover, the belated nature of capitalist development resulted in the coextensive implementation of formal subsumption with more advanced practices in the capitalist mode of production. In fact, the colonial circumstances sharply reinforced the utilization of older labor practices and surely encouraged resituating them within a process now seeking to generate surplus value with more recent technological innovations that would contribute to the further centralization and integration of operations within the mode of production. Even though the colonial economy may have inflected a less developed form of capitalism, as Banaji asserts, it was still largely in the hands of colonizers who represented a mature capitalist system and whose own policies of domination often worked to benefit domestic capitalists as they deepened the indebtedness of small cultivators. What the colonial situation openly revealed was the simultaneity of the "formal subsumption of labour . . . as a *particular* form alongside the specifically capitalist mode of production in its developed form."[48] In this connection, Banaji elsewhere granted that it was in the "backward countries subjugated to world economy as colonies that the process of mediation of capitalist . . . relations of production by archaic (precapitalist) forms of subjection of labour assumed historically unprecedented dimensions."[49] I would further add that this was true of all countries classified as "latecomers" and illustrated the case Marx already recorded in his letters to Vera Zasulich: "If the admirers of the capitalist system in Russia deny that such a combination (of the traditional peasant commune with modern technology) is possible, let them prove that Russia had to undergo an incubation period of mechanical production in order to make use of machinery! Let them explain to me how they managed, in just a few days, as it were, to introduce the machinery of exchange (banks, credit companies, etc.), which was the work of centuries in the West?"[50] Banaji was already alerted to the presence of new forces of production in India, despite its colonial status. The same could be said of China and parts of Africa. Many new technological and infrastructural developments like the construction of a system of railroads and transport and their proximity to market towns and later larger centers of population and a communication network of telegraph lines added as much to the centralization of the state as it did to the advancement of capitalism through forms of exploitation.[51]

Accordingly, Deccan capitalist wealth was dominated by usurers, merchants, shopkeepers and lesser handlers of money capital, and protobankers, who were engaged in fostering the circulation process in a system where industrial capital remained on the horizon. The penetration and expansion of commodity production provided the premise for continuing state exploitation. For the British, it proved beneficial to have this expansion "mediated through the interventions of the monied capitalists."[52] Peasants, who comprised the immediate owners of commodity production, would receive advances, in view of acquiring greater indebtedness, caused by bad crop years and the pressure exerted on waning resources allotted for subsistence. In return, the peasants were obliged to repay their creditors the whole crop to cover the exorbitant interest charged for the loan. Peasant indebtedness ended in loss of control over reproduction; repayment represented a form of surplus value that went to the creditor. Even when the debts were repaid, the small cultivators would still be deprived of the necessary means of subsistence and reproduction for the next growing cycle and fall deeper into a vicious circle of dependency.[53]

The same process of commodity production invaded larger towns in the region, and the proletarianizing observed in the countryside began to affect "smaller artisans."[54] Moneylenders took possession of handloom weavers, extending to them advances for necessary materials, means of production like silk and yarn that triggered the taking over of the product as repayment. This problem was exacerbated by the rise in subsistence costs in the Deccan towns spurred by the development of railroads, as well as increasing demand stimulated by times of scarcity and famine.[55] Recalling comparable circumstances in Europe's late Middle Ages, Banaji adds that the "monied capitalists would be compelled to intensify the rate of exploitation of household labour, producing more absolute surplus value,"[56] an experience that unfolded in nineteenth-century Japan as well, once industrialization started and the "medieval villages" and household manufacturing were increasingly attached to a money economy. Banaji reminded his adversaries that "downgrading" the appearance of capitalist relations in India meant disavowing the "prevalence of capitalist forms of exploitation," "however undeveloped the stage of bourgeois production . . . they express."[57] He is correct to label this denial as a contradiction that flies in the face of Marx's proposition that "formal subsumption of labour under capital . . . can be found as a *particular* form alongside the specifically capitalist mode of production in its developed form, because although the latter entails the former, the *converse does not necessarily obtain*." But, in this instance, Banaji appears to be emphasizing the importance of how formal subsumption does not need real subsumption even though real subsumption requires formal subsumption. Banaji continues: "That is to say, the formal subsumption of labour under capital can be found even in the absence of the developed form of the capitalist mode of production positing large-scale industry, social forces of production, etc."[58] What Marx was explaining and actually emphasizing by this parenthetic passage was only that formal subsumption did not need real subsumption. Actually the thrust of the passage proposes that with formal subsumption the particular form can be found alongside the capitalist mode of production in its *developed* form and, at the same, in its absence.[59] It is hard know what has shadowed this move apart from Banaji's desire to reinforce the stagist character of formal subsumption and to reinforce its historical closure to open the way for its succession by a developed mode of production announcing the stage of real subsumption. Much of Banaji's admirable analysis is shackled to the conviction that formal subsumption was "a stage of development" observed in the Deccan, which would have remained constrained by its historical moment and presumably surpassed by more developed forms. But this conviction is contradicted by Banaji's own acknowledgment of the flexibility of the form and Marx's silence on its supposed function in a progressive historical trajectory. To ignore its capacity to coexist alongside whatever specifically developed capitalism instead of becoming a relic reminder of a passed historical moment not only misses Marx's own recommendation but also ignores the role of the form in producing unevenness and its ability for disturbing the claims of temporal linearity split up by distinct stages (and transition). Separating formal subsumption from developed capitalism as discrete stages produces imaginary "historical situations," whereby the absence of a "capitalist mode of production on a national scale" will still enable the wide-scale establishment of dominant capitalist relations of exploitation and authorize the inclusion of "preformal" forms, which will lead to formal subsumption. The script for this scenario proposes that the "monied capitalist would gain control over the entire means of subsistence and production of this enterprise," thus constraining reproduction of the production process to a dependence on the availability of advances. The small producer still nominally controls his "means of subsistence" but would be subjected to intense capitalist exploitation. What is interesting about resuscitating distinctions Marx apparently

224 COLONIAL/POSTCOLONIAL

took little notice of is that it permits Banaji to supply yet another "stage" to
the stage represented by formal subsumption, which he, not Marx, has
named "preformal": a prestage that would be succeeded by a more advanced
moment of subsumption in a moving and linear trajectory. Any appeal to the
figuration of stages consisting of starts and stops commits analysis to a larger
conception of time and the certain path of its movement toward the realization of a final goal whose futural destination must remain abstract. In his
essay "Modes of Production in a Materialist Conception of History," moreover, published in the same year as his essay on the Deccan (1977), Banaji
condemned "the linear notion of historical time" as a "subsidiary characteristic of vulgar historical materialism."[60] Reliance on stagism can lead only
to a linear trajectory. Banaji's observation concerning the particularity of
capitalist development, its singularity and specificity, and the abstract temporality of world capitalism assimilating and effacing these evolved differences is of inestimable importance. Such assimilation ends in subordinating
the historicity of local development, already a mixture of different practices
imprinted with their historical times, to a relentless linearity that will over-
ride the differences and their times. Because of this insight, it is necessary
to examine what kind of temporality he would consider once Marxism is
released from the abstract categories of linear, stagist, and progressive time
that became the vocation of a "vulgar historical materialism" and an alternative to bourgeois modernization theory in the Cold War struggle.

Banaji sidesteps considerations of historical time for actively intervening
in arguments of an earlier generation that concentrated on the status of modes
of production and whether colonialism was constituted of dual economies
or represented an incipient capitalism. Specifically, this discussion revolved
around the axis of an "entrenched" tradition in Marxism that addressed the
following situation: circumstances where modes of production that coexisted with capital were diminished in importance and reduced to the rank
of "'specific' forms of subjugation of labour" demanded by "industrial accumulation" rather than actively participating in expanding commercial
activity. Put in another way, the issue involved determining, within a world
economy, whether coexisting modes of production functioned in a subordinate position to industrial capitalism as reservoirs of subjugated labor exploited when the need arose, "deprived of their own laws of motion, vege-
tating on the periphery of an industrialising Europe like a vast reserve of

labour power."[61] It is not my purpose to enter into this now distant contro-versy but only to call forth Banaji's preoccupation with the modes(s) of pro-duction and its consequences for considerations of historical time. His deci-sion to emphasize problems related to modes of production shifted his inquiry away from reflections on time, despite his dismissal of linearity, for space; that is to say, his analysis of how small cultivators in India's Deccan were subjected to an evolving capitalism, through the agency of formal sub-sumption, and his critical views on the mode of production and the eager-ness of interpreters to identify these figures with specific social formations spoke directly to the colonial situation. Both his essay on the Deccan and his larger concern with the mode of production made it clear why he backed off from envisaging colonies as examples of dual economies or imagined colo-nial history as representing a specific colonial mode of production. Rather, he saw the simple independent commodity production of the traditional-patri-archal systems maintaining its identity yet mediating the establishment of capitalist social production—an operation necessitating the "necessary illu-sion" of the form, as Marx affirmed, to remain intact as if it was still embed-ded in the older mode of production when it was already dominated by capi-talism. According to Banaji, this was particularly true of colonialism and was manifest in the "crystallization" of economies throughout much of the colonial world, as displayed by the disregard for capitalism's appetite for tak-ing over what it found useful.[62] Stopping short of this, the mutation of tem-poral forms occasioned by capital's logic of development meant casting the complex mix of times into the straitjacket of linear and stagist time, the so-cial time marked by clock and calendar that would designate only the repeti-tive moments of capital's circuit from production to reproduction. It would additionally invite the identification of the mode of production with the fixed countenance of space—a timeless void filled with space, which is what happened with postcolonial theory, once it was vocalized in the writings of Kalyan Sanyal and Dipesh Chakrabarty.

Postcoloniality and the Cultural Dominant

Both thinkers posited the formation of a timeless, spatial mode of produc-tion, which Kalyan Sanyal named as "postcolonial" and Dipesh Chakra-barty identified with the larger abstract temporality of modernity, what he eventually envisioned as an "alternative modernity." Sanyal's purpose was to show how capital in India produced precapitalism instead of exceeding it, whereas Chakrabarty envisioned the possibility of an authentic "history" and temporality within capitalism capable of escaping the domination of abstract labor. Unlike Banaji, both were willing to ignore the possibilities offered by the operation of formal subsumption in order to see in it something else, such as a process unaffected by capitalism. By misrecognizing the operation of formal subsumption and its appropriation of what it considered useful from the precapitalist past, each would transmute historically derived practices into ahistorical components of an irreducible cultural essence that defied both history's and time's erosions and asymmetries.

What Sanyal and Chakrabarty shared was an antipathy for the stain of "historicism," a contamination so corrosive that it impelled each to disconnect the precapitalist experience from its succeeding stage of capitalist development. It was a common strategy grounded in identifying Marx with precisely the vulgate discourse of historical materialism Banaji went to such great effort to put into question. Nevertheless, both seemed to agree on capital's reliance on noncapitalism—for Sanyal, a Luxemburgian reading of the relationship between capitalism and its outside, what he named as a "wasteland" that put into question capitalism's claim to universality. In this scenario, capitalism arose from the refuse of primitive accumulation rather than from its logic of accumulation that the capitalist will directly need to sustain its continuity.[63] This wasteland of dispossession, accordingly, supplied the site targeted for development. But it is one mediated by a logic derived from postcolonial circumstances (not colonial history). Sanyal's principal concern was to liberate Third World (postcolonial) economies from the constraint imposed on them from the outside by historicism and stagism, with their historical hinge supplied by the category of "transition," which, he believed, was at the heart of Western Marxism. The problem that generated this desire to eliminate stagism and the central role performed by transition dedicated to facilitating movement from one destination to the next was a misplaced version of Marxism, which Sanyal, along with many others, perceived as simply a Western imposition to coerce and corral the authentic historical experience of India and Third World countries into a narrative compound not of their own making. Beyond this, his scheme to rid the Third World of the "curse" of historicism raised the question of time and history he never addressed. The very decision to identify primitive accumulation and noncapital in the postcolonial world orchestrated a collision of different, multiple times, which Sanyal failed to notice in his preference for seeing the postcolonial mode of production as an exceptional spatial expression excluding time and history.

It was the postcolonial impulse to exceptionalize culture exemplified in Dipesh Chakrabarty's discourse that paradoxically led to restoring the privilege of the West. This desire grew out of an early work on labor history that concentrated on jute mill workers in Bengal: *Rethinking Working-Class History: Bengal 1890 to 1940*. The purpose of the book was to show that when Marx assigned to the working class the role of history's agent, he also implied that since the worker, as one of the personifications of capitalism (but not quite like the capitalist, actually the personification of labor in the capital-labor dyad, according to Marx), belonged to a class situated within bourgeois social relationships.[64] The argument depended on the conviction that as long as the worker had internalized a "formal freedom," quoting Marx, that was "realized" by a "a real person" and not an abstraction, he was competent to engage in exchange. But in the context of this passage, Marx is not necessarily speaking of the laborer as wage earner but only as the owner of labor power, whereby "he sells the particular expenditure of force to a particular capitalist, whom he confronts as an independent *individual*." Marx clearly recognized that "this is not his relation to the existence of capital as capital, i.e., the capitalist class,"[65] acknowledging that this circumstance changes once the worker is incorporated into the wage form and the matrix of abstraction. The passage is really concerned with the initial moment the worker sells his labor power, after which the relationship changes and thereafter is mediated by the force of law supporting the capitalist. The idea of formal freedom may have been enjoyed by precapitalist workers, who were members of the guild, but Chakrabarty's jute mill workers belong to a capitalist factory organization, not a medieval artisanal guild. Marx described the distinction in the following way: "labour as *use-value* for capital . . . is not the character of the craftsmen and guild members," and labour related to capitalism "loses all the characteristics of art" as it becomes more abstract and mechanical.[66] By overlooking these distinctions, Chakrabarty is able to propose that capitalist organization cannot be envisioned apart from the role played by bourgeois—that is, English—culture. We know that Marx used

England only as an example, as he put it, and that a good deal of his writing was not insensitive to the mediating force of local and received cultures. This move permits Chakrabarty to demonstrate how a "particular working class— the jute mill workers of Calcutta—" belonged not to a "bourgeois society" but rather to a precapitalist one, whose cultural experience would affect the status of "discipline," "authority," "solidarity," and "organization" differently in the constitution of an Indian working class by fostering received forms of consciousness and solidary relationships.[67] While the point here is to show that the universalist claims associated with categories like capital and labor "offer no master narrative of the history of 'consciousness' or 'culture,'" Chakrabarty has reinvented the operation of formal subsumption without naming it as such. In a later essay, as I will show, he rejects the concept because of its historicist and stagist contamination. The work on the jute mill workers is rich with examples of how precapitalist cultural practices and habits intermingle with the operations on the shop floor to continue playing a vital role in a modern capitalist workplace in India. This sensitivity to the combining of old labor practices with religious customs with new procedures in the factory signifies an exemplary instance of what might be found in any number of the world's regions where capitalism had established its program of production. Where this interpretation falters is its failure to recognize that these received cultural practices not only were found useful to capitalism's process of production and pursuit of capitalist value but were also undoubtedly subordinated to the new demands and were often altered to meet the new requirements. By the same token that the guild worker bore no resemblance to the wage earner, the wage earner was vastly different from the skilled artisan; they belonged to systems as different as art and economics, as Marx suggested.

What has troubled writers like Chakrabarty has been both the stigma of unevenness that has classified societies like India as underdeveloped and the projection of claims of universalism that have been forcibly imposed on different temporal regimes and cultural experiences, compelling them, as Amilcar Cabral would have said, to live in another's historical regime. These societies exemplified determined efforts to avoid the burden of sharing a compulsory unitary resemblance that capitalism frequently demanded as imperatives of its production processor. Modern social science in the West has usually followed a Weberian scenario that has reduced forms of cognition and conduct to the determination of a specific cultural endowment made up of elements of the Judeo-Christian religious traditions. Western economic rationality has come to be seen as the result of a specific cultural experience. Yet it could be equally argued that cultural experience is mediated by specific modes of production, which are foremost constituted of certain conceptions of time and temporal organization related to how production and reproduction are carried out in social formations. If the former—Weberian strategy—is employed, it leads to culturalism as an *actant* and privileges a static spatial countenance, whereas the latter assigns culture in the social formation to the register of a practice among others integrated into the temporally oriented processes of work, production, and reproduction. In this connection, it should be recognized that labor time is "the site of an opposition between abstraction of dead labour and the concreteness of living labour, between homogeneous duration and variable landscape."[68] With Chakrabarty, as shall see, there is the Marxian abstract time of labor, which is temporalized in the present, and a Heideggerian conceptualization that sees time temporalized in the future, anticipating and authenticating Being's itinerary toward death.[69] Armed with this sense of a duality of times, Chakrabarty is able to posit the coexistence of abstract time and valorize a specific cultural moment manifest as "historical difference," emerging from within capital logic itself. The former is called "History I" and represents the abstractions associated with capital, especially the agency of abstract labor and time, which also includes the idealistic theories of the Enlightenment relating to the individual; the latter, "History II," stems from subjective immediacy of the world of social reality. This failure of History I to totalize represented the incapacity of abstract labor (time) to completely assimilate forms of work and make them fully correspond to satisfying socially necessary labor, leaving open the possibility of what Bruno Gulli, after Marx, has called "living labor," that is, "labor returning to itself."[70] This should not be taken to simply mean a juxtaposition or opposition between idealism and materialism, since the action of culture, as such, involves claims to materiality, as much as a society organized on the basis of production is implicated in all kinds of activities that involve the nonmaterial and idealities. But it should be noted that extracting historical difference from abstract labor simply reflected Heidegger's move to excavate Being's temporality from an inauthentic everyday ordinary time.

In this sense, Chakrabarty is right to worry about how singularities in the "life-world" become grist for sociological generalities and lose something in the translation. Yet the category of the life-world or everyday, as it was called in different societies, a temporal concept with spatial properties performing as a chronotope, might offer a more modest unit as candidate for comparability. As for the claims of History II, it should be recognized that it is based on Being's historicality, which is actually prior to the production of history itself. Such historicality risked permanent and stationary immobility since it reflected Being in its primordial authenticity. It is interesting to note in this bifurcation a kinship with Walter Benjamin's division between *innere Erfahrung* and *Erleben*, where the former signifies a deeper experience mediated by memory and thought while the latter refers to more immediate experiences encountered in everyday life.

As I suggested, Chakrabarty's search for historical difference focused on how the central capitalist category of abstract labor split into irreparable contradiction that opened the way for the possible appearance of difference. The point was to show that mature capitalism, as represented by the reign of "abstract labor," disassembled in the face of a basic indeterminacy. Clearly, Chakrabarty was resorting to a strategy premised on the certainty that any textual claim to unity and coherence veiled an inherent instability and therefore invited the imperative to make visible its undecidability. Yet this deconstructionist strategy was an attempt to show that real subsumption had not totalized everything. What is interesting about this move is Chakrabarty's assumption that subsumption and its completion is the problem and that his discovery of difference within a totalizing abstraction of labor time spares it from this fate. The problem with this attempt to move from within capitalism rather than from the perspective of its outside is that it seeks to recover an irreducible cultural wholeness that would be haunted by the same ghost of indeterminacy. It also both projects a desire to show how capitalism's claim to realizing a totalizing and seamless coherence by eliminating traces of older forms of life fails to conceal its incapacity to achieve completion and hazards approval of a conservative political impulse in its valorization of the enduring and unchanging power of cultural tradition. In a sense this strategy resembles, in more sophisticated form, the earlier attempt by Chinese and Japanese to discount Western technology as mere utility that would have no effect on the capacity of a traditional ethical endowment to persist, even though it was capable of adopting from an alien culture. It is particularly odd to assume that capitalism has realized the state of real subsumption and the completion of the commodity relation in India. If it is difficult to know what logic has encouraged Chakrabarty to reach this conclusion, it is even more puzzling to explain why he bypassed the logic of formal subsumption, which remained within the precinct of capital, through which he could have achieved the same result in teasing out moments of difference.

Chakrabarty's main target has been historicism, which, for him and many others, has relativized all certainties in its way, leveling all heterogeneous temporalities in its path and erasing the material remnants of histories that either did not lead to the emergence of capitalism or were incorporated into its matrix to lose their temporal identities.[71] This is particularly true of conceptions of historical unevenness, which are recuperated for historicism as instances of the necessity of fixing a stage in a trajectory of catching up rather than witnessing the coexistence or co-evality of different temporalities. Chakrabarty's arguments here rest on understating how Marx envisaged the conduct of formal subsumption: instead of seeing it as a form rather than a chronologically measured stage in the development of capitalism, he has proceeded to the more mature status of real subsumption, that is, the final achievement of the commodity relation. In this way, he has, I believe, recuperated the most extreme forms of "Western Marxism" and its claim that capitalism has occupied every aspect of everyday life.

In carrying out this maneuver, he has separated the "historicist transition" from the earlier stage. But this "historicist" emplotment is a fantasy and has little to do with Marx's formulation. The argument has been built on an obsessive acceptance of a Cold War caricature of Marx that relies on Second Internationalist "stage theory" supplemented with Stalinist revisions based on the itinerary of development extracted from European history. As a form, formal subsumption is not constrained to a specific moment that will be succeeded by a more advanced form once its productivity is played out but rather possesses the capacity to accompany that process and interact with it at any time in its development. And because it does not necessarily lead to a more mature "stage," it cannot be consigned to the category of "transition" to provide the necessary bridge to a fuller capitalism that will be enlisted as evidence of historicism. For Chakrabarty, the "remnants" he identifies as feudal survivors, which are in reality historical temporal forms in the present, become instances reminding him of backwardness, usually associated with the Third World, and thus recall the stain of a permanent stigma that equates difference with unevenness and inferiority, without considering that both have been manifest everywhere, despite the ideological claims of Western developmentalist theories of makeover. In a sense, his critique of historicism ends up reaffirming its putative veracity. His rejection of the "remnants" as historical temporal forms as merely residues of historicism works to bolster the very historicism he seeks to overcome by affirming its significance within the historical itinerary of stagism rather than its relationship to a form—formal subsumption—that had always managed to exceed the history generating its specific moment.

What Chakrabarty is pointing to are "antecedents" of capital, which do not perform the labor of contributing to capitalism's "own life-process."[72] At the same time, he argues that anything that does not contribute to productive labor and thus to the instrumentalization of creating surplus value echoes the faint audibility of another past and experience that offers the guarantee of an unchanging space of freedom and enjoyment as relief in the dour world of capitalist calculation and sameness. But if "abstract labor" has been the condition of "unfreedom," then its really radical other, that is, radical difference, would be the freedom of living labor, the prospect of returning labor to itself, which means exceeding the deadening constraints imposed by real subsumption and not returning to home, to "one's native place," as Japanese folklorists dreamed of reaching. It is hard not to conclude that the rescuing of these antecedent pasts simply represents another form of bourgeois romanticism promising the "fullness" Marx had already unveiled in *Grundrisse*.[73] With his mining expedition, Chakrabarty aims to bring to the surface the figure of historical difference from an undecidability lurking in the depths of abstract labor; perhaps a more correct description of this is to make reappear a veiled contradiction that was always there. We can assume from his prior work on Bengali jute mill workers that capitalist practices were already installed in factories alongside older practices and conventions that belonged to past modes of production. In this earlier study, there is no reason to assume that Chakrabarty has proposed the achievement of real subsumption. In his later reflections he has somewhat changed his mind, now convinced that the empowerment of capital logic and especially the sovereignty of abstract labor is so great that the signs of difference have been eliminated. In this endeavor, he has simply homogenized both the West and its other, in this case India, in its difference. To make the argument, Chakrabarty actually overstates the power of abstract labor by making it the great leveler of all differences. But in his earlier work he had acknowledged an arrangement of labor (ratified in other essays) that clearly showed that while wage labor and commodification existed, it was accompanied and mediated by the utilization of other, nonlabor practices related to religion (culture) that were clearly important to the workers and, in some cases, must have come from an earlier moment when they were considered integral to and inseparable from their work. Chakrabarty could have focused on the regime of formal subsumption rather than presuming an all-consuming and conquering commodity form and come up with the same argument rather than a circuitous exposition of how abstract labor fails to conceal its undecidability to make room for historical difference produced by the indeterminacy informing it. The conduct of formal subsumption introduces abstraction in the labor process with the exchange of labor capacity for wages, yet it also diminishes this process by taking over practices it finds in the subsequent process of reproducing them. The very space for historical difference Chakrabarty wants to squeeze out of abstract labor is already present in the process of formal subsumption and the contradiction he sees in abstract labor is at its core. With this in view, he could have redeemed historical difference by starting from the historical itself instead of the full maturation of the commodity form encased by abstract labor. The problem with starting from the category of abstract labor and its corresponding presumption of real subsumption is that it allowed him to relate back to the image of an abstract human supposedly produced by the Enlightenment, which may or may not be some qualitative figure possessing rights, who serves as a template for Marx's conceptualization of wage labor. This move led to Chakrabarty's rejection of capital's claim to universalism. But these are really different impulses generating his discourse. It may well be that he has also inflated the claims associated with universalism in the effort to rescue difference for cultural identity, what he described as "a politics of human belonging and diversity" residing within Marx's analysis of capital.[74] Diversity was already present in Marx's analytic, but human belonging—the quest for home— comes from Heidegger and a turmoil-ridden Weimar Germany seeking a way to return to "home." Chakrabarty announced that he wanted to put Marx and Heidegger into a "conversation," but I am afraid the interlocutors are really talking past each other. The difference was too great: Marx was concerned with a temporality that derived from the present, from the activity of labor itself, whereas Heidegger conceived of a temporality that came from the future; Marx secularized everyday time, while Heidegger "resacralized" time as Being's destiny toward death; and the authentic "historicality of Being" could not be conflated with the movement of class struggle.[75] The identification of an "abstract human" with "abstract labor" simply is a mis-identification of Marx, while equating Heidegger's quest for "home' as an expression of universalism needs further explanation that must take into account a fundamental differentiation between the universal and the unitary.

It is entirely likely that Chakrabarty wanted to retain Marx at the same time he wished to hang on to "difference" because the resistance it makes possible is, rightly, "something that can happen only *within* the time horizon of capital, and yet it has to be thought of as something that disrupts the unity of that time."[76] But that disruption of time introduced by the intervention and co-evality of another temporality—the fracturing of the historical present—is what defined the conduct of the form of formal subsumption from the outset, constituted of the inventory of historical presuppositions and antecedents that lay behind capitalism. The very unevenness formal subsumption introduced into every present already signaled the continuing disunity of time. The history that embodied that possibility of temporal heterogeneity was repressed by capital logic and ultimately displaced to a national time and its commitment to serial homogeneity, which was simply another form of repetition. It would appear periodically in times of crisis to dramatize the unevenness of relations, between and within nations, but it has always been made to appear manifest only in the world beyond Euro-America as a signature of underdevelopment, which has become the mirror of our collective nature, present and future. As I suggested earlier, Lukács already envisioned contradictions of unevenness when he recognized that the proletariat was still capable, despite being enmeshed in the objective conditions of manual labor, to resist reification in their soul and save their humanity.[77] The difference was not going back to a home that never existed but moving in time to one that has yet to be reached.

AFTERWORD

world history and the everyday

By way of a concluding afterword, I would like to draw attention to at least two consequences of the narrative I have presented in this study. Postcolonialism, in a certain sense, represents the end of the quest that had been a genuinely internationalist movement preoccupied with the classical concerns of the founders of historical materialism and its focus on labor and the conduct of capitalism's developmental process as it encountered regional and local circumstances over diverse moments since the nineteenth century. With postcolonialism's return to the cultural dominant and the singularity of culture regions came a lessening concern for both the production process, which remained capitalistic despite its "Western" associations, and the reduction of internationalism to a new provincialism. The turn to the program of an "alternate modernity" forfeited the earlier possibilities for worldliness and foreclosed the prior concern for political economy for considerations of culture. In this regard, postcoloniality paradoxically resembled a distant inheritor of the legacy of Western Marxism, insofar as it turned Marxian-derived strategies inward (and away from Marxism) toward contemplating the uniquely irreducible character of specific cultural endowments.

When the chronicler of Western Marxism Perry Anderson observed how historical materialism had failed principally because of the defeat of the working classes and the subsequent disappearance of "confidence" and "optimism" of the founders, compounded by a "weariness" prompted by the recognized loss of universalistic aspirations, he proposed that it was time to undertake an imminent criticism of its own history. His recommendation was for historical materialism to revive its "full powers" in order to overcome the debilitating parochialism that had already conspired to undermine its best purpose.[1] Anderson sadly acknowledged it had yet to recover these powers—which he described in a later book that seemed to celebrate a Marxian revival dedicated to a renewed critical analysis of contemporary capitalism, offering a more hopeful forecast of its future.[2] But it seems to me that what this renewal lacked was precisely what the older "Western Marxism" overlooked when it responded to defeat by drawing back to make a provincial culture serve as a universal standard for the rest of the world to follow. In this respect, Western Marxism owed more to Max Weber's cultural analysis than it was willing to admit, inasmuch it was promoting a unique cultural configuration as a model of imitation. My argument in this study has been that such a revival was always available, even when it appeared that the state was not going to wither away, imprinted in all those efforts on the "periphery" of the industrial West that sought to make sense of their time and place through the prism provided by Marx and Engels. The revived efflorescence of Marxism that Anderson reported in his book *In the Tracks of Historical Materialism* (1983) was occurring at the high point of the Cold War and served as much to fortify the cultural unity of the West as it did to call critical attention to its deficiencies. Whatever else the moment of revival meant, Anderson's accounting of it enlisted examples exclusively from Europe, the United States, and Great Britain but remained silent on the world outside this "unity." After the collapse of the Berlin Wall and the mercurial speed with which new economies emerged in China, India, Brazil, and South Korea trumpeting the triumph of a globalized neoliberalism, the move toward culture, especially in consumption, was even more observable. This particular emphasis was adorned by appeals to cultural exceptionalism as explanations for the success of these newer capitalist economies, a strategy pioneered years earlier by Japan. Despite postcoloniality's rejection of capitalism's imposed domination in India, its recommendations never resulted in its disestablishment or even the suggestion of some new economic form but instead led to recruiting arguments based on the power of cultural uniqueness to account for meteoric success that was instrumentalized by some kind of bureaucratic politics easing the way and masking the burden of greater unevenness, inequality, and environmental destruction.

The second consequence of this study has been directed to showing how these various encounters between local and a worldly capitalism produced the possibility of what Marx called "world history" linked to the everyday. This too seems also to have been eventually trumped by neoliberalism. When Marx raised the prospect of the formation of a genuine world history, as an alternative to a Hegelian universalist history, he emphasized the importance of transmuting a purely "local being" into a "universal being" that would lead to the universalization of the particular and the localization of the universal. Much of this shift away from Hegel's philosophy of history was occasioned by the expanding formation of the world market already in process of establishing a complex network of communications, economy, and "intercourse" binding regions to it—in other words, a real, material history that was already being enacted and lived on a world scale. Unlike Hegel's universalistic history, Marx placed great stress on the importance of local roots and the reasons they no longer could remain isolated and secluded from the world at large. Yet, as we have seen, the universalism of capitalism was already tinted in combined tones by its retention and incorporation of older forms of life and practices put to use in the production process. The world of capitalism may have constituted a worldly and universal referent, but it was by no means unitary, since it comprised multiple developmental routes mediated by their local circumstance, histories, and times by which such a process was carried out. In other words, the world of capitalism was already a world made up of regions seeking their own capitalist development.

One of the principle ways that tightened the connection between local and universal came with the reorganization of time into the workday, with its remainder becoming what is known as the everyday. If initially the workday, with its complex averaging of necessary labor time, synchronized the largest portion of the twenty-four-hour day, its leftover was filled with heterogeneous practices and uneven and untimely temporalities, nonsynchronisms amid a social life based on a new conception of contemporaneity dominated by work routinized by clock and calendar. This remainder, constituting the flashpoint of struggle between capitalism, which always sought to lengthen the hours of work, and workers, who tried to shorten them, was seen by Marx as necessary "disposable time," when workers would reproduce their labor power, resort to pleasures, and even raise themselves culturally. In this way, the "local being" to which Marx referred was transformed into the everyday—the time and place of work, as well as where people lived out their lives navigating through different temporalities that industrial production in innumerable ways constantly connected with the wider world. It has been the purpose of my argument to show not only the persisting concern for labor and the production process in diverse regions but how the everyday encompassing work became the site where a worldly capitalism was encountered and imprinted on the local, embracing and embodying it yet at the same being mediated by it. But, it need be said, this narrative unfolding intersected with the moment Western Marxism was turning inward and exclusionary, when its own "renewal" and "settling of accounts" with its own theoretical tradition might have looked beyond its own provincialized horizon to minimally remind itself of its separation from the original Marxian vocation of worldliness, the universalizing of the particular and the gathering up of the local in the universal, signifying a genuine coming together of theory and practice. Although the narrative of the diverse developmental routes is implicitly comparative, active pursuit of the "imperative of comparison" as a way of unifying Marxism could have pointed toward an attempt to satisfy Western Marxism's preoccupation with philosophy and culture by connecting it to production, labor, and time or bringing the two halves together.

It was precisely this view of Europe, along with a critique unveiling its claims of universalism as the product of a provincial culture, that Japanese thinkers before World War II presciently articulated to prefigure the development of a later critical tradition coming from Asia and Africa that ultimately found expression in the formation of postcolonial discourse. It is thus ironic that the effort to realize a program leading to a world history promising to unite the particular with the universal came first from the West's periphery and was undertaken in Japan in the decade of the 1930s by philosophers of Kyoto Imperial University, known as the Kyoto School of Philosophy. Even though this project failed, what these philosophers sought to envision was a figure of world history that would account for the excluded particularities that had remained shadowed by the universalistic claims projected by imperial domination and colonial oppression. In this endeavor, Kyoto philosophers saw their present as the propitious moment to engage its demands to find the basis of a new civilizational unity in the form of an overcoming for a new present future. In their time, they were driven to identify a dangerous presence in the present: a deteriorating world situation requiring immediate resolution. In this environment, philosophy moved to emphasizing the importance of the phenomenological "now" and was positioned to provide a diagnosis leading to the transmutation of the present into its anticipated future. It should be stated that these philosophers were avid readers of Christopher Dawson, Nicholas Berdyaev, Arnold Toynbee, and all those who, on the eve of World War II, were searching for a form of unity that would overcome the accelerated fragmentation marking the conjuncture that eventually culminated in global conflict. It is not at all coincidental that Kyoto philosophy aimed at envisioning a proper world history in their present as a condition of imagining a future released from it. Hence, their intervention acknowledged that the present (late 1930s) provided the occasion for Japan to realize its world historical mission, ultimately embodied in the formation of the East Asia Co-Prosperity Sphere, designed to relieve Asia of white man's imperialism and secure a new destiny once the present had been overcome. In the perspective of its most original thinker, Miki Kiyoshi, the regional figure would be characterized by a restoration of what he called an "Oriental gemeinschaft" based on the principle of "cooperativism" uniting all Asians.

Neither Kyoto philosophy nor Miki envisaged a present as conceptualized by Marx, a form of self-temporalization begun in a present with the process of production and reproduction and the continuous appearance of uneven rhythms syncopating and accenting political struggles. Rather, their choice of a present signaled the moment of a future anterior, when the present's expectations spring from a not-yet-realized possibility that announces the transitional moment of overcoming to a future present. Moreover, Miki defined the everyday and world history in such a way that there could never be a dialectical relationship between the particular and universal. Since the everyday was characterized by a scarcity of events and world history defined as the stage for world eventfulness, the former—the everyday—would always remain concealed in the eclipse of the latter—world history. Needless to say, there is an insurmountable world of difference between a history dominated by desire and the future and one produced by the constant struggles in the present. For Kyoto philosophers, this meant overcoming the "modern" present for one no longer burdened by its reliance on the West and its economic domination, capable of transforming Asia into unified community.

While the Kyoto vision of world history leaned toward defining Japan's historic destiny, and its readiness to replace the older stage dominated by the reign of the world market as the arena of the nation-state, this path lay with the regional organization of the East Asian Co-Prosperity Sphere, which ultimately sought to replace white man's domination with its own version. Kyoto philosophers mistakenly proposed that subjectivity ultimately rested with "moralistic energy" and the subject of the ethnic folk, just as the "communal body" (*kyōdotai*), with its fascist overtones, proclaimed the establishment of a new form of association. In a different conjuncture, this response from the periphery was transmuted into the register of the alternative modernity of postcolonial discourse, with its own discovery of folk subjectivity in the voiceless subaltern and its irreducible culture of difference. Yet, perhaps, the possibility of reaching this "polyphonic" and "polyrhythmic" sense of an ideal unity was put best by Ernst Bloch after World War II in a work that attested to his own discovery of the world at large:

The firmer the refusal of a purely Western emphasis and of one laid solely upon development to date (to say nothing of discredited imperialism), all the stronger is the help afforded by a utopian, open and in itself experimental orientation. Only thus can hundreds of cultures flow into the unity of the human race; a unity that only then takes shape in non-linear time, and with an historical direction that is not fixed and monadic.[3]

NOTES

Introduction

1. Perry Anderson, *Considerations of Western Marxism* (London: Verso, 1976). According to Anderson, the turn away from economics to considerations of culture reflected the failure and defeat of Marxism in the interwar period. The reduction of Marxism to the "West" meant it was "less than Marxism to the extent that it was Western. Historical materialism can exercise its full powers only when it is free from parochialism, of any kind. It has yet to recover them" (94).

2. Karl Marx, *Capital: A Critique of Political Economy*, trans. David Fernbach (London: Penguin, 1991), 3:966.

3. Massimiliano Tomba, *Marx's Temporalities*, trans. Peter D. Thomas and Sara R. Ferris (Leiden: Brill, 2013), ix.

4. Ibid., 62, 61, 74. See also Karl Marx, *Grundrisse*, trans. with a foreword by Martin Nicolaus (London: Penguin, 1993), 83.

5. This is clearly implied in Marx's letter to Engels (October 8, 1858) in which he asserted that the

   proper task of bourgeois society is the creation . . . and of the production based on that market. Since the world is round, the colonization of California and Australia and the opening up of China and Japan would seem to have completed the process. For us, the difficult question is this: on the Continent evolution is imminent and will, moreover, instantly assume a socialist character. Will it not necessarily be crushed in this little corner of the earth, since the *movement* of bourgeois society is still in the *ascendant* over a far greater area. (Karl Marx and Frederick Engels, *Collected Works* [hereafter *MECW*] [London: Lawrence and Wishart, 2010], 40:346–47)

6. Maurice Merleau-Ponty, *Adventures of the Dialectic*, trans. Joseph Bien (Evanston, Ill.: Northwestern University Press, 1973), 59–61.

7. This is the principal argument proposed in Tomba, *Marx's Temporalities*, esp. 60–91.

8. Jairus Banaji, "Introduction: Themes in Historical Materialism," in *Theory as History: Essays on Modes of Production and Exploitation* (Chicago: Haymarket, 2011), 9.

9. Karl Marx, *Capital: A Critique of Political Economy*, trans. Ben Fowkes (London: Penguin, 1990), 1:876.

10. Kevin Anderson, *Marx at the Margins: On Nationalism, Ethnicity, and Non-Western Societies* (Chicago: University of Chicago Press, 2010), 79.

11. Theodore Shanin, *Late Marx and the Russian Road: Marx and the Peripheries of Capitalism* (New York: Monthly Review Press, 1983), 136.

12. Jairus Banaji, "Modes of Production: A Synthesis," in *Theory as History*, 349.

13. Ibid., 20.

14. Ibid., 350.

15. Ibid.

16. Marx, *Capital*, 1:727. The argument, which I will discuss, was made by Rosa Luxemburg. See Peter Hudis and Kevin B. Anderson, introduction to *The Rosa Luxemburg Reader*, ed. Peter Hudis and Kevin B. Anderson (New York: Monthly Review Press, 2004), 19.

17. Marx, *Grundrisse*, 853; *MECW*, 34:93–104. For additional examples of how old practices outlive their originating moment, see Marx, *Capital*, 3:440–55, 728–48, 754.

18. Marx, *Capital*, 1:1019.

19. V. I. Lenin, *The Development of Capitalism in Russia*, in *Collected Works* (London: Lawrence and Wishart, 1960), 3:197. See also 200, where "corvee economy . . . passes imperceptibly into the capitalist system."

20. Tomba, *Marx's Temporalities*, xii.

21. Shanin, *Late Marx and the Russian Road*, 106, 107.

22. Karl Marx, "The British Rule in India," in *Dispatches for the New York Tribune: Selected Journalism of Karl Marx*, selected with an introduction by James Ledbetter (London: Penguin, 2007), 218–19.

23. Marx, *Grundrisse*, 488.

24. Marx, *Capital*, 1:876.
25. Karl Marx and Frederick Engels, *The German Ideology*, in *Collected Works* (New York: International, 1976), 5:85. It is interesting to note the relationship of Marx's conceptualization of an "illusory community," the state, to Benedict Anderson's later refiguration of the "imagined community" and his valorization of the nation.
26. Marx, *Capital*, 1:915, 918.
27. Marx, *Grundrisse*, 508.
28. Marx and Engels, *German Ideology*, 51.
29. Ibid., 49.

1. Marx, Time, History

1. Reinhart Kosellek, *Zeitschichten, Studien zur Historik* (Frankfurt: Suhrkamp, 2000).
2. Watsuji Tetsurō (1889–1960), a conservative Japanese philosopher, studied briefly with Martin Heidegger. Watsuji's best-known work, *A Climate*, was published before World War II and provided a geographically determined explanation of why Japan and the Japanese were able to embody decisive elements of East and West. Watsuji inverted Heidegger's emphasis on Being's authentic historicality (time) by proposing the importance of environment—climate and place (space)—as a determining mediation in shaping human and specifically Japanese life. He went on to write important books on social ethics and morality centered on contrasting Japan's tradition of community/familistic social values to Western individualism.
3. Stavros Tombazos, *Le temps dans l'analyse économique, les catégories du temps dans Le Capital* (Paris: Editions Société des Saisons, 1994); Peter Osborne, *The Politics of Time: Modernity and Avant-Garde* (London: Verso, 1995).
4. Antonio Negri, *Time for Revolution*, trans. Matteo Mandarini (New York: Continuum, 2005), 35.
5. Daniel Ben-Said, *Marx for Our Times: Adventures and Misadventures of a Critique*, trans. Gregory Elliott (London: Verso, 2009), 82.
6. Karl Marx, *Capital: A Critique of Political Economy*, trans. Ben Fowkes (London: Penguin, 1990), 1:91.
7. Osborne, *Politics of Time*, 23–29.
8. Chris Arthur, *The New Dialectic and Marx's Capital* (Leiden: Brill, 2004), 120–21.
9. Georgio Agamben, *Infancy and History: On the Destruction of Experience*, trans. Liz Heron (London: Verso, 1993), 91.

10. Tombazos, *Le temps dans l'analyse économique*, 9.

11. Ibid., 12ff.

12. Massimiliano Tomba, *Marx's Temporalities*, trans. Peter D. Thomas and Sara R. Ferris (Leiden: Brill, 2013), 136.

13. Eelco Runia, *Moved by the Past: Historical Discontinuity and Mutation* (New York: Columbia University Press, 2014), 49. In this respect, Runia proposes that historiography's real vocation is "metonymics," inasmuch as it is really occupied with a "transfer of presence," which often appears by its absence, by presenting an absence in the present. In this sense, the operation of formal subsumption relocates a practice from another context into a new one, to reveal the missing (or absent) past in the present.

14. Tombazos, *Le temps dans l'analyse économique*, 11–12.

15. Karl Marx, *Theories of Surplus Value* (Amherst, N.Y.: Prometheus, 2000), 3:468. See also Karl Marx, *Capital: A Critique of Political Economy*, trans. David Fernbach (London: Penguin, 1991), 3:735, 744.

16. Karl Marx, *Grundrisse*, trans. with a foreword by Martin Nicolaus (London: Penguin, 1993), 105.

17. Ibid., 102.

18. Ibid., 508.

19. Tomba, *Marx's Temporalities*, 40.

20. Karl Marx, *The Eighteenth Brumaire of Louis Bonaparte* (New York: International, 1994), 17.

21. Pierre Macherey, *Petits riens, ornières et dérives du quotidian* (Paris: Le Bord de l'eau, 2009).

22. It could also be argued that the first volume of *Capital* involves another conception of history in chapter 10, "The Working Day." In this account, Marx presents the advent of factory legislation limiting child labor that instantiated the appearance of political struggle. See Ben-Said, *Marx for Our Times*, 27, 86–87.

23. Tomba, *Marx's Temporalities*, 101–3.

24. Arthur, *New Dialectic and Marx's Capital*, 28, 34 (italics in original).

25. Jason Read, *The Micro-Politics of Capital: Marx and the Prehistory of the Present* (Albany: State University of New York Press, 2003), 34.

26. Ibid., 35.

27. It should be pointed out in this connection that Uno's theorization of *muri* grew out of Marx's explanation of the contingent history that accounted for the separation of cultivators from their means of subsistence and the accumulated hoard that became the basis of primitive accumulation. This conception of noncausal "causation" was the principle that permitted Max Weber to bring together capitalism and certain forms of protestantism. Like Uno's con-

ception of the commodification of labor that advanced the observation that labor was a commodity that could not be made, it just appeared as a contingent occurrence and was therefore "unrational."

28. Marx, *Capital*, 1:255; Ben-Said, *Marx for Our Times*, 253.

29. Marx, *Capital*, 1:255; see also 3:400–401.

30. Marx, *Capital*, 1:267; also Marx, *Theories of Surplus Value*, 3:468.

31. Marx, *Capital*, 1:889.

32. Marx, *Theories of Surplus Value*, 3:491. Marx referred to this as the "*dissolution process*," "the *parting process*," of the preceding mode of production. "This is the period of its *historical process*" and where labor thereby separates itself from previous conditions of labor (468–69).

33. Marx, *Grundrisse*, 83–84. Samir Amin, in a similar vein, proposed that the "market alienation" substituted the economy for nature as the external agent driving social evolution (*Eurocentrism*, trans. Russell Moore and James Membrez [New York: Monthly Review Press, 2009], 229).

34. Ben-Said, *Marx for Our Times*, 58).

35. G. W. F. Hegel, introduction to *Lectures on the Philosophy of World History*, trans. H. B. Nisbet (Cambridge: Cambridge University Press, 1998), 145–47.

36. Ernst Bloch, *The Heritage of Our Times*, trans. Neville Plaice and Stephen Plaice (Berkeley: University of California Press, 1991), 90, 92.

37. Marx, *Capital*, 1:526; see also 529–31.

38. Ibid., 1019–38; *MECW* 34:424.

39. Marx, *Grundrisse*, 508.

40. Ibid., 104.

41. Ibid., 508–9.

42. Marx, *Capital*, 1:900.

43. Ibid., 909.

44. *MECW*, 34:118.

45. Marx, *Grundrisse*, 297.

46. Ibid., 508.

47. *MECW*, 34:425–26.

48. Ibid., 486.

49. Marx, *Grundrisse*, 105–6 (italics added).

50. Marx, *Capital*, 1:931.

51. Ibid., 919–22.

52. Michael Perelman, *The Invention of Capitalism: Classical Political Economy and the Secret History of Primitive Accumulation* (Durham, N.C.: Duke University Press, 2000), 25–37.

53. Marx, *Capital*, 3:742.

54. Theodore Shanin, *Late Marx and the Russian Road: Marx and the Peripheries of Capitalism* (New York: Monthly Review Press, 1983), 103.

55. Ibid., 106.

56. Marx, *Grundrisse*, 109.

57. Ben-Said, *Marx for Our Times*, 21.

58. Marx, *Grundrisse*, 460.

59. Karl Marx and Frederick Engels, *The German Ideology*, in *MECW*, 5:50.

60. Marx, *Grundrisse*, 107.

61. See Marx's critique of Proudhon's method of a history that takes place not in the order of time but in the "succession of ideas in the understanding" (*The Poverty of Philosophy*, trans. H. Quelch [Amherst, N.Y.: Prometheus, 1995], 118–32).

62. For a brilliant accounting of this historiographic shift, which I have relied on, see Ben-Said, *Marx for Our Times*, 9–39.

63. Karl Marx and Frederick Engels, *The German Ideology*, in *Collected Works* (New York: International, 1976), 5:172.

64. Ibid., 55.

65. Ibid., 50.

66. Karl Marx, "A Contribution to the Critique of Hegel's Philosophy of Right," 249, quoted in Ben-Said, *Marx for Our Times*, 24.

67. Marx and Engels, *German Ideology*, 49.

68. Ben-Said rightly wonders what has driven "the disproportion between the endless commentaries on the putative 'Marxist philosophy' and the scant attention paid to [the] conceptual revolution" and concludes that such a lapse was "cause for surprise" (*Marx for Our Times*, 35).

69. Marx and Engels, *German Ideology*, 49.

70. Walter Benjamin, *The Arcades Project*, trans. Howard Eiland and Kevin McLaughlin (Cambridge, Mass.: Harvard University Press, 1999), 388–89.

71. Ben-Said, *Marx for Our Times*, 35, 82.

72. Marx, *Grundrisse*, 460.

73. Ibid., 460–61.

74. Ibid., 460.

75. Marx, *Theories of Surplus Value*, 3:491–92.

76. Kevin Anderson, *Marx at the Margins: On Nationalism, Ethnicity, and Non-Western Societies* (Chicago: University of Chicago Press, 2010).

77. Marx, *Grundrisse*, 107.

78. Lawrence Krader, *The Asiatic Mode of Production: Sources, Development, and Critique in the Writings of Karl Marx* (Assen: Van Gorcum, 1975), 137, and intro-

duction to *The Ethnological Notebooks of Karl Marx*, ed. Lawrence Krader (Assen: Van Gorcum, 1973); Anderson, *Marx at the Margins*, 154–95.

79. Marx, *Grundisse*, 107. For a different translation of this passage, see Krader, *Asiatic Mode of Production*, 107.

80. Marx, *Grundisse*, 107.

81. Ibid., 97.

82. Ibid., 472.

83. Krader, *Asiatic Mode of Production*, 138.

84. Marx, *Capital*, 3:772; Krader, *Asiatic Mode of Production*, 138.

85. Marx, *Capital*, 3:773.

86. Anderson, *Marx at the Margins*, 162–63.

87. Marx, *Grundrisse*, 465.

88. Ibid., 471.

89. Ibid., 472.

90. Ibid., 483.

91. Ibid., 493.

92. Ibid., 472, 486; see also Anderson, *Marx at the Margins*, 161.

93. Ibid., 472.

94. Ibid., 473.

95. Ibid.

96. Ibid., 475.

97. Perry Anderson, *Lineages of the Absolutist State* (London: Verso, 1979), 481, 488. Anderson, in contrast to a number of other earlier interpreters, takes these letters seriously and refers to them, as does Kojin Karatani, *The Structure of World History: From Modes of Production to Modes of Exchange*, trans. Michael Bourdaghs (Durham, N.C.: Duke University Press, 2013). In most accounts that interminably dwell on the transition from feudalism to capitalism, there is no mention of these letters; their absence is present in all those strong theoretical readings of Marx that have posited the completion of the commodity relation as a fait accompli.

98. Shanin, *Late Marx and the Russian Road*, 112.

99. Ibid., 102, 101.

100. Ibid., 111.

101. Ibid., 110.

102. Ibid., 112–13.

103. Ibid., 106.

104. Ibid., 103.

105. Jairus Banaji, "Capitalist Domination and the Small Peasantry: The Deccan Districts in the Late Nineteenth Century," in *Theory as History: Essays on Modes of Production and Exploitation* (Chicago: Haymarket, 2011), 307.

106. *MECW* 34:93.

107. Ibid., 432–33.

108. Ibid., 106.

109. Ibid., 95.

110. Ibid.

111. Marx, *Grundisse*, 240–49.

112. Banaji, "Capitalist Domination and the Small Peasantry," 280; *MECW* 34:431, 435.

113. Slavoj Žižek, *The Sublime Object of Ideology* (London: Verso, 2001), 11.

114. Marx, *Capital*, 1:1019.

115. Marx, *Grundisse*, 296.

116. Marx, *Capital*, 1:1019.

117. Louis Althusser, *Sur la reproduction* (Paris: Presses Universitaires de France, 1995), 43.

118. Tomba, *Marx's Temporalities*, 103, 144ff.

119. Ibid., 103.

120. Marx, *Capital*, 3:452–53. This passage is probably more Engels than Marx, in its eagerness to see capitalism develop without the ambiguities of formal subsumption into real subsumption, and is actually contradicted by Marx's observations in "Results of the Immediate Process of Production" and his notebooks. That it acknowledges the role played by formal subsumption in blocking the full realization of capital is, however, the important point.

121. Marx, *Grundrisse*, 512 (italics added).

122. Marx, *Capital*, 1:91.

123. Ibid., 1019.

124. Ibid., 1023.

125. Ibid.

126. Ibid., 645.

127. Marx, *Capital*, 3:914.

128. *MECW*, 34:448.

129. Marx, *Capital*, 1:645. See also Massimiliano Tomba, "Historical Temporalities of Capital: An Anti-Historicist Perspective," *HM* 17 (2009): 63.

130. *MECW*, 34:117 (italics added).

131. Ibid., 118.

132. Read, *Micro-Politics of Capital*, 108.

133. Marx, *Capital*, 1:727; see also Rosa Luxemburg, "The Historical Conditions of Accumulation," in *The Rosa Luxemburg Reader*, ed. Peter Hudis and Kevin B. Anderson (New York: Monthly Review Press, 2004), 34.

134. Marx, *Grundrisse*, 278 (italics added).

135. Ibid., 460.

136. Vincent Geoghegan, *Ernst Bloch* (London: Routledge, 1996), 109.

2. Marxism's Eastward Migration

1. Walter Benjamin, "On the Concept of History," in *Walter Benjamin: Selected Writings*, vol. 4, *1938–1940*, ed. Howard Eiland and Michael W. Jennings (Cambridge, Mass: Belknap Press of Harvard University Press, 2003), 393.

2. Daniel Ben-Said, *Marx for Our Times: Adventures and Misadventures of a Critique*, trans. Gregory Elliott (London: Verso, 2009), 27.

3. Hayden White, *Metahistory: The Historical Imagination of Nineteenth Century Europe* (Baltimore: Johns Hopkins University Press, 1973), 285–330. White's use of metonymy's power of relationality confirms Engels's earlier observation that Marx was disposed to write in the active voice, describing events as they unfolded, to signify an expression of radicalism. See Eelco Runia, *Moved by the Past: Discontinuity and Historical Mutation* (New York: Columbia University Press, 2014), 49–83.

4. Theodore Shanin, *Late Marx and the Russian Road: Marx and the Peripheries of Capitalism* (New York: Monthly Review Press, 1983), 114.

5. Karl Marx, *Grundrisse*, trans. with a foreword by Martin Nicolaus (London: Penguin, 1993), 539–40.

6. Karl Marx, *Capital: A Critique of Political Economy*, trans. Ben Fowkes (London: Penguin, 1990), 1:876.

7. Karl Marx and Frederick Engels, *The German Ideology*, in *Collected Works* (New York: International, 1976), 5:73.

8. The *narodniki* was a populist movement formed in Russia in 1861 in response to the emancipation of the serfs in that year. Its theoretical forbearers were intellectuals like Alexander Herzen (1812–1870), Nicolai Chernyashevky (1842–1904), and Nikolai Mikayalovsky (1841–1902), and its followers believed that the peasantry could be mobilized to over throw the monarchy. It took its name from the call enjoining the middle class "to go to the people" and envisioned the rural village as the germinal cell of Russian socialism. It was at a *narodniki* meeting that Lenin met his future adversary Peter Struve (1870–1944), who originally was interested in Marxism but became a prominent proponent of liberalism and outspoken opponent of Bolshevism. Lenin's first

critique of the *narodniki* discourse was the "The Heritage We Renounce" (1897), which was written at the end of his exile and attacked the populists for petit bourgeois romanticism.

9. V. I. Lenin, "What the 'Friends of the People' Are and How They Fight the Social-Democrats," in *Collected Works* (London: Lawrence and Wishart, 1960), 1:290–91.

10. V. I. Lenin, "The Economic Content of Narodism and the Criticism of It in Mr. Struve's Book," in ibid., 415.

11. Ibid., 426.

12. This is the argument of Lenin's penetrating critique of *narodism* as a form of petit bourgeois ideology, personified by one of its prominent ideologists, Peter Struve. See ibid., 340–507; also V. I. Lenin, "The Heritage We Renounce," in *Collected Works* (London: Lawrence and Wishart, 1962), 2:508–9, 516.

13. Lenin, "Economic Content of Narodism," 379; see also 404. "Mr. Struve says: 'Thus Mr. Yuzhakov quite clearly documents the Slavophil roots of Narodism . . .'; and later, summarizing his exposition of the sociological ideas of Narodism, he adds that the belief in 'Russia's exceptional development' constitutes a 'historical tie between Slavophilism and Narodism.'" Lenin was convinced that it "represented the interests of and ideas of the Russian small producer . . . the contradiction between the interests of labour and of *capital*."

14. Ibid., 365.

15. Ibid., 380.

16. Ibid., 436.

17. Ibid., 426.

18. Ibid., 427.

19. Ibid., 485.

20. Lenin, "What the 'Friends of the People' Are," 217.

21. V. I. Lenin, *The Development of Capitalism in Russia*, in *Collected Works* (London: Lawrence and Wishart, 1960), 3:31.

22. Ibid.

23. Ibid., 32–33.

24. Ibid., 33.

25. Ibid., 194.

26. Ibid., 212.

27. Ibid., 214–15.

28. Lenin, "Economic Content of Narodism," 466.

29. Ibid., 467.

30. Ibid., 479.

31. Lenin, *Development of Capitalism in Russia*, 172.

32. Ibid., 205.

33. Ibid., 181; see also 191–215; and V. I. Lenin, *The Development of Capitalism in Russia*, in *Essential Works of Lenin*, ed. Henry M. Christian (New York: Dover, 1987), 27.

34. Lenin, *Development of Capitalism in Russia*, 197.

35. Ibid., 198.

36. Ibid., 200.

37. Ibid., 204.

38. Rosa Luxemburg, "The Industrial Development of Poland," in *The Complete Works of Rosa Luxemburg*, ed. Peter Hudis (London: Verso, 2013), 1:41–42. In this, her inaugural essay, Luxemburg draws a comparison between Polish workers, male and female, and Russian workers and concludes that labor time was significantly longer and wages were lower than average in Poland. Yet, in the competitive struggle between Polish and Russian workers, the former were more productive.

39. Lenin, *Development of Capitalism in Russia*, 215–19.

40. Lenin, "Heritage We Renounce," 510–13.

41. Ibid., 510.

42. Lenin, *Development of Capitalism in Russia*, 215.

43. Ibid., 217.

44. Ibid., 218.

45. Lenin, "Heritage We Renounce," 510–11. Lenin does not elaborate further here, but it seems important to suggest that a piece-rate program would induce the worker to work faster to produce more and was still different from averaging the magnitude of socially necessary time. Its capacity for both intensive expansion of production and exploitation was as great. Apart from early essays on shortening the length of the workday, Lenin is not particularly sensitive to the larger questions related to time.

46. Lenin, *Development of Capitalism in Russia*, 219.

47. The idea relating financial capital to the fate of remnants was suggested to me by Ken Kawashima, letter to author, 2010.

48. Rosa Luxemburg, *The Accumulation of Capital*, trans. Agnes Schwarzschild (London: Routledge, 2003), 332.

49. Ibid., 330.

50. Marx, *Capital*, 1:714.

51. Ibid., 716.

52. Ibid., 775.

53. Ibid., 876

54. For Luxemburg's argument concerning Marx's diagram on expanded reproduction, see *Accumulation of Capital*, 309–27.

55. Ibid., 332.

56. Luxemburg, "Industrial Development of Poland," 9.

57. Luxemburg, *Accumulation of Capital*, xiii.

58. Rosa Luxemburg, "Introduction to Political Economy," in *Complete Works*,
1:295–96.

59. Kevin Anderson, *Marx at the Margins: On Nationalism, Ethnicity, and Non-
Western Societies* (Chicago: University of Chicago Press, 2010), 173–80. For the
evidence and a persuasive argument of how, in the French translation of volume I of *Capital*, Marx qualified the example of England as the classic case and
made clear that the development of capitalism was possible elsewhere and
could be carried out according to different routes, see 272n.20.

60. Luxemburg, *Accumulation of Capital*, 338.

61. Ibid., 338.

62. Ibid., 296–97.

63. Ibid., 297.

64. Ibid., 313.

65. Ibid., 330.

66. Ibid., 426.

67. Ibid., 433.

68. Ibid., 329.

69. Ibid., 328.

70. Ibid., 348–49.

71. Ibid., 350.

72. In Chinua Achebe's novel *Arrow of God*, the collision and resulting violence is
sparked by a clash of competing systems of time accountancy.

73. Luxemburg, *Accumulation of Capital*, 351.

74. *Mark* was an ancient form of communal organization derived from Roman
times that describes the earliest Germanic village communities.

75. Rosa Luxemburg, "The Dissolution of Primitive Communism: From the An-
cient Germans and the Incas to India, Russia, and Southern Africa," in *The
Rosa Luxemburg Reader*, ed. Peter Hudis and Kevin B. Anderson (New York:
Monthly Review Press, 2004), 75.

76. Ibid., 79.

77. Ibid., 82.

78. Ibid., 95.
79. Luxemburg, "Introduction to Political Economy," 226.
80. Luxemburg, "Dissolution of Primitive Communism," 101.
81. It is customary to separate combined from unevenness, as recently suggested by Neil Davidson, *How Revolutionary Were the Bourgeois Revolutions?* (Chicago: Haymarket, 2012), and others, which therefore allows an argument where unevenness might be positioned as a causal agent in bringing about a revolutionary transformation while combined development is seen as an effect of the revolution. This might be good sociology in its fidelity to privileging strict classifications, but it is not very good history. While it is true that the Japanese state after 1868, as one example, resorted to forms of combined development—the example of Okinawa in the 1880s being the first instance of this strategy—it still produced unevenness at the core of the arrangement since older practices fused with newer ones were serving the pursuit of value under the subordination of capitalism. Combinations need not be *evenly* constituted mergers. See ibid., 323.
82. Luxemburg, "Dissolution of Primitive Communism," 109.
83. Ibid., 110.
84. Luxemburg, *Accumulation of Capital*, 330, 332.
85. Ibid., 337–38 (italics added).
86. Ibid., 338.
87. Quoted in Davidson, *How Revolutionary Were the Bourgeois Revolutions?*, 292.
88. Ibid.
89. Ibid.
90. Ibid., 292–93.
91. Luxemburg, *Accumulation of Capital*, 424.
92. Ibid., 338–39.
93. Marx, *Capital*, 1:784.
94. Ibid., 790.
95. Luxemburg, *Accumulation of Capital*, 339.
96. Ibid., 343.
97. Ibid., 345.
98. Ibid., 346.
99. Michael Löwy, *The Politics of Combined and Uneven Development: The Theory of Permanent Revolution* (London: Verso, 1981), 50–51.
100. Leon Trotsky, *History of the Russian Revolution*, trans. Max Eastman (Chicago: Haymarket, 2008), 3, 333.
101. Löwy, *Politics of Combined and Uneven Development*, 87.

254 2. MARXISM'S EASTWARD MIGRATION

102. Ibid., 89.

103. Trotsky, *History of the Russian Revolution*, 7.

104. Ibid., 4–5; see also 39.

105. My thanks to Andy Liu for this observation.

106. Georg Lukács, *History and Class Consciousness: Studies in Marxist Dialectics*, trans. Rodney Livingstone (Cambridge, Mass.: MIT Press, 1971), 91.

107. Ibid., 93.

108. Ibid.

109. Ibid., 204.

110. I am indebted to Jack Wilson for reminding me of this Althusserian critique of Lukács's conception of reification, which rightly has little or no room for the operation of formal subsumption. But what Lukács was doing in the quoted passages was really following Marx's own distinction between capitalism's "life process" and the "antecedent life processes" that predated capitalism. The proposal that seeks to explain how older practices appeared to have derived from capitalism still calls attention to the operation of formal subsumption. In the end, Lukács was undoubtedly shadowing Marx, who, in both *Theories of Surplus Value* and volume 3 of *Capital*, quoted earlier, stated that older economic practices continue to retain their original identities in capitalism even though they assume the form of capital par excellence (3:744).

3. Opening to the Global South

1. José Carlos Mariátegui, "The Problem of Race in Latin America," in *José Carlos Mariátegui: An Anthology*, ed. and trans. Harry E. Vanden and Marc Becker (New York: Monthly Review Press, 2011), 324.

2. Ibid., 316.

3. I would guess that this might have been true of Italy as well, but I have no real knowledge to support this contention. This was certainly the case in areas such as South Asia, Indonesia, China, and Japan. In the last, the Japan Communist Party remained loyal to Soviet directives until the Hungarian uprising after World War II.

4. Walter Adamson, *Hegemony and Revolution: A Study of Antonio Gramsci's Political and Cultural Theory* (Berkeley: University of California Press, 1983), 188.

5. Marx and Engels's *The German Ideology* must be seen as the paradigmatic exposition of unevenness and unequal development, even though it has rarely, if ever, been grasped in this register. Gramsci's *The Southern Question* was an attempt to cut through the screen of ideology that kept North and South separated, while Tōsaka Jun's classic *The Japanese Ideology* (1935) returned to the

construction of archaism in his present and the role played by philosophic heremeneutics in the formation of a "Japanese-style fascism." See Ken C. Kawashima, Fabian Schafer, and Robert Stolz, eds., *Tosaka Jun: A Critical Reader* (Ithaca, N.Y.: East Asia Program, Cornell University, 2013); and Harry Harootunian, *Overcome by Modernity: History, Culture and Community in Interwar Japan* (Princeton, N.J.: Princeton University Press, 2000), esp. 118–49.

6. Antonio Gramsci, *The Southern Question*, trans. with an introduction by Pasquale Verdicchio (West Lafayette, Ind.: Bordighera, 1995), 29.

7. Ibid., 16, from the Turin statement.

8. Ibid., 41.

9. Ibid.

10. Ibid., 20.

11. Ibid., 27.

12. Ibid., 28.

13. Ibid., 36.

14. Ibid., 37.

15. Ibid., 43.

16. In these passages on Italian southern ideology, there are interesting points of contact with the ideology of the American South's white planter class and its residues after the Civil War that widen the basis of comparative study of the southern question.

17. Gramsci, *Southern Question*, 45.

18. Ibid., 47.

19. Carlo Levi, *Christ Stopped at Eboli*, trans. Frances Frenaye (New York: Farrar, Straus and Giroux, 2008), 1–3.

20. Antonio Gramsci, *Selections from the Prison Notebooks*, ed. and trans. Quinton Hoare and Geoffrey Nowell-Smith (London: Lawrence and Wishart, 1971), 59.

21. Antonio Gramsci, *Prison Notebooks*, ed. and trans. Joseph Buttigieg (New York: Columbia University Press, 2007), 3:257.

22. Ibid., 252.

23. Neil Davidson, *How Bourgeois Were the Bourgeois Revolutions?* (Chicago: Haymarket, 2012), 316.

24. Antonio Gramsci, *Prison Notebooks*, ed. and trans. Joseph Buttigieg (New York: Columbia University Press, 1996), 2:207.

25. Davidson, *How Bourgeois Were the Bourgeois Revolutions?*, 317.

26. Antonio Gramsci, *Antonio Gramsci: Further Selections from the Prison Notebooks*, trans. and ed. Derek Boothman (Minneapolis: University of Minnesota Press, 1995), 277.

27. Ibid., 374–75.

28. Geoff Waite, *Nietzsche's Corps/e: Aesthetics, Politics, Prophecy, or, the Spectacular Technoculture of Everyday Life* (Durham, N.C.: Duke University Press, 1996), 83; Peter Szondi, *Theory of Modern Drama*, trans. Michael Hays (Minneapolis: University Minnesota Press, 1984), 96; Kojin Karatani, *History and Repetition*, trans. with an introduction by Seiji M. Lippit (New York: Columbia University Press, 2012), 1–25.

29. Peter D. Thomas, *The Gramscian Moment: Philosophy, Hegemony, and Marxism* (Chicago: Haymarket, 2012), 154n.55.

30. Karl Marx, *Grundrisse*, trans. with a foreword by Martin Nicolaus (London: Penguin, 1993), 106.

31. Davidson, *How Bourgeois Were the Bourgeois Revolutions?*, 322.

32. Thomas, *Gramscian Moment*, 282–84.

33. Ibid., 282.

34. Ibid., 284.

35. Ibid., 283.

36. José Carlos Mariátegui, "The Land Problem," in *José Carlos Mariátegui*, 84.

37. Ibid., 84–85.

38. José Carlos Mariátegui, "Anniversary and Balance Sheet," in *José Carlos Mariátegui*, 128.

39. José Carlos Mariátegui, "Theory," in *José Carlos Mariátegui*, 126.

40. Ibid.

41. José Carlos Mariátegui, "On the Indigenous Problem," in *José Carlos Mariátegui*, 150.

42. It is interesting to notice that West African revolutionary Amilcar Cabral proposed, during the post–World War II struggle against Portuguese colonization, the importance of living African histories rather than an imposed European narrative. Even before World War II, Japanese philosophers of the Kyoto School, who were far from being revolutionary, had already seen that much of the world's peoples had been subordinated to a history and its trajectory that belonged to Europe instead of their own country or region.

43. Mariátegui, "Problem of Race in Latin America," 308.

44. Mariátegui, "Theory," 125.

45. Ibid.

46. José Carlos Mariátegui, "The World Crisis and the Peruvian Proletariat," in *José Carlos Mariátegui*, 296. With his privileging of the present as the unit of analyzing contemporary history, Mariátegui was pointing to a new form of historical writing, undoubtedly derived from Marx's *Eighteenth Brumaire of*

Louis Bonaparte, which he was putting into practice. Thinkers like Georg Lukács saw how reification had "grotesquely" afflicted journalism. "Here it is," he wrote, "subjectivity itself, knowledge, temperament and powers of expression that are reduced to an abstract mechanism functioning autonomously and divorced from the personality of their 'owner' . . . and subject matter at hand. The journalist's 'lack of conviction,' the prostitution of experience and beliefs, is comprehensible only as the apogee of reification" (*History and Class Consciousness: Studies in Marxist Dialectics*, trans. Rodney Livingstone [Cambridge, Mass.: MIT Press, 1971], 100). In a later passage, Lukács compared history in bourgeois thought with the worst kind of "provincial journalism" because of its inability to "consider *the problem of the present as a historical problem*" (157). The Japanese philosopher Tōsaka Jun was convinced that most daily journalism was driven by a hermeneutic shaped by "print capital" and was imprisoned by an immediacy (resembling Lukács's complaint) that prevented the recognition of mediations (the "non-immediate") as a condition sociohistorical critique. See Tosaka Jun, "The Academy and Journalism," in *Tosaka Jun*, 36–49. Closer to our own time, there is the example of Jean-Paul Sartre, who has carried on this tradition.

47. Mariátegui, "World Crisis and the Peruvian Proletariat," 296.
48. Ibid.
49. Ibid., 297.
50. Ibid., 302.
51. Ibid.
52. Mariátegui, "Land Problem," 69.
53. Ibid.
54. Mariátegui, "The Economic Factor in Peruvian History," in *José Carlos Mariátegui*, 118.
55. Mariátegui, "Land Problem," 69.
56. Ibid., 70.
57. Ibid.
58. Ibid., 71.
59. Ibid., 72.
60. Ibid.
61. Ibid., 73.
62. Ibid.
63. José Carlos Mariátegui, "National Progress and Human Capital," in *José Carlos Mariátegui*, 156, and "Land Problem," 75.
64. Mariátegui, "Land Problem," 75.

65. José Carlos Mariátegui, "Peru's Principal Problem," in *José Carlos Mariátegu*, 140, and "On the Indigenous Problem," 147.
66. José Carlos Mariátegui, "On the Character of Peruvian Society," *José Carlos Mariátegui*, 246.
67. Ibid., 245.
68. Ibid., 248.
69. Mariátegui, "Land Problem," 111.
70. Mariátegui, "On the Character of Peruvian Society," 251, and "Land Problem," 103.
71. Mariátegui, "On the Character of Peruvian Society," 249.
72. Ibid., 251.
73. Mariátegui, "Land Problem," 104.
74. Ibid., 107.
75. Ibid.
76. Ibid., 112.
77. Ibid., 115.
78. Mariátegui, "Problem of Race in Latin America," 310.
79. Ibid., 316.
80. Ibid., 317.
81. Mariátegui, "Anniversary and Balance Sheet," 130.

4. Theorizing Late Development and the "Persistence of Feudal Remnants"

1. Perry Anderson, *Lineages of the Absolutist State* (London: Verso, 1979), 484.
2. Ibid. Anderson states that in later considerations found in *Grundrisse*, Marx extended the scope of the Asiatic mode of production to include archaic communities throughout regions beyond Asia. But in these passages, as I have already shown, he settled on the communal nature of such societies to which, still later, he returned as a possible model of contemporary national economic development, the subject of his letters to Vera Zasulich, reinforced by the appearance of the Paris Commune and his later ethnological notes.
3. Karl Marx, "History of the Opium Trade [I]," in *Dispatches for the New York Tribune: Selected Journalism of Karl Marx*, selected with an introduction by James Ledbetter (London: Penguin, 2007), 27.
4. Ibid.
5. Karl Marx, "The Future Results of British Rule in India," in *Dispatches for the New York Tribune*, 219.

6. M. Codes, "The Reaffirmation of Unilinealism," which encapsulated what came to be known as Comintern policy, in *The Asiatic Mode of Production, Science and Politics*, ed. Anne M. Bailey and Joseph R. Llobera (London: Routledge, 1981), 99–105.

7. Hani Gorō, *Rekishiron chosakushū* (Tokyo: Aoki shoten, 1969), 4:185.

8. Ibid., 186.

9. My thanks to Osamu Nakano for this citation.

10. Arif Dirlik, *Revolution and History: Origins of Marxist Historiography, 1919–1939* (Berkeley: University of California Press, 1979).

11. Ibid., 50.

12. Ibid., 181.

13. Ibid., 182.

14. Quoted in Rebecca Karl, "The Economic as Lived Experience: Semi-colonialism" (manuscript), 1.

15. On this paradoxical revival of the defunct AMP in the 1980s, see Timothy Brook, "Introduction," in *The Asiatic Mode of Production in China*, ed. Timothy Brook (Armonk, N.Y.: Sharpe, 1989), 17, 16. The restoration of the lingering figure of the Asiatic mode of production in the 1980s had a great deal to do with the role played by the state and the expansion of bureaucratic capitalism and the continuing process of exceptionalizing China.

16. Karl Marx, *Capital: A Critique of Political Economy*, trans. Ben Fowkes (London: Penguin, 1990), 1:175; see also 172–73.

17. Brook, "Introduction," 17.

18. Ibid., 18.

19. Wang Yanan, *Zhongguo jingji yuanlun* (Principles of the Chinese economy, 1947), in *Wang Yanan wenji* (Collected works of Wang Yanan) (Fuzhou: Fujian Jiaoyu chubanshe, 1988), 3:30; trans. Andy Liu, 3.

20. Karl, "Economic as Lived Experience," 10, 16.

21. V. I. Lenin, *Imperialism, the Highest Stage of Capitalism*, in *Essential Works of Lenin*, ed. Henry M. Christian (New York: Dover, 1987), 215–16.

22. Ibid., 226–28.

23. Ibid., 230.

24. Ibid., 231.

25. Ibid.

26. Wang, *Zhongguo jingji yuanlun*, 28; Liu, 2.

27. Ibid.

28. Ibid., 27; Liu, 1.

29. Marx, *Capital*, 1:91.
30. Wang, *Zhongguo jingji yuanlun*, 29; Liu, 3.
31. Ibid., 30–32; Liu, 3–4.
32. Quoted in Karl, "Economic as Lived Experience," 13.
33. Wang, *Zhongguo jingji yuanlun*, 37; Liu, 7.
34. Ibid., 157; Liu, 11.
35. Ibid.
36. For this, I am indebted to Gavin Walker's illuminating account in *The Sublime Perversion of Capital: Marxist Thought and the Politics of History in Modern Japan* (Durham, N.C.: Duke University Press, forthcoming).
37. Andrew E. Barshay, *The Social Sciences in Modern Japan: The Marxian and Modernist Traditions* (Berkeley: University of California Press, 2004), 77–92.
38. Yamada Moritarō, *Nihon shihonshugi bunseki* (Analysis of Japanese capitalism) (Tokyo: Iwanami shoten, 1934), 168–69.
39. Ibid., 172.
40. Ibid., 173.
41. Ibid.; Marx, *Capital*, 1:345.
42. Yamada, *Nihon shihonshugi bunseki*, 3, 173.
43. Ibid., 7–12.
44. Ibid., v.
45. Ibid., 4–5.
46. Ibid., 3.
47. Ibid., 47.
48 Ibid.
49. Ibid., 45–46.
50. Ibid., 50.
51. Ibid., 76.
52. Ibid., 72.
53. Uno Kōzō, "Nōgyō mondai joron" (Introduction to the agrarian problem), in *Uno Kōzō chosakushū* (Selected writings of Uno Kōzō) (Tokyo: Iwanami shoten, 1974), 8:156, also 26. I have also consulted Gavin Walker's translation of this text in manuscript form.
54. Ibid., 156.
55. Yamada, *Nihon shihonshugi bunseki*, 80–81.
56. Ibid., 83.
57. Ibid., 172.
58. Uno, "Nōgyō mondai joron," 9–10.
59. Ibid., 152–56.

60. Ibid., 13.
61. Ibid., 16.
62. Ibid., 17.
63. Ibid.
64. Ibid., 19.
65. Ibid., 37.
66. Ibid.
67. Ibid., 38.
68. Ibid., 41.
69. Ibid., 54–55.
70. Ibid., 55.
71. Ibid.
72. Ibid., 43.
73. In a long, critical footnote, Uno criticizes Koike Motoyuki, juxtaposing his argument that locates the roots of feudality in the tradition of the small cultivator's management and its incapacity to evolve new relations of production to Koike's interpretation that lodged the persistence of the "feudality of thinking, sentiment and custom in the continuation of ground rent" (ibid., 18–19).
74. Ibid., 57.
75. Ibid.
76. Ibid.
77. Marx, *Capital*, 1:878, no. 3.
78. Uno, "Nōgyō mondai joron," 58.
79. Ibid., 59.
80. Ibid., 81.

5. Colonial/Postcolonial

1. Neil Lazarus, "The Fetish of the 'West' in Postcolonial Theory," in *Marxism, Modernity and Postcolonial Studies,* ed. Crystal Bartolovich and Neil Lazarus (Cambridge: Cambridge University Press, 2002), 55.
2. Leela Gandhi, *Postcolonial Theory: A Critical Introduction* (New York: Columbia University Press, 1998), 5–19.
3. Claude Meillassoux, *Maidens, Meal and Money: Capitalism and the Domestic Community* (Cambridge: Cambridge University Press, 1981), 91.
4. Ibid.
5. Ibid., 87–88.
6. Ibid., 34.
7. Ibid., 39.

262 5. COLONIAL/POSTCOLONIAL

8. Ibid., 49.
9. Ibid.
10. Ibid., 92.
11. Ibid., 94.
12. Ibid., 95.
13. Ibid., 96.
14. Karl Marx, *Grundrisse*, trans. with a foreword by Martin Nicolaus (London: Penguin, 1993), 509.
15. Meillassoux, *Maidens, Meal and Money*, 96.
16. Ibid., 97.
17. Ibid.
18. Ibid., 98.
19. Ibid., 138.
20. Ibid.; see also 105.
21. Ibid., 107.
22. Ibid., 110.
23. Ibid., 111.
24. Jairus Banaji, "Capitalist Domination and the Small Peasantry: The Deccan Districts in the Late Nineteenth Century," in *Theory as History: Essays on Modes of Production and Exploitation* (Chicago: Haymarket, 2011), 325.
25. Kalyan Sanyal, *Rethinking Capitalist Development: Primitive Accumulation, Governmentality and Post-Colonial Capitalism* (London: Routledge, 2006), 31.
26. Ibid., 32.
27. Banaji, "Capitalist Domination and the Small Peasantry," 325–26.
28. Ibid., 277.
29. Ibid., 278.
30. Ibid., 279.
31. Kevin Anderson, *Marx at the Margins: On Nationalism, Ethnicity, and Non-Western Societies* (Chicago: University of Chicago Press, 2010), 211; Lawrence Krader, *The Asiatic Mode of Production: Sources, Development, and Critique in the Writings of Karl Marx* (Assen: Van Gorcum, 1975), 202.
32. My thanks to Norihiko Tsuneishi for this observation.
33. Banaji, "Capitalist Domination and the Small Peasantry," 279.
34. Ibid., 280.
35. Marx, *Grundrisse*, 278 (italics added)..
36. Ibid., 505.
37. Ibid., 509.
38. Ibid.

39. Karl Marx, *Capital: A Critique of Political Economy*, trans. Ben Fowkes (London: Penguin, 1990), 1:645. This reference to formal and real subsumption was probably the initial formulation, provided in a context dedicated to explaining absolute and relative surplus value. In later formulations, like the appendix, Marx is more specific, and the implied stagism appears more recessive and certainly less definitive and important than explaining how both can co-exist and the subsidiary forms of formal subsumption.

40. Ibid., 1024, 1034.

41. Banaji, "Capitalist Domination and the Small Peasantry," 281.

42. Ibid.

43. Ibid., 281–82.

44. Ibid., 285.

45. Ibid., 288.

46. Ibid., 330.

47. Ibid., 332.

48. Marx, *Capital*, 1:1019.

49. Jairus Banaji, "Modes of Production in a Materialist Conception of History," in *Theory as History*, 62.

50. Theodore Shanin, *Late Marx and the Russian Road: Marx and the Peripheries of Capitalism* (New York: Monthly Review Press, 1983), 103.

51. Banaji, "Capitalist Domination and the Small Peasantry," 315.

52. Ibid., 301.

53. Ibid., 305.

54. Ibid., 324.

55. Ibid.

56. Ibid., 325.

57. Ibid., 329.

58. Ibid.

59. Marx, *Capital*, 1:1019.

60. Banaji, "Modes of Production in a Materialist Conception of History," 61.

61. Ibid., 66.

62. Ibid., 99.

63. Sanyal, *Rethinking Capitalist Development*, 67.

64. Dipesh Chakrabarty, *Rethinking Working-Class History: Bengal 1890 to 1940* (Princeton, N.J.: Princeton University Press, 1989), 3.

65. Marx, *Grundrisse*, 464.

66. Ibid., 297.

67. Chakrabarty, *Rethinking Working-Class History*, 4.

68. Daniel Ben-Said, *Marx for Our Times: Adventures and Misadventures of a Critique*, trans. Gregory Elliott (London: Verso, 2009), 86.

69. Ibid., 82.

70. Bruno Gulli, *Labor of Fire: The Ontology of Labor Between Economy and Culture* (Philadelphia: Temple University Press, 2005); Chakrabarty, *Rethinking Working-Class History*, 17, and *Deprovincializing Europe: Postcolonial Thought and Historical Difference* (Princeton, N.J.: Princeton University Press, 2000), esp. chap. 2.

71. Chakrabarty, *Rethinking Working-Class History*, 63–65.

72. Ibid., 63.

73. Marx, *Grundrisse*, 162.

74. Chakrabarty, *Rethinking Working-Class History*, 67.

75. Ben-Said, *Marx for Our Times*, 82–83.

76. Ibid., 95.

77. Georg Lukács, *History and Class Consciousness: Studies in Marxist Dialectics*, trans. Rodney Livingstone (Cambridge, Mass.: MIT Press, 1971), 172.

Afterword

1. Perry Anderson, *Considerations of Western Marxism* (London: Verso, 1976), 89–94.

2. Perry Anderson, *In the Tracks of Historical Materialism* (London: Verso, 1983), 9–31.

3. Ernst Bloch, *A Philosophy of the Future*, trans. John Cumming (1961; New York: Herder and Herder, 1970), 140–41.

INDEX

value, as abstraction, introduction of in origin of capitalism, 57–58

wage labor: and commodity form, 37; introduction of, 33, 39–40, 47, 48, 50, 61–62, 75, 76–77, 92; nondifferentiation in, 58; and workday versus disposable time, 61
Wakefield, Edward, 3
Wallerstein, Immanuel, 220
Wang Yanan: on Asiatic mode of production model, 155, 158, 159, 161; on comprador-bureaucratic class, 162, 164, 168, 169, 170, 171, 173, 174; issues addressed by, 165–66; on local variations in historical development, 135, 171; on origin and development of Chinese feudalism, 171; on shared interests of imperialists and Chinese class allies, 168–69

ON SEMIFEUDALISM IN CHINA: as consequence of colonialism, 167–68, 169; critique of, 170–74; and dual economy of primitive and capitalist accumulation, 163–64, 168, 169, 173, 174, 213; and Marxist temporal unilinearism, 169–71, 174; as model for all backward countries, 169, 174; and stunting of economic growth, 162–64, 165, 166, 167–68, 169–70, 172–73
Watsuji Tetsurō, 21, 194, 243n.2
wealth, precapitalist accumulations of, 39
Weber, Max, 5, 15, 18–19, 228–29, 236, 244n.27
West Africa, colonial: formal subsumption in, 201; unwillingness

to undermine domestic economy in, 208–10
West Africa, postcolonial, restoration of domestic economies in, 201
Western Marxism: aura of exceptionalism of, 76; and Cold War, 3–4, 5; and commodity form, dominance of, 112; exclusion of Third World Marxism from, 3–4; focus on force of commodity form in, 1; hegemony of, 1; history as unilinear in, 2; postcolonial theory as paradoxical inheritor of, 235; presumed completion of real subsumption in, 1–5, 71, 73; and progressive developmentalism, 5–6, 12; and promotion of Western model, 236; as provincialization of Marxism, 1

CULTURAL CRITIQUE IN, 1, 4, 241n.1; and abandonment of expected withering of state, 73; and presumed completion of real subsumption, 4; and progressive developmentalism, 5–6, 12
White, Hayden, 249n.3
Wittfogel, Karl, 166
work, versus nonwork, lack of sharp distinction between in early capitalism, 62, 118
workday: in agricultural versus factory work, 203; clashes surrounding, 31; creation of, 61, 76–77; and technology, 37; and world history linked to the everyday, 237
world history: and capitalism's appropriation of material forms of archaic systems, 237; as collectivity of individual cases, 20; Kyoto